Study Guide for Kalat's
Biological
Psychology
Sixth Edition

Elaine M. Hull
State University of New York at Buffalo

Brooks/Cole Publishing Company

I(T)P® An International Thomson Publishing Company

Pacific Grove • Albany • Belmont • Bonn • Boston • Cincinnati • Detroit • Johannesburg • London
Madrid• Melbourne • Mexico City • New York • Paris • Singapore • Tokyo • Toronto • Washington

Senior Assistant Editor: *Faith Stoddard*
Editorial Assistant: *Stephanie M. Anderson*
Marketing Team: *Lauren Harp, Alicia Barelli, and Romy Taormina*
Art Coordinator: *Lisa Torri*
Production Coordinator: *Mary Vezilich*
Printing and Binding: *Patterson Printing*
Cover Design: *Roy R. Neuhaus*
Cover Photo: Collection of Howard Berkowitz/Jane Wooster Scott/SuperStock

For more information, contact:

BROOKS/COLE PUBLISHING
511 Forest Lodge Road
Pacific Grove, CA 93950
USA

International Thomson Editores
Seneca 53
Col. Polanco
11560 México, D. F., México

International Thomson Publishing Europe
Berkshire House 168-173
High Holborn
London WC1V 7AA
England

International Thomson Publishing Japan
Hirakawacho Kyowa Building, 3F 418
2-2-1 Hirakawacho
Chiyoda-ku, Tokyo 102
Japan

Thomas Nelson Australia
102 Dodds Street
South Melbourne, 3205
Victoria, Australia

International Thomson Publishing Asia
221 Henderson Road
#05-10 Henderson Building
Singapore 0315

Nelson Canada
1120 Birchmount Road
Scarborough, Ontario
Canada M1K 5G4

International Thomson Publishing GmbH
Königswinterer Strasse
53227 Bonn
Germany

Printed in the United States of America

5   4   3

ISBN 0-534-35034-8

PREFACE

When a book is as well written as Kalat's *Biological Psychology*, everything fits together logically and "makes sense." It is easy to acquire a feeling of understanding. However, the sense of security produced by passive understanding is frequently shattered by an exam that requires recall and active reconstruction of the material. One of the earliest psychological principles of learning is that recognition is easier than recall and that passively following an argument is easier than actively reconstructing it. Unfortunately, passively understood material does not become part of us in the same way that actively manipulated material does.

The role of this study guide is to stimulate your active assimilation of the material in Kalat's textbook. Each chapter of the text has its own introductory and concluding summaries and a number of review and discussion questions. Thus the initial reading and review of each chapter is directed by the text itself. The study guide is designed for more comprehensive, indepth review. The Introduction provides a brief review of each chapter to refresh your memory at the beginning of a study session. Key Terms and Concepts provide a quick overview of the material in outline form. Make sure that each term is familiar, and note its relationship to the overall structure of the chapter. Short-Answer Questions are designed to help you organize information pertinent to specific problems. These questions are listed under headings that refer to the main divisions of the chapter. If you have difficulty answering a question fully, refer to the appropriate section of the text to find the answer. The Multiple-Choice Questions check your knowledge of detail and emphasize points that are easy to get confused. Some may seem picky, but it is better to encounter the confusing detail here rather than on an exam. Answers are listed at the end of the section. A number of chapters have graphics to be labeled or to be used in answering accompanying questions. Each graphic is adapted from or taken directly from the text; you can refer to the appropriate drawing in the text if you have difficulty labeling it. Some chapters have Helpful Hints that suggest analogies or mnemonic devices to help you understand or remember factual information. Finally, there are nine crossword puzzles, each covering one or two chapters. I hope that these provide an enjoyable way to solidify and test your knowledge of the information. The answers are given at the end of the Study Guide.

Biological psychology is full of detailed experimental knowledge and also of contradictions and perplexities. It also has important general concepts and broad philosophical implications. The concepts and generalizations are hollow without an interesting conceptual framework and some detailed knowledge. A student once asked how anyone could stand to teach a course in which so much is unknown. However, this is a problem only if you expect the body to work in a simple, stereotyped way. Fortunately, there is considerable orderliness about the body, and equally fortunately, there is a great deal of adaptability that gives rise to unresolved questions and apparent conflicts. The study of brain and behavior may well be the most exciting frontier of knowledge. In contrast to the consternation of the student who wanted knowledge handed out in tidy packets, many others have found that their biological psychology course did more to challenge and enrich their basic philosophy of life than did any other course. I hope that this text and study guide will help make your experiences with biological psychology more like those of the latter students than like those of the former.

Thanks to James Kalat, author of *Biological Psychology*, to Jim Brace-Thompson, the Psychology Editor for Brooks/Cole ITT Publishing Company, and to Faith Stoddard, Senior Acquisitions Editor for the Study Guide. My special thanks go to my husband, Richard T. Hull, a veteran crossword puzzle fan, for his help with the puzzles and many other aspects of this project.

Elaine M. Hull

CONTENTS

1

HUMAN BEHAVIOR IN THE CONTEXT OF THE ANIMAL KINGDOM

INTRODUCTION

Biological psychology is the study of the physiological, ontogenetic (developmental), evolutionary, and functional explanations of behavior. Bird song provides an example of the four types of explanation. Increased testosterone levels during mating season cause a brain area that is important for singing to increase in size, providing a physiological mechanism for singing. Ontogenetic explanations focus on genes, nutrition, and experience during an early sensitive period, when the bird learns the appropriate species-typical song. Evolutionary explanations discuss the selection of traits, including the neural substrates of behavior, in terms of their adaptive value to the organism. If an organism is better able to reproduce because of a certain trait, that trait will be passed on to its offspring, whose reproduction will in turn be facilitated. Functional explanations describe the advantages conferred by each trait. For example, a male bird's song attracts a female and deters competition from other males.

Genes are the units of heredity; they maintain their structural identity from one generation to another. Chromosomes and the genes they contain come in pairs, one from each parent. An individual with identical genes of a given pair is said to be homozygous for that gene; an individual with an unmatched pair of genes is heterozygous for that gene. Genes may be dominant or recessive, or they may show more complex effects, including partial penetrance (producing effects under some but not all conditions). Sex-linked genes are usually found on the X chromosome; any characteristic produced by a recessive X-linked gene will be observed primarily in males, who do not have a second X chromosome to overrule the recessive gene. Genetic variation is produced by recombination of genes during sexual reproduction and by random mutations. Most mutations are maladaptive and produce recessive genes. Such mutations are not likely to produce harmful effects unless both parents have the same mutant genes.

Heritability is a correlation coefficient that describes the extent to which variations in a characteristic are due to genetic, as opposed to environmental, variations. It is determined either by comparing the resemblance between monozygotic (identical) twins with that between dizygotic (fraternal) twins or by comparing the resemblance of adopted children to their adoptive vs. biological parents. Even traits with high heritability in "standard" conditions may be influenced by environmental interventions. For example, phenylketonuria (PKU) results from a recessive gene that prevents metabolism of the amino acid phenylalanine. The resulting high levels of phenylalanine lead to brain malformations and mental retardation. However, a diet low in phenylalanine can greatly reduce the abnormalities. Genetic influences on behavior may be either relatively direct, via production of proteins (including enzymes) that increase the probability of certain behaviors, or indirect, by affecting liver enzymes or height or physical activity, for example.

DNA (deoxyribonucleic acid) serves as a template for the synthesis of messenger RNA (ribonucleic acid), which in turn provides a template for the production of structural proteins and enzymes. It is now possible to identify the exact location of genes on chromosomes. Knowing a gene's location can enable detection of harmful conditions before symptoms begin. It may also help us determine the defective protein produced by that gene, and thereby aid in the search for better treatments. On the other hand, employers and insurance companies may refuse to hire or insure individuals with known defective genes.

Evolution is a change over generations in the frequencies of various genes in a population. Genes that confer a reproductive advantage will become more prevalent in later generations. Evolution does not necessarily imply improvement, since previous success does not guarantee future success in a changing world. Humans have not stopped evolving; medical treatments and welfare programs may increase survival, but may not enhance an individual's reproductive success. Neither use nor disuse of a given structure or behavior can cause an evolutionary increase or decrease in that feature. Evolution is based on the benefit for genes, not for individuals or species. Genes for altruistic behavior, for example, may be favored by reciprocal altruism or by kin selection. Sociobiology seeks functional explanations for the evolution of social behaviors. However, these explanations are often speculative. Furthermore, even if genes do predispose us towards certain behavior patterns, we still have flexibility in acting on those predispositions.

The issue of animal experimentation has become controversial. The usefulness of animal research rests both on the similarity across species of many biological functions and on the difficulty or impossibility of conducting such research on humans. Some animal rights activists, the "abolitionists", believe that all animals have the same rights as humans and should never be used by humans for any purpose. "Minimalists" agree that some animal research is necessary, but that it should be minimized. Valuable clinical treatments of human disorders have been gleaned from animal experiments. However, even though experimenters attempt to minimize pain, and even though animal care committees (which include veterinarians and community members as well as scientists) oversee the research, a certain amount of distress accompanies much animal experimentation. In this case, as in many other ethical issues, it is difficult to gain resolution of the competing values.

KEY TERMS AND CONCEPTS

1. Biological explanations of behavior
   Physiological explanation
      Testosterone and bird song: increase in size of a brain area
   Ontogenetic explanation
      Sensitive period: must hear song early in life, but won't sing till next year
   Evolutionary explanations
      Common ancestor
   Functional explanations
      Male sings to attract mate and defend territory
      No need for organism to understand function

2. The genetics and evolution of behavior
   The genetics of behavior
      Mendelian genetics
         Genes: units of heredity that maintain structural identity and do not
            blend with one another
         Chromosomes
         Homozygous vs. heterozygous
         Dominant vs. recessive
         Partial penetrance
         Crossing over
         Sex-linked and sex-limited genes
            X and Y chromosomes

2

Sources of variation
    Recombination
    Mutation
Heritability
    Monozygotic (identical) twins
    Dizygotic (fraternal) twins
    Phenylketonuria (PKU)
        Inability to metabolize phenylalanine
        Brain malformations, mental retardation, irritability
        Modified by low phenylalanine diet
How genes affect behavior
    Increasing production of a protein
    Indirect effects
        Alcohol abuse: enzyme that converts acetaldehyde to acetic acid
        Change in one behavior due to change in another behavior
The biochemistry of genetics
    Deoxyribonucleic acid (DNA)
        Bases: guanine, cytosine, adenine, thymine
        Skeleton: phosphate and deoxyribose
    Template for ribonucleic acid (RNA)
        Bases: guanine, cytosine, adenine, uracil
        Skeleton: phosphate and ribose
        Messenger RNA (mRNA)
    Translation of mRNA
        Structural proteins or enzymes
    Location of genes on chromosomes
        Detect harmful condition before symptoms begin
        Determine protein produced by gene
The evolution of behavior
    Genes associated with reproductive success
    Artificial selection
Common misunderstandings about evolution
    Does evolution mean improvement?
    Have humans stopped evolving?
    Does use or disuse cause evolutionary change in that feature?
        Lamarckian evolution
    Does evolution benefit individual or species?
        Altruistic behavior
        Group selection
        Reciprocal altruism
        Kin selection
Sociobiology
    Functional explanations
    Criticisms
        Explanations often speculative
        The way things are is not necessarily the way they should be

3. The use of animals in research
    Reasons for animal research
        Similar mechanisms of behavior
        Exaggerated processes
        Curiosity about animals
        Clues to human evolution
        Can't experiment on humans
    The ethical debate

3

Animal research leads to useful discoveries.
Minimalists vs. abolitionists
    Minimalists: weigh value of research vs. distress to animal
    Abolitionists: equal rights for animals; no animal research
    Abolitionists vs. environmental protection groups
Substantial government regulation
    Institutional Animal Care and Use Committees
    National standards of care
Dispute between one ethical position and another
    "Do no harm" vs. "A little harm leads to a greater good."

SHORT-ANSWER QUESTIONS

1. *Biological explanations of behavior*
   a. What are the four major types of explanation of behavior sought by biological psychologists?

   b. What is the effect of testosterone on the brain of male songbirds? of female songbirds?

   c. What is an ontogenetic explanation?

   d. What is an example of an evolutionary explanation?

   e. What are the two functions of the male bird's song? What should we infer about the male's understanding of his behavior?

4

2. *The genetics and evolution of behavior*
   a. Briefly, what is a gene?

   b. What does it mean for an individual to be homozygous for a particular gene?

   c. What is a dominant gene? When can the effects of a recessive gene be seen?

   d. What is partial penetrance of a gene?

   e. What is the result of "crossing over" of two aligned chromosomes?

   f. On which chromosome are almost all sex-linked genes?

g. What is a sex-limited gene? On which chromosomes may it occur? Why are its effects usually limited to one sex?

h. What are two sources of genetic variation?

i. How is heritability of a trait determined?

j. What is phenylketonuria (PKU)? How can its effects be modified?

k. What are some of the ways in which genes may influence behavior?

l. Briefly explain the roles of DNA and RNA in protein synthesis.

m. What are some advantages and disadvantages of identifying the location of certain genes on chromosomes?

n. Does evolution always imply improvement? Why or why not?

o. Have humans stopped evolving?

p. How can a gene that promotes altruistic behavior be maintained in evolution, if it places its possessor in danger?

q. What kinds of issues do sociobiologists seek to explain? What are two criticisms of sociobiological explanations?

3. *The use of animals in research*
    a. What are five reasons biological psychologists study nonhuman animals?

b.   What are some of the useful discoveries that have been based on animal research?

c.   Compare the positions of the "minimalists" and the "abolitionists" with regard to the conduct of animal research.

d.   What is the role of Laboratory Animal Care Committees? What groups are represented in their membership?

POSTTEST

Multiple-Choice Questions

1.   Which of the following is *not* a major category of biological explanation?
    a.   physiological explanations
    b.   ontogenetic explanations
    c.   evolutionary explanations
    d.   mental explanations

2.   Most adult male songbirds
    a.   sing throughout the year and throughout wide territories.
    b.   sing when testosterone levels are high enough to increase the size and activity of a brain area that is critical for singing.
    c.   sing because they know that their songs will attract females and deter male competitors.
    d.   sing the correct song, even if they have never heard the song.

3.   An individual with a pair of identical genes at a given site on a pair of chromosomes
    a.   is homozygous for that gene.
    b.   is heterozygous for that gene.
    c.   must have crossing over at that gene.
    d.   must have partial penetrance for that gene.

8

4. Genes that affect an individual's life under certain conditions, but not others, are said to
   a. be homozygous genes.
   b. be heterozygous genes.
   c. have partial penetrance.
   d. have crossing over at those genes.

5. Sex-linked genes are usually
   a. genes on autosomal chromosomes that are expressed only under hormonal conditions that are usually found only in one sex.
   b. genes on autosomal chromosomes that are expressed in both sexes.
   c. genes on the X chromosome, which cannot be overridden by a second X chromosome in males.
   d. genes that most frequently engage in crossing over.

6. Mutations
   a. result from the recombination of genes from the two parents.
   b. are random genetic changes that are usually maladaptive.
   c. are so rare that they hardly ever affect inheritance.
   d. are more likely to produce harmful effects in offspring if the two parents are not closely related; therefore, people should marry their close relatives.

7. Phenylketonuria (PKU)
   a. has high heritability under normal conditions.
   b. results from inability to metabolize phenylalanine, which results in high levels of that amino acid, which in turn results in brain damage and mental retardation.
   c. effects can be minimized by a low phenylalanine diet.
   d. all of the above.

8. The order of bases on DNA
   a. determines the order of bases on RNA, which in turn determines the order of amino acids in proteins.
   b. directly determines the order of amino acids in proteins, which in turn determines the order of bases in RNA.
   c. is less important for genetic function than is the sequence of deoxyribose sugar molecules.
   d. is more important for determining the shapes of carbohydrates and fats than of proteins.

9. The survival of genes for altruistic behavior can be explained by
   a. either reciprocal altruism or kin selection.
   b. the fact that altruism is only a little harmful to the individual.
   c. the fact that altruism benefits the species, though it may harm the individual.
   d. All of the above are equally good explanations.

10. Animal research
    a. yields no useful discoveries.
    b. is regulated by Institutional Animal Care and Use Committees, which are composed of veterinarians, community representatives, and scientists.
    c. depends entirely on the wisdom and good intentions of individual researchers for maintaining good care of the animals.
    d. all of the above.

11. "Abolitionist" animal advocates
    a. agree that some animal research is acceptable if an important goal can be achieved with minimal suffering.
    b. maintain that use of primates in experimentation should be abolished, but that "lower" animals may be used.
    c. maintain that all animal experimentation, as well as any other use of animals, should be totally eliminated.
    d. are also called "minimalists".

Answers to Multiple-Choice Questions

1. d   5. c   9. a
2. b   6. b   10. b
3. a   7. d   11. c
4. c   8. a

2 NERVE CELLS AND NERVE IMPULSES

INTRODUCTION

Neurons, like all animal cells, are bounded by a fatty membrane, which restricts the flow of chemicals into and out of the cell. Animal cells also contain structures, such as a nucleus, ribosomes, mitochondria, lysosomes, and a Golgi complex, that are important for various genetic, synthetic, and metabolic functions. A neuron is composed of (1) dendrites, which receive stimulation from other cells; (2) the soma or cell body, which contains the genetic and metabolic machinery and also conducts stimulation to the axon; and (3) the axon, which carries the nerve impulse to other neurons, frequently across long distances. Neurons may be classified as receptors, or sensory neurons, which are highly sensitive to specific external stimuli; motor neurons, which stimulate muscles and glands; and interneurons, which communicate with other neurons. One can infer a great deal about a neuron's function from its shape. For example, a neuron that integrates input from many sources has many branching dendrites. Some small interneurons have axons and dendrites that branch diffusely, but only within a small radius. The nervous system also contains a great many support cells called glia, which provide support functions and participate indirectly in neural communication.

Most of the adult vertebrate brain cannot develop new neurons; however, neurons can change their shapes and connections. The cell loss and dendritic shrinkage that result from aging are partly compensated by increased dendritic branching in alert elderly people, but there is decreased branching in senile elderly people.

A blood-brain barrier prevents many substances, including most viruses and bacteria as well as most forms of nutrition, from entering the brain. In most parts of the brain, glucose is the only nutrient that can cross the barrier in significant amounts. Therefore, the brain is highly dependent on glucose and on thiamine, which is needed to metabolize glucose. Fat soluble molecules and small uncharged molecules can cross the barrier freely. The barrier depends on tight junctions between endothelial cells lining the capillaries.

The ability of a neuron to respond quickly to stimulation depends on the resting potential. A metabolically active sodium-potassium pump establishes concentration gradients by transporting sodium (Na^+) ions out of the cell and potassium (K^+) ions into the cell. There is a resultant negative charge inside the cell, because three sodium ions are pumped out for every two potassium ions pumped in. Selective permeability of the membrane increases this potential by allowing potassium ions to flow out, down their concentration gradient; the loss of the positive potassium ions leaves the inside of the neuron even more negative. The relative impermeability of sodium results in minimal inflow of positive ions to offset the potassium outflow. The concentration and electrical gradients exert opposing influences on potassium. The electrical gradient (the negative charge inside the cell) attracts more potassium inside the cell than would be there if the concentration gradient were the only influence. Sodium ions, however, are attracted to the inside by both the electrical and concentration gradients. Therefore, if the sodium channels were opened, there would be considerable impetus for sodium to flow into the cell.

A neuron may receive input that either hyperpolarizes it (makes the inside more negative) or depolarizes it (makes the inside less negative). If the membrane is depolarized to a threshold level, it briefly loses its ability to exclude sodium ions, and these ions rush in through voltage-activated sodium channels. They cause the inside of the neuron to become positive, at which point the membrane quickly becomes impermeable to sodium again. However, as the neuron becomes more depolarized, voltage-activated potassium channels open, resulting in even greater permeability than usual to potassium, which is repelled out of the neuron by both the positive electrical gradient and its own concentration gradient. The exit of the positively charged potassium ions returns the neuron approximately to its previous resting potential. This rapid exchange of ions is called the action potential. All action potentials of a given neuron are approximately equal in size and shape, regardless of the size of the depolarization that gave rise to them. This principle is called the all-or-none law. Immediately after an action potential, a neuron is resistant to reexcitation. During the 1 millisecond absolute refractory period, no stimulus can initiate a new impulse; during the subsequent relative refractory period of about 4 milliseconds, slight hyperpolarization resulting from potassium outflow makes it more difficult, but possible, to produce an action potential.

Once an action potential occurs, entering sodium ions spread to adjacent portions of membrane, thereby depolarizing these areas to their threshold and allowing sodium to rush in there. Thus the action potential is regenerated at each succeeding area of the axon until it reaches the end. The regenerative flow of ions across the membrane is slower than electrical conduction within the axon. In some axons, 1-mm-long segments of myelin (a fatty insulating substance) are wrapped around the axon, with short uncovered segments (nodes of Ranvier) in between. The action potential is conducted passively with some decrement under the myelin sheath. There is still sufficient potential to depolarize the next node of Ranvier to its threshold, and the action potential is regenerated at full strength at each node. The impulse appears to "jump" from node to node. This mode of transmission is called saltatory conduction and is much faster than transmission without myelin. It forces the action potential to use the faster electrical conduction within the axon for a longer distance before engaging in the slower regenerative flow across the membrane. Very small local neurons use only graded potentials, not action potentials, because they transmit information over very short distances.

KEY TERMS AND CONCEPTS

The cells of the nervous system
1.   Neurons and glia
      The structures of an animal cell
            Membrane
                  Two layers of fat molecules
                  Protein channels
            Cytoplasm
            Nucleus
            Mitochondria
            Ribosomes
            Endoplasmic reticulum
            Lysosomes
            Golgi complex
      The structure of a neuron
            Cell body or soma
            Dendrites
                  Dendritic spines
            Axon
                  Axon hillock
                  Myelin sheath
                  Presynaptic terminal or end bulb

   Synapse
  Variations among neurons
   Receptor or sensory neuron
   Motor neuron
   Interneuron
   Additional terms
    Afferent
    Efferent
    Intrinsic
Glia
  Absorb, store and transfer chemicals, remove waste
   Astrocytes
  Form myelin sheaths
   Oligodendrocytes: brain and spinal cord
   Schwann cells: periphery
  Guide neurons
   Radial glia, during development
   Schwann cells, during regeneration of peripheral axons
  Contribute to structural changes in neurons

2. Structural changes in neurons and glia
Neurons
  General inability to divide
   Exceptions: olfactory receptors, song-producing areas of canaries, areas
    of rat brain
  Potential for dendritic branching
Glia
  Ability to divide
  Origin of cancer
Aging: loss of neurons and some shrinking of dendrites
  Normal elderly people: shorter dendrites but more branches
  Senile elderly people: Short, poorly branched dendrites

3. The blood-brain barrier
Why we need a blood-brain barrier
  Natural killer cells
  Virus infected cells
How the blood-brain barrier works
  Endothelial cells of capillaries
  Chemicals that can cross passively
   Small uncharged molecules
   Fat soluble molecules
  Active transport system
   Glucose
   Amino acids

4. The nourishment of vertebrate neurons
Dependence on glucose
  Due to blood-brain barrier
Requirement for thiamine (vitamin B_1)
  Deficiency leads to Korsakoff's syndrome

The nerve impulse
1. The resting potential of the neuron
   Phospholipid membrane with embedded proteins
   Polarization
   Concentration gradient
       More sodium outside
       More potassium inside
       Chloride and large negatively charged proteins inside
       Microelectrode

   The forces behind the resting potential
       Selective permeability
           Ion channels
       Sodium-potassium pump
           Active transport
       Electrical gradient vs. concentration gradient
   Why a resting potential? Strong, fast response

2. The action potential
   Hyperpolarization
   Depolarization
   Threshold
   All-or-none law
   The molecular basis
       Voltage-activated channels
       Sodium inflow
       Potassium outflow
       Drug effects
           Scorpion venom: opens sodium channels and closes potassium channels
           Local anesthetic: blocks sodium channels
           General anesthetic: opens potassium channels
   The refractory period
       Absolute refractory period
       Relative refractory period

3. Propagation of the action potential
   Axon hillock
   Successive depolarization of adjacent areas
   Regenerative ion flow slower than current spread in axon

4. The myelin sheath and saltatory conduction
   Myelinated axons
   Nodes of Ranvier
   Saltatory conduction
       Increases speed by increasing distance current spreads within axon
       Conserves energy by decreasing sites of sodium inflow
   Multiple sclerosis

5. Signaling without action potentials
   Local neuron
   Graded potentials
       Depolarization
       Hyperpolarization

SHORT-ANSWER QUESTIONS

The cells of the nervous system

1. *Neurons and glia*

   a. What did Ramon y Cajal demonstrate?

   b. List the major structures of animal cells and give the main function of each.

   c. What are the main subdivisions of the neuron and the function of each?

   d. List seven anatomical distinctions between dendrites and axons.

   e. What is the myelin sheath?

   f. What is the function of the presynaptic terminal or end bulb?

g. List the three major types of neurons and tell what each is specialized to do. What is another term for sensory neuron?

h. What do the terms *afferent* and *efferent* mean? Can an axon be both afferent and efferent? Explain.

i. What is an intrinsic neuron?

j. How do glia differ from neurons?

k. What are four functions of glia?

l. What two kinds of glia form myelin sheaths?

m. What is the function of radial glia? What related function do Schwann cells perform?

n. What kind of glia exchanges chemicals with adjacent neurons?

2. *Structural changes in neurons and glia*
    a. What are some exceptions to the general principle that vertebrate neurons are not replaced after they die?

    b. What type of cell is most likely to be involved in brain cancer? Why?

    c. Does the microscopic anatomy of dendrites change in normal adults?

    d. How do the brains of normal, alert old people differ from those of middle-aged people? How do the brains of senile old people differ?

3. *The blood-brain barrier*
    a. Why do we need a blood-brain barrier? Why don't we have a similar barrier around other body organs?

    b. What happens if a virus does enter the nervous system?

    c. Describe the arrangement of the endothelial cells that form the blood-brain barrier?

    d. What types of chemicals can cross the blood-brain barrier freely?

    e. Give one reason why heroin produces stronger effects than does morphine.

    f. What is the role of the active transport system? What two types of chemicals are transported in this way?

4. *The nourishment of vertebrate neurons*
    a. What is the major fuel of neurons?

    b. Why can't most parts of the adult brain use fuels other than glucose?

    c. Why is a shortage of glucose usually not a problem?

    d. Why is a diet low in thiamine a problem?

The nerve impulse
1. *The resting potential*
    a. What is the composition of the membrane covering the neuron? Describe its structure.

    b. How is the electrical potential across the membrane measured?

c.   What is meant by selective permeability of the membrane? Which chemicals can cross the membrane and which ones cannot?

d.   What is the sodium-potassium pump? How does its exchange of sodium and potassium ions lead directly to a small electrical potential across the membrane?

e.   How does the selective permeability of the membrane increase the electrical potential?

f.   Describe the competing forces acting on potassium ions? Why don't all the potassium ions surrounding a neuron migrate inside the cell to cancel the negative charge there?

g.   What is the advantage of expending energy during the "resting" state to establish concentration gradients for sodium and potassium?

2.   *The action potential*
   a.   What happens to the electrical potential of a cell if a negative charge is applied? What is this change called?

b. What happens to the potential if a brief, small positive current is applied? What is this change called?

c. What happens to the potential if a threshold depolarization is applied?

d. What is the all-or-none law? How may a neuron signal "greater than"?

e. What does the term "voltage-activated sodium channels" mean?

f. What causes the initial rapid increase in positivity of the action potential? Why doesn't the potential stop at 0 rather than actually reversing polarity?

g. What accounts for the ensuing repolarization? Why does this hyperpolarize slightly, rather than stopping at the previous resting potential ?

h.   What effect does scorpion venom have on the membrane?

i.   What is the effect of local anesthetic drugs like
     Novocain and Xylocaine?

j.   What is the effect of general anesthetics?

k.   What is the absolute refractory period?

l.   What is the relative refractory period?

3. *Propagation of the action potential*
    a.   How does an action potential propagate down an axon?

4. *The myelin sheath and saltatory conduction*
    a. What is the major advantage of the myelin sheath, and how is this advantage conferred?

    b. What is meant by saltatory conduction?

5. *Signaling without action potentials*
    a. In what ways is transmission by local neurons different from the usual conduction by axons? Why is this local transmission restricted to very short distances?

POSTTEST

Multiple-Choice Questions

1. The membrane of a cell consists primarily of
    a. two layers of protein molecules.
    b. two layers of fat molecules.
    c. two layers of carbohydrate molecules.
    d. one layer of fat molecules adjacent to a layer of protein molecules.

2. Which of the following is the site of protein synthesis in cells?
    a. nucleus.
    b. mitochondria.
    c. ribosomes.
    d. lysosomes.

3. Which of the following is the site of chemical reactions that produce energy for the cell?
    a. nucleus.
    b. mitochondria.
    c. ribosomes.
    d. lysosomes.

4. Which part of the neuron is specialized to carry electrical activity toward the cell body?
   a. dendrites.
   b. soma.
   c. axon.
   d. end bulbs.

5. Dendritic spines
   a. are structures inside the dendrite that give it rigidity.
   b. are the sites of all synapses on a neuron.
   c. are long outgrowths that stretch for several millimeters.
   d. may play an important role in forming memories.

6. Receptor neurons
   a. are sometimes called efferent neurons.
   b. are highly sensitive to specific types of stimulation.
   c. have dendrites and axons that reside entirely within a sensory structure.
   d. more than one of the above.

7. Intrinsic neurons
   a. are afferent to a given structure.
   b. are efferent to a given structure.
   c. have dendrites and axons confined within a structure.
   d. have multiple axons extending to numerous structures.

8. Glia
   a. are larger as well as more numerous than neurons.
   b. are found in only a few areas of the brain.
   c. are able to divide, unlike most neurons.
   d. form synaptic connections with neurons and other glia.

9. Which of the following is *not* a function of glia?
   a. guiding the migration of neurons and the growth of their axons and dendrites
   b. exchanging chemicals with adjacent neurons
   c. forming myelin sheaths
   d. transmitting information over long distances to other cells

10. Senility is associated with
    a. deficiencies in dendritic branching.
    b. increased dendritic branching.
    c. decreased numbers of glia.
    d. deficient patterns of axon branching.

11. The blood-brain barrier
    a. is formed by Schwann cells.
    b. allows some substances to pass freely, others to pass poorly, and still others to not pass through at all.
    c. is completely impermeable to all substances.
    d. keeps the blood from washing away neurons.

12. Which of the following is true of the blood-brain barrier?
    a. Electrically charged molecules are the only molecules that can cross.
    b. Fat soluble molecules cannot cross at all.
    c. It results from tight junctions between endothelial cells.
    d. An active transport system pumps blood across the barrier.

13. If a virus enters the brain,
    a. it survives in the infected neuron.
    b. a particle of it is exposed through the neuron's membrane so that the infected cell can be killed.
    c. it is immediately removed by glia before it can enter a neuron.
    d. it is impossible for any virus ever to enter the brain.

14. Adult neurons
    a. are like all other cells of the body in depending heavily on glucose.
    b. depend heavily on glucose because they do not have enzymes to metabolize other nutrients.
    c. depend heavily on glucose because other nutrients cannot cross the blood-brain barrier in significant amounts.
    d. cannot use glucose because they do not receive enough oxygen or thiamine through the blood-brain barrier to metabolize it.

15. Potassium
    a. is found mostly outside the neuron.
    b. is pumped into the resting neuron by the sodium-potassium pump, but some flows out as a result of the concentration gradient.
    c. is actively pumped outside the neuron during the action potential.
    d. more than one of the above.

16. The sodium-potassium pump
    a. creates a negative potential inside the neuron by removing 3 sodium ions for every 2 potassium ions that it brings in.
    b. creates a negative potential inside the neuron by removing 2 sodium ions for every 3 potassium ions that it brings in.
    c. creates a positive potential inside the neuron by removing 3 sodium ions for every 2 potassium ions that it brings in.
    d. is basically a passive mechanism that requires no metabolic energy.

17. The resting potential
    a. prepares the neuron to respond rapidly to a stimulus.
    b. is negative inside the neuron relative to the outside.
    c. can be measured as the voltage difference between a microelectrode inside the neuron and a reference electrode outside the neuron.
    d. all of the above.

18. Sodium ions
    a. are found largely inside the neuron during the resting state because they are attracted in by the negative charge there.
    b. are found largely inside the neuron during the resting state because they are actively pumped in.
    c. are found largely outside the neuron during the resting state because they are actively pumped out, and the membrane is largely impermeable to their reentry.
    d. are actively repelled by the electrical charge of the neuron's resting potential.

19. Hyperpolarization
    a. refers to a shift in the cell's potential in a more negative direction.
    b. refers to a shift in the cell's potential in a positive direction.
    c. can trigger an action potential if it is large enough.
    d. occurs in an all-or-none fashion.

20. Depolarization of a neuron can be accomplished by having
    a. a negative ion, such as chloride (Cl^-), flow into the cell.
    b. potassium (K^+) ions flow out of the cell.
    c. sodium (Na^+) ions flow into the cell.
    d. sodium ions flow out of the cell.

21. The all-or-none law
    a. applies only to potentials in dendrites.
    b. states that the size and shape of the action potential are independent of the intensity of the stimulus that initiated it.
    c. makes it impossible for the nervous system to signal intensity of a stimulus.
    d. more than one of the above.

22. When a neuron receives a threshold depolarization
    a. the membrane becomes highly permeable to sodium ions for a brief time.
    b. so much sodium comes in that it almost completely depletes the extracellular fluid of sodium.
    c. sodium flows in only until the potential across the membrane is zero.
    d. an action potential occurs, the size of which reflects the size of the stimulus that gave rise to it.

23. The down slope of the action potential graph
    a. is largely a result of sodium ions being pumped back out again.
    b. is the result of potassium ions flowing in briefly.
    c. is the result of sodium ions flowing in briefly.
    d. usually passes the level of the resting potential, resulting in a brief hyperpolarization, due to potassium freely leaving the cell.

24. Which of the following is true?
    a. Local anesthetics block nerve transmission by blocking sodium channels.
    b. Scorpion venom also blocks sodium channels.
    c. General anesthetics keep sodium channels open and close potassium channels.
    d. All of the above are true.

25. The absolute refractory period
    a. is the time during which a stimulus must exceed the usual threshold in order to produce an action potential.
    b. is the time during which a neuron is more excitable than usual.
    c. sets a maximum on the firing frequency of a neuron.
    d. more than one of the above.

26. Propagation of an action potential
    a. is analogous to the flow of electrons down a wire.
    b. is almost instantaneous.
    c. is inherently unidirectional because positive charges can flow only in one direction.
    d. depends on passive diffusion of sodium ions inside the axon, which depolarize the neighboring areas to their threshold.

27. Myelin sheaths
    a. are interrupted about every 1 mm by a short unmyelinated segment.
    b. would be much more efficient if they were not interrupted with a lot of leaky nodes.
    c. are less effective in speeding transmission than a simple increase in axon size.
    d. none of the above.

28. Saltatory conduction refers to
    a. the salt ions used in the action potential.
    b. the jumping in of sodium ions once the sodium channels are opened.
    c. the impulse jumping from one node of Ranvier to the next.
    d. the impulse jumping from one myelin sheath to the next.

29. Myelin sheaths
    a. slow conduction of the impulse by blocking sodium's entry to the cell; their advantage lies in making the impulse all-or-none.
    b. are destroyed in multiple sclerosis.
    c. are found on dendrites.
    d. are found on cell bodies.

30. The nodes of Ranvier
    a. are interruptions of the myelin sheath at about 1 mm intervals.
    b. are sites of abundant sodium channels.
    c. are sites where an action potential is regenerated.
    d. all of the above.

31. Local neurons utilize
    a. action potentials to transmit information over long distances.
    b. action potentials to transmit information over short distances.
    c. graded potentials to convey information over short distances.
    d. graded potentials to convey information over long distances.

Answers to Multiple-Choice Questions

1. b	7. c	13. a	19. a	25. c	31. c
2. c	8. c	14. c	20. c	26. d	
3. b	9. d	15. b	21. b	27. a	
4. a	10. a	16. a	22. a	28. c	
5. d	11. b	17. d	23. d	29. b	
6. b	12. c	18. c	24. a	30. d	

Helpful Hints

1. To remember the relative locations of sodium and potassium ions during the resting potential, remember that sodium (Na^+) is "Not allowed" inside the neuron and potassium (K^+) is labeled "Keep."

2. To appreciate the difference between fast electrical conduction inside the membrane and slow regenerative potentials across the membrane, think of ions simply elbowing their like-charged neighbors a short distance away inside the membrane, while sodium and potassium ions have to swim their equivalent of the length of a pool to cross the membrane.

Diagrams

1. Label the following structures on the diagram of a motor neuron below: axon, axon hillock, dendrites, myelin sheath, node of Ranvier, nucleus, soma, presynaptic terminals, muscle fiber.

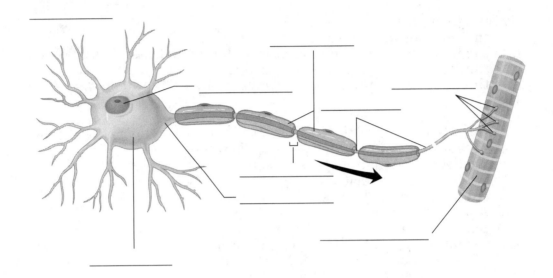

2. In the diagram of neurons A and B below, label the directions as either afferent or efferent.

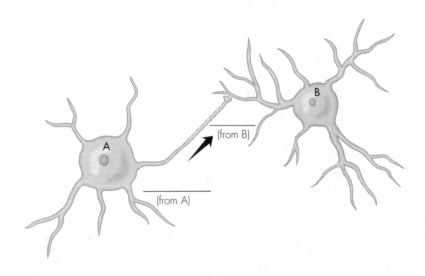

(from B)

(from A)

3. Label the four types of glia cells.

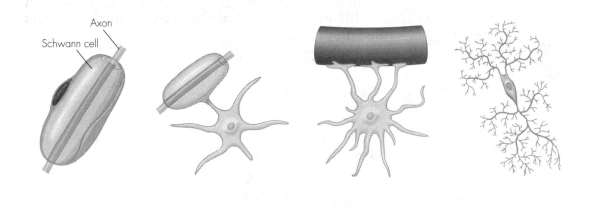

_____   _____   _____   _____

4. Label the blanks below as either Na⁺ or K⁺.

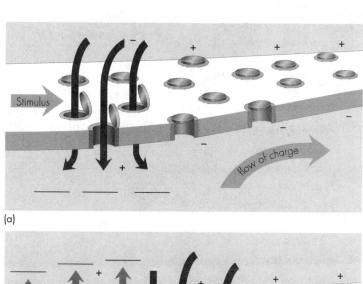

(a)

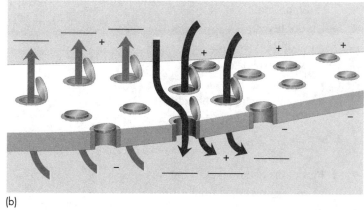

(b)

GENES, CELLS, AND BEHAVIOR

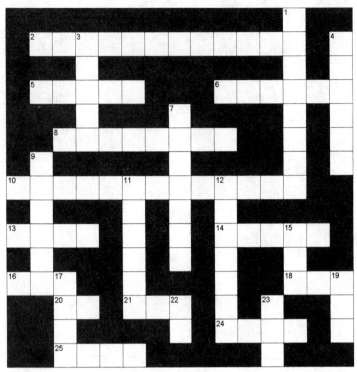

Constructed by Elaine M. Hull using Plexus Word Weaver®

Across

2 A hormone secreted in greater quantities in males than in females

5 Type of acid used as a transmitter or part of peptides

6 Potentials that vary in magnitude

8 Part of refractory period during which it is more difficult, but not impossible, to initiate a new action potential

10 Make more negative

13 Support cells in the nervous system

14 Aspect of impulse increased by myelin sheath

16 Single strand transcribed from DNA (abbr.)

18 Common name for lipids

20 Sex chromosomes of a male mammal

21 ___-linked gene, a gene on the X or Y (usually X) chromosome

24 Unit of heredity

25 ____ of Ranvier, area between myelin sheaths where action potential regenerates its full amplitude

Down

1 Part of the neuron that receives stimulation from other cells

3 Short dendritic outgrowth

4 Type of glia that guides neurons in development

7 Part of axon where action potential begins

9 Insulating sheath

11 Ion pumped into cell (abbr.)

12 Cell at -70mV is said to be this

15 Direction away from a structure (abbr.)

17 Part of the neuron that carries impulses to other neurons

19 Number of layers of phospholipid molecules in cell membrane

22 Sex chromosomes of a female mammal

23 Blueprint for RNA (abbr.)

3

SYNAPSES AND DRUGS

INTRODUCTION

C. S. Sherrington inferred from careful behavioral observations that neurons do not merge with each other but communicate across tiny gaps called synapses. Reflex arcs that have one or more synapses are slower than simple transmission along the same distance of unbroken axon. Sherrington also inferred that complex integration of stimuli, including spatial and temporal summation of both excitation and inhibition, occurs at synapses. Most of his inferences were later confirmed by electrophysiological recordings using microelectrodes inserted inside neurons. Inhibitory postsynaptic potentials (IPSPs) hyperpolarize the postsynaptic cell, making it more difficult to produce an action potential. Excitatory postsynaptic potentials (EPSPs) depolarize the postsynaptic neuron and may summate spatially and temporally with other EPSPs to reach triggering threshold for an action potential.

EPSPs and IPSPs result from the release of neurotransmitters from presynaptic terminals. The neurotransmitter diffuses to and combines with receptor sites on the postsynaptic neuron, giving rise to either ionotropic or metabotropic changes that produce the postsynaptic potentials. The neurotransmitter then detaches from its receptor and is either reabsorbed by the presynaptic terminal and reused or broken by enzymes into inactive components. Different neurotransmitters have different modes of inactivation, but some form of inactivation is critical to prevent the neurotransmitter from having a prolonged effect on the postsynaptic neuron, which would make it incapable of responding to new stimuli. The effect on the postsynaptic cell depends on the type and amount of neurotransmitter, the nature and number of receptors, the amount of deactivating enzyme present at the synapse, the rate of reuptake, and probably other factors. Neuromodulators are substances that alter the effects of neurotransmitters at nearby cells, frequently having no effect by themselves. Each neuron is thought to release the same neurotransmitter or combination of neurotransmitters at all of its terminals. Although each particular synapse is always excitatory or always inhibitory, each neuron receives many synapses, some of which are excitatory and some of which are inhibitory. Some synaptic mechanisms involve a brief flow of ions; others affect metabolic processes and are of slower onset and longer duration. However, all neurotransmitters must be inactivated, either by reuptake into presynaptic terminals or by enzymes. The most widely studied neurotransmitter systems are those of acetylcholine, dopamine, norepinephrine, epinephrine, serotonin, glutamate, glycine, gamma-aminobutyric acid (GABA), beta-endorphin, the enkephalins, purines (especially adenosine), and nitric oxide. Levels of some neurotransmitters can be affected by diet.

Drugs typically either impede or facilitate chemical transmission at a given type of synapse. They may either block or activate a certain type of receptor, or they may affect release, reuptake, or enzyme inactivation of the neurotransmitter. Since different neurotransmitters have different behavioral and physiological effects, we can frequently predict the effect of a drug on behavior or physiology if we know its synaptic effect. However, there are individual differences in the effectiveness and side effects of drugs, due in part to differences in the numbers and distributions of the subtypes of receptors affected by the drug.

Most abused drugs and most reinforcing activities, including electrical self-stimulation of the brain, are linked to inhibition of the nucleus accumbens, usually by dopamine. Stimulant drugs, such as amphetamine, cocaine, and methylphenidate

31

(Ritalin), either increase the release of dopamine or block its reuptake. Nicotine acts on nicotinic receptors to increase dopamine release in the nucleus accumbens. Opiates, such as morphine and "endogenous morphines" (endorphins), increase the release of dopamine indirectly, by inhibiting inhibitory GABA neurons that would otherwise inhibit dopamine release. Some people with an altered form of the dopamine D_2 receptor exhibit a "reward deficiency syndrome," which increases the likelihood of a variety of unrestrained pleasure-seeking behaviors.

Several drugs do not depend on dopamine synapses for their reinforcing effects. For example, some effects of opiates are not reversed by dopamine antagonists. Phencyclidine (PCP or "angel dust") produces reinforcing effects by inhibiting glutamate receptors in the nucleus accumbens, rather than by stimulating dopamine synapses. Marijuana and other cannabinoids mimic the effects of anandamide, a neurotransmitter that inhibits activity at serotonin $5-HT_3$ synapses located primarily in the hippocampus, basal ganglia, and cerebellum. Hallucinogenic drugs, such as LSD and mescaline, bind to serotonin receptors, especially the $5-HT_2$ subtype. MDMA ("ecstasy") stimulates dopamine release at low doses, but at high doses it stimulates and even destroys serotonin receptors. Caffeine constricts blood vessels and also interferes with the inhibitory effects of adenosine on dopamine and glutamate release. Alcohol inhibits brain activity through general effects, such as decreasing sodium influx and expanding neuronal membranes, and also by decreasing serotonin activity and facilitating $GABA_A$ receptors. There is a genetic predisposition for alcohol abuse. Some factors that may mediate this predisposition include altered forms of D_2 or D_4 dopamine receptors, greater then average relief from anxiety or increases in endorphins after drinking alcohol, and underestimation of one's own intoxication. Antabuse (disulfiram) is used to treat alcoholism; it inactivates acetaldehyde dehydrogenase, the enzyme that converts acetaldehyde (the toxic metabolic product of alcohol) to acetic acid (a source of energy). A person who drinks after taking Antabuse will become sick. However, many persons who use Antabuse never drink, and therefore never become ill; they use Antabuse as a daily reminder not to drink alcohol. Better understanding of the actions of drugs can both enhance our ability to treat various disorders, including drug addiction, and increase our understanding of normal brain function.

KEY TERMS AND CONCEPTS

The concept of the synapse
1. The properties of synapses
    Charles Sherrington's inferences
        Reflex arc
        Coordinated flexing and extending
    Speed of a reflex and delayed transmission
    Temporal summation
        John Eccles
        Microelectrode
        Excitatory postsynaptic potential (EPSP)
    Spatial summation
    Inhibitory synapses
        Inhibitory postsynaptic potential (IPSP)

2. The relationship among EPSP, IPSP, and action potential
    Location of synapse
    Spontaneous firing rate

3.　The neuron as decision maker
　　Disinhibition

Chemical events at the synapse
1.　The discovery that most synaptic transmission is chemical
　　T. R. Elliott
　　　　Adrenalin
　　　　Sympathetic nervous system
　　O. Loewi
　　　　Vagus nerve
　　　　Accelerator nerve

2.　The sequence of chemical events at a synapse
　　Types of neurotransmitters
　　　　Amino acids
　　　　Peptides
　　　　Acetylcholine
　　　　Monoamines
　　　　Purines (including adenosine)
　　　　Gases (including nitric oxide)
　　Synthesis of transmitters
　　　　Role of diet
　　　　Acetylcholine
　　　　　　Choline
　　　　　　Lecithin
　　　　Dopamine, norepinephrine, epinephrine
　　　　　　Catecholamines
　　　　　　Phenylalanine and tyrosine
　　　　Serotonin
　　　　　　Tryptophan
　　　　　　Role of insulin
　　Transport of transmitters
　　Release and diffusion of transmitters
　　　　Vesicles
　　　　Voltage-dependent calcium gates
　　　　Quantum
　　　　Dale's law (Dale's principle)
　　　　　　Combination of transmitters
　　Activation of receptors of the postsynaptic cell
　　　　Ionotropic effects (rapid, short-lived)
　　　　　　Glutamate
　　　　　　GABA
　　　　　　Acetylcholine (nicotinic)
　　　　Metabotropic effects and second messenger systems (slow, long-lasting)
　　　　　　G-protein (coupled to GTP)
　　　　　　Cyclic AMP
　　　　Neuromodulators, including peptides
　　　　　　Conditional effect
　　Presynaptic receptors
　　　　Autoreceptor
　　　　Heteroreceptor
　　Inactivation and reuptake of neurotransmitters
　　　　Acetylcholinesterase
　　　　Reuptake
　　　　　　Transporters

COMT (catechol-o-methyltransferase)
MAO (monoamine oxidase)

3.   Neurotransmitters and behavior
      Multiple receptor types

Synapses, drugs, and behavior
1.   How drugs can affect synapses
      Agonist
      Antagonist
      Increase or decrease synthesis
            Alpha-methyl-para-tyrosine (AMPT)
      Increase or decrease release
            Reserpine: makes vesicles leaky
            Amphetamine: increases release
      Stimulate or block presynaptic receptors
      Increase or decrease reuptake
            Amphetamine
            Tricyclic antidepressants
      Block enzymes that inactivate
            Monoamine oxidase (MAO) inhibitors
      Attach directly to receptors
            Affinity
            Efficacy
      Complications
            Multiple receptor types
            Multiple effects

2.   Synapses, reinforcement and addiction
      Nucleus accumbens
            Dopamine: inhibitory transmitter
            Glutamate: excitatory transmitter
      Electrical self-stimulation of the brain
            James Olds and Peter Milner
            Dopamine D_2, D_3, and D_4 receptors
      Effects of stimulant drugs on dopamine synapses
            Amphetamine: increases release of dopamine and other neurotransmitters
                  via reversal of reuptake mechanism
            Cocaine: blocks reuptake of dopamine, norepinephrine, and serotonin
            Rebound "crash"
            Methylphenidate (Ritalin): blocks reuptake of dopamine
                  Attention deficit disorder (ADD)
            Dopamine: mostly inhibitory, decreases "noise"
      Synaptic effects of other abused drugs
            Nicotine (nicotinic receptors): increases dopamine release in nucleus
                  accumbens
            Morphine and other opiates (endorphin receptors)
                  Increase dopamine release indirectly, by inhibiting GABA release
                  Also act independently of dopamine
            Phencyclidine (PCP): inhibits glutamate receptors in nucleus accumbens
      Variations in synapses and variations in personality
            Serotonin at 5-HT_3 receptors: nausea
                  Ondansetron: blocks nausea
            Dopamine D_2 receptor: alcoholism and "reward deficiency syndrome"
            Dopamine D_4 receptor: "novelty seeking"

34

Some other self-administered drugs
    Opiates
        Endorphins: endogenous morphines
    Marijuana (cannabinoids)
        Fat soluble: slow release
        Anandamide receptors in hippocampus, basal ganglia and cerebellum
        Inhibits nausea by inhibiting $5\text{-}HT_3$ receptors
    Hallucinogenic drugs (LSD, mescaline)
        $5\text{-}HT_2$ receptors
    MDMA ("ecstasy")
        Low dose: stimulates dopamine release
        High dose: stimulates and destroys serotonin synapses
    Caffeine
        Increases heart rate but constricts blood vessels
        Blocks adenosine's inhibition of glutamate and dopamine release,
            thereby increasing their release
    Alcohol
        Decreases dendritic branching
        Impairs reasoning and memory
        Inhibits flow of sodium and other processes
        Decreases serotonin activity
        Facilitates $GABA_A$ receptor
        Risk factors for alcohol abuse
            Genetic predisposition
            Underestimation of intoxication
        Alcohol consumption and alcohol metabolism
            Ethyl alcohol --> acetaldehyde --> acetic acid
            Acetaldehyde dehydrogenase
            Disulfiram (Antabuse)

SHORT-ANSWER QUESTIONS

The concept of the synapse
1.   *The properties of synapses*
    a.   What is a reflex?

    b.   What experimental evidence did Sherrington have for synaptic delay? for temporal summation?

c. What evidence did he have for spatial summation? for coordinated excitation and inhibition?

d. Describe John Eccles's experimental support for Sherrington's inferences.

e. What is an EPSP, and what ionic flow is largely responsible for it?

f. What is an IPSP, and what ionic flows can produce it?

2. *The relationship among EPSP, IPSP, and action potential*
   a. Why may some synapses have a greater influence than others?

   b. What influence do EPSPs and IPSPs have on neurons with a spontaneous rate of firing?

3.   *The neuron as decision maker*
  a.   What factors influence a cell's "decision" whether or not to produce an action potential?

Chemical events at the synapse
1.   *The discovery that most synaptic transmission is chemical*
  a.   What did T. R. Elliott propose?

  b.   Describe Loewi's experiment with the two frogs' hearts.

2.   *The sequence of chemical events at a synapse*
  a.   What are the six major events, in sequence, at a synapse?

  b.   List the major neurotransmitters.

  c.   How is nitric oxide unlike most other neurotransmitters?

d.   How is the synthesis of peptide neurotransmitters different from that of most other neurotransmitters?

e.   List the three catecholamines in the order of their synthesis. What determines which one will be released by a given neuron?

f.   How might one increase the amount of acetylcholine in the brain? the catecholamines? serotonin?

g.   How quickly can neurotransmitter molecules be transported down the axon to the terminal? Why is this a special problem for peptide neurotransmitters?

h.   What is a quantum? Give one possible basis for quantal release of transmitter. How strong is the evidence for this mechanism of quantal release?

i.   What generalization can be drawn regarding the release of various transmitters at the terminals of a given neuron?

j. Contrast ionotropic and metabotropic synaptic mechanisms. List three ionotropic neurotransmitter receptors.

k. Discuss the role of second messengers in producing the metabotropic effects of transmitters. What kinds of changes can they exert?

l. What is a G-protein? What is the "first messenger"? What is one common second messenger?

m. What is a neuromodulator? How does a neuromodulator differ from most neurotransmitters?

n. What is the function of presynaptic receptors? What is an autoreceptor? What is a heteroreceptor?

o. How are ACh, 5-HT, and the catecholamines inactivated? Why is inactivation important?

3. *Neurotransmitters and behavior*
    a. Why should there be multiple receptor types for each neurotransmitter?

Synapses, drugs, and behavior
1. *How drugs can affect synapses*
    a. List five ways in which drugs may affect synaptic action.

    b. What is an agonist? an antagonist?

    c. How can one drug be an agonist at a given receptor, while another drug, with similar affinity for that receptor, is an antagonist?

    d. What is the effect of the drug AMPT (alpha-methyl-para-tyrosine)? of tricyclic antidepressants?

2. *Synapses, reinforcement and addiction*
    a. Which brain area seems to be especially important for reinforcement and addiction? What is the effect of dopamine on neurons there?

b. How were the brain mechanisms of pleasure and reinforcement discovered?

c. Is dopamine release always associated with pleasure?

d. What is the effect of amphetamine on synapses? on psychological state?

e. Compare the effects of cocaine with those of amphetamine. What are the similarities and differences?

f. Why do amphetamine and cocaine users frequently report a "crash" a couple of hours after taking the drugs?

g. Why is methylphenidate (Ritalin) usually not abused?

h.   What is the basis of nicotine's reinforcing effects? Are all cholinergic drugs reinforcing?

i.   Which neurotransmitter seems to have effects that are opposite those of dopamine in the nucleus accumbens? Which abused drug inhibits certain receptors for this neurotransmitter?

4.   *Some other self-administered drugs*
     a.   What is an endorphin? What may account for opiates' addictive property?

     b.   How do opiates increase the release of dopamine? How do we know that not all opiate effects are produced by increasing dopamine release?

     c.   What is the main psychoactive chemical in marijuana? Why do marijuana users not experience a sudden "crash" several hours after taking the drug, as do amphetamine and cocaine users?

     d.   Which brain chemical binds to cannabinoid receptors? How does it decrease nausea?

e. Where in the brain are cannabinoid receptors located? Why do large doses of marijuana not threaten breathing or heartbeat?

f. Which receptor does LSD stimulate? Can we explain the effects of LSD on behavior?

g. What are the physiological effects of MDMA ("Ecstasy")?

h. How does caffeine stimulate the nervous system? What is a major effect of adenosine?

i. What are two effects of alcohol on membranes? What type of receptor is made more responsive by alcohol?

j. Describe the metabolism of alcohol. What are two reasons why Antabuse (disulfiram) may inhibit drinking?

POSTTEST

Multiple-Choice Questions

1. C. S. Sherrington
    a. did extensive electrophysiological recording of synaptic events.
    b. inferred the existence and properties of synapses from behavioral experiments on reflexes in dogs.
    c. was a student of John Eccles.
    d. found that conduction along a single axon is slower than through a reflex arc.

2. Which of the following was *not* one of Sherrington's findings?
    a. The speed of conduction through a reflex arc was significantly slower than the known speed of conduction along an axon.
    b. Repeating a subthreshold pinch several times in rapid succession elicited leg flexion.
    c. Simultaneous subthreshold pinches in different parts of the foot elicited flexion.
    d. Reflex arcs are limited to one limb and are always excitatory.

3. Electrophysiological recording from a single neuron
    a. utilizes a microelectrode inserted into the neuron and a reference electrode outside the neuron.
    b. supported Sherrington's inferences.
    c. is a field pioneered by John Eccles.
    d. all of the above.

4. IPSPs
    a. may summate to generate an action potential.
    b. are always hyperpolarizing under natural conditions.
    c. are characterized mainly by an influx of sodium ions.
    d. are characterized by a large influx of sodium and a smaller influx of potassium.

5. Which of the following is true?
    a. The size of EPSPs is the same at all excitatory synapses.
    b. The primary means of inactivation for all transmitter substances is degradation by an enzyme.
    c. The size, duration, and direction (that is, hyperpolarizing or depolarizing) of a postsynaptic potential are functions of the type and amount of transmitter released, the type and number of receptor sites present, the amount of deactivating enzyme present at the synapse, the rate of reuptake, and perhaps other factors.
    d. A given neuron may release either an excitatory or an inhibitory transmitter (at different times), depending on whether it was excited or inhibited by a previous neuron.

6. EPSPs and action potentials are *similar* in that
    a. sodium is the major ion producing a depolarization in both.
    b. sodium is the major ion producing a hyperpolarization in both.
    c. potassium is the major ion producing a depolarization in both.
    d. both decay as a function of time and space, decreasing in magnitude as they travel along the membrane.

7. EPSPs
   a. result from a flow of potassium (K⁺) and chloride (Cl⁻) ions.
   a. result from a flow of potassium (K^+) and chloride (Cl^-) ions.
   b. are always depolarizing in natural conditions.
   c. are always large enough to cause the postsynaptic cell to reach triggering threshold for an action potential; otherwise there would be too much uncertainty in the nervous system.
   d. are the same as action potentials.

8. EPSPs and IPSPs
   a. may alter a neuron's spontaneous firing rate.
   b. are more effective if they are located at the end of dendrites, rather than on the cell body.
   c. usually occur one at a time, so that the neuron does not get "confused."
   d. all of the above.

9. T. R. Elliott discovered that
   a. adrenalin slowed a frog's heart.
   b. adrenalin could mimic the effects of the sympathetic nervous system.
   c. synaptic transmission is electrical rather than chemical.
   d. all of the above.

10. Otto Loewi discovered that a substance collected from the vagus nerve innervating one frog's heart and transferred to a second frog's heart
   a. slowed the second frog's heart.
   b. speeded the second frog's heart.
   c. either speeded or slowed the second frog's heart, depending on the quantity applied.
   d. had no effect, thereby showing that synaptic transmission is not chemically mediated.

11. The level of acetylcholine in the brain can be increased by increasing dietary intake of
   a. acetylcholine.
   b. tyrosine.
   c. choline.
   d. tryptophan.

12. The level of serotonin in the brain can be increased by eating a meal that has protein and is also high in
   a. choline.
   b. tyrosine.
   c. fat.
   d. carbohydrates.

13. The speed of transport of substances down an axon
   a. is fast enough that even the longest axons require only a few minutes for substances synthesized in the nucleus to reach the terminal.
   b. limits the availability of acetylcholine and the monoamines more than that of peptides.
   c. limits the availability of peptides more than that of acetylcholine and the monoamines.
   d. is a severe limitation on the availability of all neurotransmitters.

14. Calcium
    a. is kept outside the neuron by voltage-dependent calcium gates when the membrane is at rest.
    b. enters the terminal when the voltage-dependent calcium gates are opened by an action potential.
    c. causes the release of neurotransmitter.
    d. all of the above.

15. Vesicles
    a. are near-spherical packets filled with neurotransmitter.
    b. are especially important for storing nitric oxide.
    c. are now known to be the only anatomical basis for the quantal release of transmitter.
    d. store only excitatory neurotransmitters; inhibitory neurotransmitters are never stored in vesicles.

16. Each terminal of a given axon
    a. releases a different combination of neurotransmitters in order to provide a rich repertoire of effects.
    b. releases the same neurotransmitter or combination of neurotransmitters as every other terminal of that axon.
    c. releases only one neurotransmitter, so as not to "confuse" the postsynaptic cell.
    d. releases all of the neurotransmitters known to exist in the brain.

17. Ionotropic synaptic mechanisms
    a. have slow-onset, long-lasting effects.
    b. use a cyclic AMP response.
    c. are exemplified by glutamate, GABA, and nicotinic acetylcholine receptors.
    d. frequently use hormones as transmitters.

18. Metabotropic synapses
    a. may have effects that significantly outlast the release of transmitter.
    b. are activated when a neurotransmitter binds to its receptor site and thereby induces a change in an intracellular part of the receptor that is coupled to a G-protein.
    c. are characterized by initiation of changes in proteins by cyclic AMP, which in turn open or close ion gates or alter the structure or metabolism of the cell.
    d. all of the above.

19. Neuromodulators
    a. frequently have an effect only when the "main" neurotransmitter is present.
    b. are carried in the blood throughout the entire body.
    c. almost always produce a major effect by themselves, in addition to their modulatory effect.
    d. usually have ionotropic effects.

20. Acetylcholinesterase
    a. promotes reuptake of ACh into cholinergic terminals, thereby inactivating it.
    b. is the enzyme that produces ACh.
    c. is the enzyme that cleaves ACh into two inactive parts.
    d. blocks reuptake of choline into cholinergic terminals.

21. Reuptake of neurotransmitter
    a. is the major method of inactivation of ACh.
    b. is the major method of inactivation of serotonin and the catecholamines.
    c. is speeded up by COMT.
    d. is completely blocked by MAO.

22. An antagonist is a drug that
    a. has no affinity for a receptor.
    b. changes EPSPs into IPSPs.
    c. mimics or strengthens the effects of a neurotransmitter.
    d. blocks the effects of a neurotransmitter.

23. Reinforcement and drug addiction are frequently associated with
    a. inhibition of certain cells in the nucleus accumbens.
    b. release of dopamine in the nucleus accumbens.
    c. decreased activity of glutamate in the nucleus accumbens.
    d. all of the above.

24. Amphetamine
    a. stimulates the release of dopamine and several other neurotransmitters.
    b. stimulates nicotinic receptors.
    c. stimulates adenosine receptors.
    d. blocks the conversion of tyrosine to dopa.

25. Cocaine
    a. blocks reuptake and enzyme degradation of glutamate, thereby prolonging its effects.
    b. blocks reuptake of dopamine, norepinephrine, and serotonin.
    c. is absorbed into fat and released slowly, thereby preventing a "crash" a few hours later.
    d. all of the above.

26. Methylphenidate (Ritalin)
    a. is frequently abused, because its effects are extremely rapid, and it therefore produces a sudden rush of excitement.
    b. inhibits certain kinds of glutamate receptors.
    c. inhibits reuptake of dopamine.
    d. is used to treat opiate addiction.

27. Nicotine
    a. stimulates nicotinic acetylcholine receptors and thereby increases dopamine release.
    b. blocks nicotinic receptors and thereby increases dopamine release.
    c. blocks dopamine receptors and thereby increases acetylcholine release.
    d. stimulates dopamine receptors directly, and thereby produces reinforcement.

28. Opiates
    a. block receptors that are stimulated by endorphins.
    b. inhibit GABA neurons and thereby increase dopamine release.
    c. inhibit dopamine neurons and thereby increase GABA release.
    d. are especially addictive when taken for medical reasons.

29. Marijuana
    a. stimulates cannabinoid receptors located primarily in the brain stem; it thereby interferes with breathing.
    b. blocks adenosine receptors.
    c. is very likely to produce a "crash" a couple of hours after its ingestion.
    d. mimics the effects of the endogenous neurotransmitter anandamide.

30. LSD
    a. stimulates the release of norepinephrine and dopamine.
    b. blocks most serotonin receptors.
    c. is an agonist at 5-HT$_2$ receptors.
    d. blocks the synthesis of serotonin.

31. Caffeine
    a. dilates blood vessels.
    b. stimulates adenosine receptors.
    c. indirectly increases the release of glutamate and dopamine.
    d. directly decreases the release of glutamate.

32. Alcohol
    a. inhibits the flow of sodium across the membrane.
    b. expands the surface of all membranes.
    c. makes GABA$_A$ receptors more responsive.
    d. all of the above.

33. Acetaldehyde dehydrogenase
    a. is the generic name for Antabuse.
    b. controls the rate of conversion of acetic acid, a toxic product of alcohol metabolism, into acetaldehyde, a source of energy.
    c. controls the rate of conversion of acetaldehyde, a toxic product of alcohol metabolism, into acetic acid, a source of energy.
    d. if present in high levels, would make us feel very ill after drinking alcohol.

Answers to Multiple-Choice Questions

1. b	7. b	13. c	19. a	25. b	31. c
2. d	8. a	14. d	20. c	26. c	32. d
3. d	9. b	15. a	21. b	27. a	33. c
4. b	10. a	16. b	22. d	28. b	
5. c	11. c	17. c	23. d	29. d	
6. a	12. d	18. d	24. a	30. c	

Diagrams

1. Label the electrical potentials shown in the graph below.

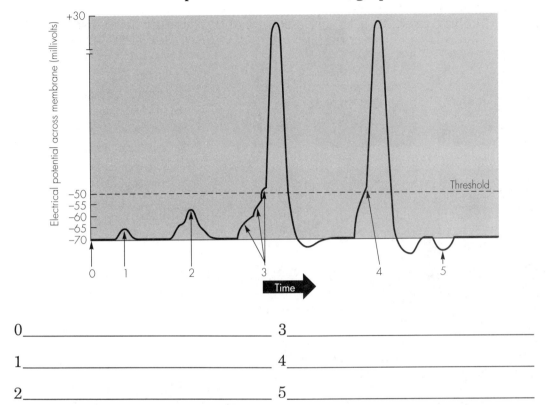

0 _____   3 _____

1 _____   4 _____

2 _____   5 _____

2. Judging from the indicated movement of ions, which synapse is excitatory and which is inhibitory? Label the components of the synapse.

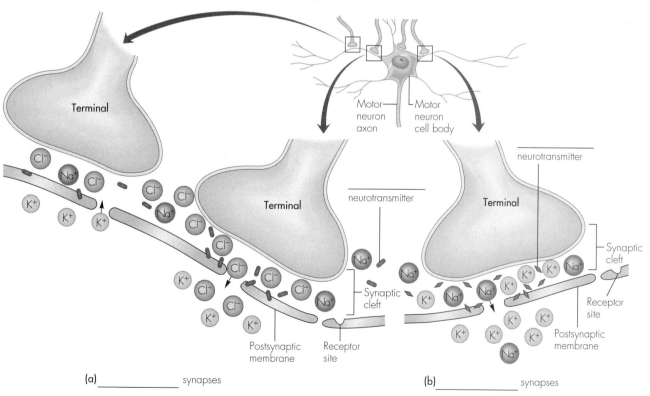

(a) _____ synapses   (b) _____ synapses

49

SYNAPSES AND DRUGS

Constructed by Elaine M. Hull using Plexus Word Weaver®

Across

1 Drug that stimulates release of dopamine, etc.

5 Drug that blocks synthesis of dopamine and norepinephrine (abbr.)

6 A monoamine transmitter made from tryptophan

8 A monoamine transmitter important for reinforcement

9 An amino acid that opens chloride channels and inhibits neurons (abbr.)

12 Packet in which transmitter molecules are stored

14 An enzyme that metabolizes monoamines (abbr.)

15 Unit of behavior studied by Sherrington

16 Temporary hyperpolarization (abbr.)

18 The tendency of a drug to bind to a certain type of receptor (abbr.)

19 _____ oxide, a gaseous transmitter

20 Temporary depolarization (abbr.)

21 Animal whose reflexes were studied by Sherrington

22 _____ acid, a metabolite of acetaldehyde, a source of energy

Down

1 A brain chemical that stimulates the same receptors as cannabinoids

2 A chain of amino acids

3 A drug that stimulates opiate receptors

4 ___otropic, a type of synapse that produces rapid effects

7 The person who proposed that each neuron releases the same transmitter from all of its terminals

10 ____receptor, on axon terminal, sensitive to its own transmitter

11 A precursor to acetylcholine

12 The nerve stimulated by Loewi, which slowed the heart

13 A drug that constricts blood vessels to the brain and interferes with adenosine's effects

17 A drug that blocks certain glutamate synapses, sometimes called "angel dust" (abbr.)

18 A disorder commonly treated with Ritalin (abbr.)

4

THE ANATOMY AND INVESTIGATION
OF THE NERVOUS SYSTEM

INTRODUCTION

The vertebrate nervous system consists of two major divisions, the central (CNS) and the peripheral (PNS) nervous systems. The CNS is composed of the brain and the spinal cord. The PNS is divided into the somatic and the autonomic nervous systems. The somatic system consists of sensory nerves that convey information from sense organs to the spinal cord, and motor nerves carrying messages from the spinal cord to muscles and glands. A pair of sensory nerves enters (one from each side) and a pair of motor nerves exits from the spinal cord through each pair of openings in the vertebral canal. The sensory nerves enter the spinal cord from the dorsal side, and the motor axons leave from the ventral side. Cell bodies of sensory neurons lie in the dorsal root ganglia; those of the motor neurons are in the spinal cord. The autonomic nervous system also sends neurons through the vertebral openings, to synapse in ganglia outside the spinal cord. Ganglia of the sympathetic division of the autonomic nervous system are arranged in an interconnected chain along the thoracic and lumbar sections of the spinal cord. Ganglia of the parasympathetic division receive input from the cranial nerves and the sacral section of the cord and are located near the organs they innervate. The interconnections of the sympathetic system promote unified action by the body in a fight-or-flight situation, whereas the relative independence of the parasympathetic innervations allows for more discrete energy-saving responses. Most of the final synapses of the sympathetic nervous system use the neurotransmitter norepinephrine, while the final parasympathetic synapses use acetylcholine.

The brain is divided into the hindbrain, the midbrain, and the forebrain. The hindbrain is composed of the medulla, the pons, and the cerebellum. The medulla contains numerous nuclei that control life-preserving reflexes. The pons has many fibers that cross from right to left, going to the cerebellum, which is directly behind the pons. The cerebellum helps control movement and may be important for organizing sensory input and shifting attention. The reticular formation and the raphe system, which increase or decrease the brain's readiness to respond to stimuli, have diffusely branching neurons throughout the medulla, pons, and midbrain and send diffusely branching axons throughout the brain. The midbrain is composed of the tectum (or roof), on which are the two superior colliculi and the two inferior colliculi, involved in sensory processing; and the tegmentum, containing extensions of neural systems of the hindbrain. The forebrain includes the limbic system, a number of interlinked structures important for motivational and emotional behaviors; the hypothalamus, important for motivational and hormonal regulation; the pituitary or master gland; the basal ganglia, which influence motor movements, emotional expression, and reasoning; the hippocampus, important in memory functions; the thalamus, which is the main source of input to the cerebral cortex; and the cerebral cortex, which surrounds the rest of the brain and is responsible for complex sensory analysis and integration, language processing, motor control, and social awareness. The ventricles are fluid-filled cavities within the brain.

The cerebral cortex consists of up to six laminae, or layers, of cell bodies parallel to the surface of the brain. The cells are organized into columns, perpendicular to the laminae; each column contains cells with similar response properties. The occipital lobe of the cerebral cortex is the site of primary visual processing. The parietal lobe processes somatosensory information and contributes to several complex processes, including identification of objects by touch, attentiveness to stimuli, and ability to use maps. The temporal lobe processes auditory information and is important for perception of complex visual patterns and comprehension of language. The frontal lobe contains the motor cortex, which controls fine movements, and prefrontal cortex, which contributes to social awareness, the expression of emotion, memory for recent details (working memory), and calculation of actions and their outcomes.

Since the brain is incredibly complex, we must use a variety of techniques to understand its function. Small areas of the brain may be stimulated or damaged, using a stereotaxic instrument and atlas for guidance; location is later confirmed by histological techniques. One method is to make an electrolytic or chemical lesion in a given structure; the resulting behavioral deficits must then be described as precisely and comprehensively as possible. A gene knock-out approach induces a mutation of a specific gene, which can affect wide-spread systems of cells. A brain structure involved with control of movement or motivation may be investigated by electrical or chemical stimulation and electrical recording, coupled with careful behavioral observation. Microdialysis allows for collection of transmitters released from a specific brain area during behavior. It is possible to label metabolic activity using autoradiography and to measure the distribution of a protein or peptide using immunohistochemistry. The structure of living human brains can be assessed using computerized axial tomography (CAT) or magnetic resonance imaging (MRI). Human brain activity can be inferred from the electroencephalograph (EEG), the magnetoencephalograph (MEG), positron-emission tomography (PET), records of regional cerebral blood flow, and functional magnetic resonance imaging (fMRI).

KEY TERMS AND CONCEPTS

The divisions of the vertebrate nervous system
1. Some terminology
    Dorsal (toward the back)
    Ventral (toward the stomach)
    Dorsal-ventral axis of human brain at right angles to dorsal-ventral axis of spinal cord
2. The spinal cord
    Sensory nerves
    Motor nerves
    Bell-Magendie Law
    Dorsal root ganglion
    Gray matter
    White matter

3. The autonomic nervous system
    Sympathetic nervous system ("fight or flight")
        Sympathetic chains of ganglia
        Thoracic and lumbar regions
        Norepinephrine
    Parasympathetic nervous system (energy conserving)
        Cranial and sacral regions
        Ganglia near organs
        Acetylcholine

4. The hindbrain (rhombencephalon)
    Brain stem
    Medulla
        Vital reflexes
        Cranial nerves
    Pons ("bridge")
        Fibers crossing
        Cranial nerves
    Reticular formation
    Raphe system
    Cerebellum
        Control of movement
        Organization of sensory information

5. The midbrain (mesencephalon)
    Tectum
        Superior and inferior colliculi
    Tegmentum
        Cranial nerves
        Reticular formation
        Substantia nigra

6. The forebrain (prosencephalon)
    Limbic system
        Olfactory bulb
        Hypothalamus
        Hippocampus
        Amygdala
        Cingulate gyrus of cerebral cortex
    Hypothalamus
        Motivated behaviors
        Control of pituitary gland
    Pituitary gland
        "Master gland"
    Basal ganglia
        Caudate nucleus
        Putamen
        Globus pallidus
        Control of movement
        Aspects of emotional expression
        Parkinson's disease
        Huntington's disease
    Hippocampus
        Fornix
        Fimbria
        Role in memory
    Thalamus
        Transmit sensory information to cortex

7. The ventricles
    Central canal
    Cerebrospinal fluid (CSF)
    Choroid plexus
    Subarachnoid space
    Meninges

Hydrocephalus

The cerebral cortex
1. Organization of the cerebral cortex
    Laminae and columns
    Sensory, motor, and association areas

2. The occipital lobe (posterior, or caudal, end of cortex)
    Primary visual cortex
        Striate cortex
        Cortical blindness

3. The parietal lobe (between occipital lobe and central sulcus)
    Central sulcus
    Postcentral gyrus
    Primary somatosensory cortex
        Two light-touch bands
        One deep-pressure band
        One light-touch and deep-pressure band
    Effects of damage
        Impaired identification of objects by touch
        Clumsiness on opposite side of body
        Inability to draw and follow maps
        Neglect of opposite side of body

4. The temporal lobe (lateral, near temples)
    Primary auditory cortex
    Language comprehension
    Complex visual patterns
    Klüver-Bucy syndrome

5. The frontal lobe (from central sulcus to anterior end of brain)
    Primary motor cortex
        Precentral gyrus
    Prefrontal cortex
        Prefrontal lobotomies
            Lack of initiative
            Failure to inhibit unacceptable impulses
            Impaired facial expression of emotion
            Impairment of some aspects of memory
        More important for working memory than reference memory
        Delayed response task
        Shifting of attention
        Calculating actions and outcomes

Investigating how the brain controls behavior
    Phrenology -- pseudoscience
1. The stereotaxic instrument
    Bregma
    Stereotaxic atlas

2. Lesions and ablations
    Methods of producing lesions and ablations
        Removal of tissue

                Electrolytic lesions
                Sham lesions
                Toxic chemicals
                        6-hydroxydopamine
                Gene knock-out
        Histological techniques
                Microtome
                Stains
                        Nissl for cell bodies
                        Weigert for axons
        Difficulties of interpretation
                Double dissociation of function

3.   Stimulating and recording brain activity
        Electrical or chemical stimulation
        Microdialysis
        Autoradiography
                Radioactive 2-deoxy-D-glucose
        Immunohistochemistry
                Antibodies chemically attached to dyes

4.   Studying the structure of living human brains
        Computerized axial tomography (CT or CAT)
        Magnetic resonance imaging (MRI)
                Nuclear magnetic resonance (NMR)

5.   Measuring human brain activity
        Electroencephalography (EEG)
                Evoked potential
        Magnetoencephalography (MEG)
        Positron-emission tomography (PET)
        Regional cerebral blood flow (rCBF)
                Potassium ions
                Nitric oxide
        Functional MRI

SHORT-ANSWER QUESTIONS

The divisions of the vertebrate nervous system
1. *The spinal cord*
    a. Draw a cross section of the spinal cord, including sensory and motor nerves, dorsal root ganglia, and dorsal and ventral directions.

b. What is the Bell-Magendie Law?

c. What makes up gray matter? white matter? Why is white matter white?

2. *The autonomic nervous system*
    a. Of what two parts does the autonomic nervous system consist? Give the location and basic function of each.

    b. Which transmitter is used by the postganglionic parasympathetic nerves? Which is used by most sympathetic postganglionic nerves?

3. *The hindbrain*
    a. What are the three components of the hindbrain? Give one "specialty" of each.

    b. List the 12 cranial nerves and note their sensory and/or motor function.

    c.   What are the anatomical location and functions of the reticular formation and the raphe system?

4.   *The midbrain*
    a.   What are the two major divisions of the midbrain? Name two structures in each division.

5.   *The forebrain*
    a.   What are the major structures comprising the limbic system? What are the general functions of this interconnected system?

    b.   Where is the hypothalamus, and what kinds of behavior does it help regulate?

    c.   Where is the pituitary? What is its function? What structure largely controls it?

    d.   Where are the basal ganglia? Which structures make up the basal ganglia? Briefly describe their function.

e. Where is the hippocampus? To what psychological process has it been linked?

f. Describe the relationship of the thalamus to the cerebral cortex.

6. *The ventricles*
   a. What are the ventricles? Where is cerebrospinal fluid (CSF) formed? In which direction does it flow? Where is it reabsorbed into blood vessels?

   b. What are the functions of CSF?

The cerebral cortex
1. *Organization of cerebral cortex*
   a. What is the relationship of gray matter to white in the cortex? Compare this relationship to that in the spinal cord.

   b. How many layers (laminae) does human neocortex have? Describe the input to lamina IV and the output from lamina V.

c. What is the relationship of columns to laminae? What can be said about all the cells within one column?

d. What is the current understanding of the relationships among sensory, motor, and association areas of cortex? What are the sources of input to association cortex?

2. *The occipital lobe*
    a. What are the location and functions of the occipital lobe?

3. *The parietal lobe*
    a. What are the location and functions of the parietal lobe?

4. *The temporal lobe*
    a. Where is the temporal lobe? What are some temporal lobe functions?

5. *The frontal lobe*
    a. What are the location and functions of the frontal lobe? Distinguish between the precentral gyrus and the prefrontal cortex.

b.   What were the results of prefrontal lobotomies?

c.   What is the difference between working memory and reference memory? Which shows greater impairment after prefrontal lesions?

d.   What is the delayed response task, and how is it affected by prefrontal lesions? Is this primarily a test of working or reference memory?

Investigating how the brain controls behavior
   a.   What was phrenology? What were its half-truths and its weaknesses?

1.   *The stereotaxic instrument*
   a.   What is a stereotaxic instrument and how is it used? What is a stereotaxic atlas?

2.   *Lesions and ablations*
   a.   What are three methods for producing lesions or ablations of specific brain areas?

b.   What is the gene knock-out approach? What is one advantage and one disadvantage of this technique?

c.   What is a microtome? For what purpose are histological stains used?

d.   What problems of interpretation do lesion experiments present?

3.   *Stimulating and recording brain activity*
     a.   What are two ways of stimulating brain activity?

     b.   What type of information does microdialysis provide? Briefly describe this technique.

     c.   What is the principle underlying immunohistochemistry? What kind of information does it provide?

4. *Studying the structure of living human brains*
   a. Describe the process of computerized axial tomography. What sort of information does it provide?

   b. Describe the process of magnetic resonance imaging.

5. *Measuring human brain activity*
   a. What does the EEG record. What are some of its uses?

   b. What is an evoked potential?

   c. What is the principle underlying magnetoencephalography (MEG)?

   d. What is the principle behind positron-emission tomography? What are some advantages and disadvantages of this technique?

e. How is regional cerebral blood flow measured? What are two chemicals that appear to increase blood flow to the most active areas of the brain?

f. How does functional MRI differ from standard MRI. What are its advantages?

POSTTEST

Multiple-Choice Questions

1. Which is true concerning the spinal cord?
   a. Sensory neurons enter on the ventral side; motor neurons exit on the dorsal side.
   b. Cell bodies of sensory neurons lie outside the CNS in the dorsal root ganglia.
   c. Cell bodies of motor neurons lie outside the CNS in the ventral root ganglia.
   d. All of the above are true.

2. The parasympathetic system
   a. is sometimes called the "fight or flight" system.
   b. has a chain of interconnected ganglia along the thoracic and lumbar regions of the spinal cord.
   c. uses norepinephrine as its transmitter to end organs, whereas the sympathetic system uses acetylcholine.
   d. is an energy-conserving system.

3. Concerning the cranial nerves
   a. the first two enter the forebrain, with nuclei in the olfactory bulb and thalamus.
   b. nerves 3-12 enter the medulla.
   c. all have both sensory and motor components.
   d. all have only sensory components.

4. The hindbrain
   a. consists of four parts: the superior and inferior colliculi, the tectum, and the tegmentum.
   b. contains the reticular formation and raphe system.
   c. controls the pituitary gland.
   d. consists of the pons, which is adjacent to the spinal cord; the medulla, which is rostral to the pons; and the cerebellum, ventral to the pons.

5. The medulla
   a. contains prominent axons crossing from one side of the brain to the other.
   b. is part of the limbic system.
   c. contains nuclei that control vital functions.
   d. is especially important for working memory.

6. The cerebellum
   a. contributes to the control of movement and the organization of sensory information that guides movement.
   b. is concerned mostly with visual location in space.
   c. is located immediately ventral to the pons.
   d. more than one of the above.

7. The components of the midbrain include
   a. the superior and inferior colliculi in the tectum, involved in sensory processing.
   b. the tegmentum, containing nuclei of the third and fourth cranial nerves, part of the reticular formation, and pathways connecting higher and lower structures.
   c. the substantia nigra, origin of a dopamine-containing pathway that deteriorates in Parkinson's disease.
   d. all of the above.

8. The limbic system
   a. is a set of isolated areas that are important for different aspects of memory.
   b. is a set of interlinked structures that are important for motivated and emotional behaviors.
   c. is another term for the basal ganglia.
   d. gets its name from the Latin word for bridge.

9. The hypothalamus
   a. contains parts of the reticular formation and raphe system.
   b. is part of the basal ganglia.
   c. is important for motivated behaviors and hormonal control.
   d. is connected only with the brain stem.

10. The basal ganglia
    a. are composed primarily of the caudate nucleus, putamen, and globus pallidus.
    b. control movement directly via axons to the spinal cord.
    c. are primarily concerned with sensory processing.
    d. all of the above.

11. The hippocampus
    a. controls breathing, heart rate, and other vital reflexes.
    b. provides the major control for the pituitary gland.
    c. is part of the basal ganglia.
    d. none of the above.

12. The thalamus contains
    a. the superior and inferior colliculi.
    b. nuclei that project to particular areas of cerebral cortex.
    c. nuclei that regulate the pituitary.
    d. nuclei having to do with motivated behaviors, such as eating, drinking, sex, fighting, arousal level, and temperature regulation.

13. Cerebrospinal fluid
    a. is formed by cells lining the four ventricles.
    b. flows from the lateral ventricles to the third and fourth ventricles, and from there either to the central canal of the spinal cord or to the subarachnoid space, where it is reabsorbed into the blood vessels.
    c. cushions the brain and provides buoyancy.
    d. all of the above.

14. The laminae of the cortex
    a. usually consist of only two layers, one of axons and one of cell bodies.
    b. are always the same thickness throughout the brain of a given species, though they may differ across species.
    c. consist of up to six layers, which vary in thickness across the various brain areas.
    d. are present only in humans; other mammals have cells and axons mixed together in the cortex.

15. Which of the following is true of cortical columns?
    a. Columns run parallel to the laminae, across the surface of the cortex.
    b. There are six columns in the human brain, and only one or two in other mammals.
    c. Cells within a column have similar response properties.
    d. The properties of cells within a column change systematically from top to bottom; cells at the top may respond to one stimulus, while those at the bottom respond to a different one.

16. Association areas of the cortex
    a. get all their input from the sensory cortex.
    b. receive input directly from the thalamus, as well as from the sensory areas of cortex.
    c. receive input only from the thalamus.
    d. are areas set aside for a special kind of "associational" information.

17. Which is true of the occipital lobe?
    a. It is located at the posterior end of the cortex and contains primary visual cortex.
    b. It is located at the sides of the brain and is concerned mostly with perception of complex visual patterns.
    c. It is located immediately behind the central sulcus and contains the postcentral gyrus.
    d. It is located at the top of the brain and contributes to somatosensory processing.

18. Which is true of the parietal lobe?
    a. It contains the primary receiving area for axons carrying touch sensations and other skin and muscle information.
    b. It has a somewhat complicated spatial representation of the body on the postcentral gyrus.
    c. Damage to it on one side sometimes produces neglect of the opposite side of the body.
    d. All of the above are true.

19. The temporal lobe
    a. is located immediately in front of the central sulcus.
    b. is involved in some complex aspects of visual processing.
    c. has as its only function the processing of simple auditory information.
    d. none of the above.

20. Damage to the frontal lobe
    a. may cause losses of initiative and of social inhibitions and produce difficulties with delayed response tasks.
    b. is still a widely used surgical technique for mental patients because of its remarkable calming and normalizing tendencies without noticeable side effects.
    c. produces drastic impairments in intelligence.
    d. all of the above.

21. A stereotaxic instrument is used for
    a. producing current to make lesions.
    b. producing evoked potentials.
    c. locating small structures deep within the brain.
    d. recording EEGs.

22. The lesion method
    a. requires careful interpretation of behavioral deficits, including multiple kinds of tests.
    b. uses histological techniques to produce lesions.
    c. is flawed because lowering the electrode kills so many neurons that it is impossible to determine whether a behavioral deficit is a result of the electrical lesion or of the extensive damage produced by the electrode on its way to the lesion site.
    d. more than one of the above.

23. Which of the following is *not* a method of producing a lesion or ablation?
    a. surgical removal of brain tissue with a knife or vacuum suction.
    b. autoradiography.
    c. administering a localized electrical current.
    d. administering a neurotoxin, such as 6-hydroxydopamine.

24. The gene knock-out approach
    a. refers to the administration of large doses of genes to knock out certain brain areas.
    b. refers to the directed mutation of a specific gene that codes for a particular protein that may be important for production of a neurotransmitter or for another cellular function.
    c. is a method used to stimulate the production of certain gene products that knock out specific behaviors.
    d. unlike other lesion techniques, has no problems of interpretation.

25. Microdialysis is used primarily to
    a. measure the release of neurotransmitters during behavior.
    b. label the production of proteins or peptides in particular types of tissues.
    c. record electrical activity of brain areas during behavior.
    d. inactivate a brain area briefly, in order to infer its function.

26. Autoradiography
    a. is used primarily to measure blood flow to various brain areas.
    b. uses the principle that atoms with odd atomic weights have inherent rotation that can be altered by a magnetic field.
    c. may use radioactively labeled 2-deoxy-D-glucose to map relative activity levels in the brain.
    d. may use radioactively labeled antibodies to locate an area that has been damaged.

27. Computerized axial tomography
    a. is preferable to other means of detecting abnormalities because it uses no dyes, X rays, or radioactive chemicals.
    b. uses an EEG record to determine regional cerebral blood flow.
    c. uses radioactive elements that emit positrons, which collide with electrons, releasing two gamma rays for each collision; these gamma rays are recorded.
    d. uses dye injected into the blood for contrast, and multiple X rays through the head at different angles; a computer then constructs an image of the brain.

28. An evoked potential
    a. is recorded from an intracellular electrode in a single neuron.
    b. is an electrical response to a sensory stimulus, recorded using an EEG apparatus.
    c. is used to produce a sham lesion.
    d. is the electrical output of the brain in the absence of external sensory stimuli.

29. Functional MRI
    a. is used to infer an increase in brain activity, because the delivery of O_2 by hemoglobin to specific brain areas can be measured.
    b. provides the same information as standard MRI, but for a larger area of the brain.
    c. is used to record electrical activity of brain areas.
    d. is used to delete genes for knock-out experiments.

Answers to Multiple-Choice Questions

1. b	6. a	11. d	16. b	21. c	26. c
2. d	7. d	12. b	17. a	22. a	27. d
3. a	8. b	13. d	18. d	23. b	28. b
4. b	9. c	14. c	19. b	24. b	29. a
5. c	10. a	15. c	20. a	25. a	

Helpful Hints

1. To remember the 12 cranial nerves, use this mnemonic device:

1.	On	(Olfactory)
2.	Old	(Optic)
3.	Olympia's	(Oculomotor)
4.	Towering	(Trochlear)
5.	Tops,	(Trigeminal)
6.	A	(Abducens)
7.	Firm,	(Facial)
8.	Staid	(Statoacoustic)
9.	German	(Glossopharengial)
10.	Viewed	(Vagus)
11.	A lot of	(Accessory)
12.	Hops	(Hypogastric)

2. To remember the functions of the hypothalamus, think of the "4 Fs": Fighting, Fleeing, Feeding, and Reproductive Behavior.

Diagrams

1. In the following diagram of a sagittal section through the human brain, label the following structures: cerebral cortex, parietal lobe, occipital lobe, frontal lobe, cingulate gyrus, corpus callosum, thalamus, hypothalamus, superior and inferior colliculi, midbrain, cerebellum, pons, pituitary gland, tissue dividing the lateral ventricles, medulla, spinal cord, central canal of the spinal cord.

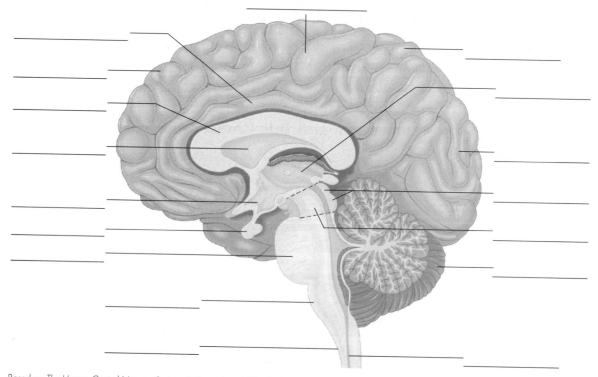

Based on *The Human Central Nervous System: A Synopsis and Atlas*, by R. Nieuwenhuys, J. Voogd, and C. van Huijzen Springer-Verlag, 1988.

2. In the following diagram of a cross section through the spinal cord, label the following directions or structures: dorsal, ventral, sensory nerve, dorsal root ganglion, motor nerve, white matter, gray matter, central canal.

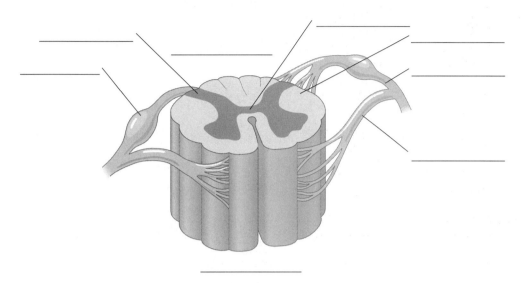

3. In the following diagram of the human cerebral cortex, label the following structures: central sulcus, precentral gyrus, postcentral gyrus, occipital lobe, frontal lobe, parietal lobe, and temporal lobe. Give the functions of each brain area.

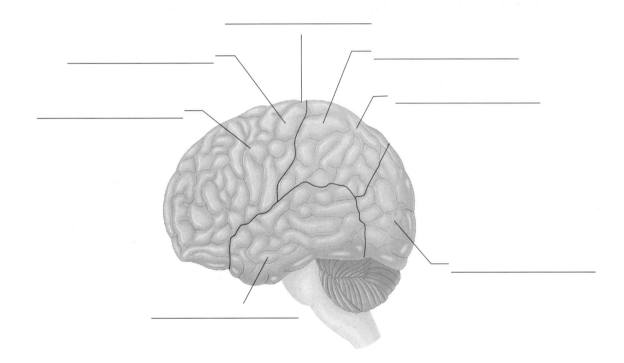

5

THE DEVELOPMENT AND
EVOLUTION OF THE BRAIN

INTRODUCTION

The central nervous system develops from two long thin lips on the surface of the embryo that merge to form a fluid-filled tube. The forward end of the tube enlarges to become the forebrain, midbrain, and hindbrain; the rest becomes the spinal cord. Cerebrospinal fluid continues to fill the central canal of the spinal cord and four hollow ventricles of the brain.

There are four major stages in the development of neurons: proliferation, migration, differentiation, and myelination. During proliferation, cells lining the ventricles divide. Some of the new cells remain in place and continue dividing, whereas others migrate beyond previous cells to their new destinations. Differentiation includes formation of the axon and dendrites and is influenced by chemical interactions with surrounding neurons. Myelination is the formation, by glial cells, of insulating sheaths around axons, which increase the speed of transmission. Brain growth consists primarily of the addition of new units, such as the glomeruli of the olfactory bulb and columns of cerebral cortex, but there may be some increase in the size of the units as well.

There is an initial overproduction of neurons; those that fail to form synapses with appropriate target cells die. The process of programmed cell death, or apoptosis, can be prevented if the neuron receives a neurotrophin from the target cell. Rita Levi-Montalcini discovered the first neurotrophin, nerve growth factor (NGF), which promotes survival of neurons of the sympathetic nervous system. Several additional neurotrophins have been discovered; different ones are effective for different kinds of axons. In addition to preventing apoptosis, neurotrophins may also enhance axonal branching and promote regrowth of axons after injury.

As the brain grows, axons must travel long distances to reach their appropriate targets. They are guided by concentration gradients of chemicals, such as the protein TOP_{DV}, which guides retinal neurons to the appropriate part of the tectum. After axons reach the general area of their target, they begin to form synapses with postsynaptic cells. These target cells receive an overabundance of synapses; they gradually strengthen some synapses and reject others. Initially, there are many tentative connections between axons and target cells; later, fewer but stronger attachments develop. The postsynaptic cell's acceptance of synapses from some axons is influenced by the chemical markers on the axon and increased attractiveness due to simultaneous activity by two or more axons. As many as half to two-thirds of neurons in certain areas fail to form any lasting synapses and, as a result, die. The overproduction of neurons and subsequent pruning of unsuccessful connections provide a process of selection of the fittest or most informative connections and enable the nervous system to compensate for variations in body size.

Environmental enrichment results in a thicker cortex, more dendritic branching, and enhanced performance on learning tasks. Effects of enrichment, or of sensory deprivation, have been observed in species as diverse as honeybees, fish, birds, rats and humans, although it is sometimes difficult to determine cause and effect relationships. The developing brain is more vulnerable than the adult brain to the effects of alcohol and other toxic chemicals, infections, hormonal imbalances, and malnutrition.

70

It is difficult to infer the evolution of brain or behavior. However, if a given structure is organized similarly in all mammals, we can infer that that genes regulating the formation of that structure were inherited from a common ancestor. Brain mass is highly correlated with both body size and the mother's basal metabolic rate. However, primates have larger brains than would be predicted by either of these factors. Although overall brain size generally correlates well with the size of its substructures, certain brain areas are larger or smaller than expected. The size of a given brain area corresponds roughly to the extent to which a species uses that area for a specific function. Both absolute brain size and brain-to-body ratio are sometimes correlated with measures of intelligence, across species and among humans. However, it is difficult to measure comparative intelligence across species. Although genetic factors contribute to variations in total brain size, improved health and nutrition probably account for the increased brain sizes in the past 200 years.

KEY TERMS AND CONCEPTS

The development of the brain
1. The growth and differentiation of the vertebrate brain
    Early development of the nervous system
        Neural tube
        Hindbrain
        Midbrain
        Forebrain
        Spinal cord
        Central canal of spinal cord
        Ventricles of brain
        Cerebrospinal fluid (CSF)
    The growth and development of neurons
        Proliferation of new cells
        Migration beyond previous cells
        Differentiation, forming axon first and then dendrites
        Myelination of some axons, continuing for years
        Organization of brain areas
            Olfactory bulb glomeruli
            Cortical columns
            Addition of new units
            Expansion of old units
    Determinants of neuron survival
        Nerve growth factor (NGF)
            Rita Levi-Montalcini
            Apoptosis
        Other neurotrophins
            Brain-derived neurotrophic factor (BDNF)
            Neurotrophins 3, 4/5, 6
        Functions of neurotrophins
            Prevent apoptosis
            Increase branching of incoming axons
            Decrease pain and increase axon regrowth after injury
        Overproduction of neurons and massive cell death
            Survival of the fittest
            Compensation for unpredictable variations in body size

71

2. Pathfinding by axons
   Chemical pathfinding by axons
      Specificity of axon connections
         Axons to extra leg of salamander
         Optic tract axons to tectum of newts and fish
      Chemical gradients
         TOP$_{DV}$
      Many tentative connections, followed by fewer but stronger ones
   Competition among axons as a general principle
      Neural Darwinism

3. Fine-tuning by experience
      Enriched environment
         Thicker cortex
         More dendritic branches
         Improved learning
      Bird song learning
         Decreases number, but increases size, of dendritic spines
      Lack of visual experience
         Kittens: anterior ectosylvian region of parietal lobe
            Normally responsive only to visual stimuli
            After visual deprivation, responsive to auditory and tactile stimuli
         Blind humans
            Parts of visual cortex become sensitive to auditory and touch stimuli
      Children with extensive early music training
         Absolute pitch
         Larger area of left temporal cortex
      Extensive experience with stringed instrument: larger area of postcentral gyrus of right hemisphere
      Combinations of chemical and experiential effects
         Chemical gradients
         Spontaneous action potentials
         Simultaneous activity of axons from nearby retinal areas
            Lateral geniculate

4. The vulnerable developing brain
      Impaired thyroid function in infancy: permanent mental retardation
      Fetal alcohol syndrome
         Short, less branched dendrites
      Rett syndrome: mental retardation in girls
         Short dendrites with few branches or spines
         Possible deficit in neurotrophins

The evolution of the brain and its capacities
1. Inferring the evolution of brain and behavior
   Limited inferences from fossils or current species
   Similarity of some areas of cortex among mammals
   Dissimilarities of other cortical areas

2. What makes the human brain special?
   Size
      Correlation of brain size with body size
      Correlation with mother's basal metabolic rate
      Primates: larger and more folded brains than predicted

72

Growth of the whole brain and its structures
    Parallel growth of different structures
    Some structures unusually large, if important to organism
Is bigger better? (And if so, why?)
    Larger brains: increased distances slow communication
    Brain-to-body ratio
    Learning one task: helps or hinders learning second task
    Concept of oddity
Brain size and IQ performance among humans
    Correlations between brain size and intelligence
    MRI
Brain size, IQ, and sex
    No consistent relationship between body size and IQ
    Women: greater neuron density in temporal cortex, larger corpus
        callosum
    Sex differences on certain tasks
Organization
    Microscopic details
    Prefrontal and auditory cortex relatively larger in humans
    Primary visual and primary motor cortex and olfactory bulb relatively
        smaller in humans
    More axons from one cortical area to another
    More axons from basal ganglia to cortex
    More widespread monoamine axons
The evolution of the brain and intelligence

SHORT-ANSWER QUESTIONS

The development of the brain
1. *The growth and differentiation of the vertebrate brain*
    a.   Describe the formation of the central nervous system in the embryo. What happens to the fluid-filled cavity?

    b.   What are the three main divisions of the brain?

c.   What are the four major stages in the development of neurons? Describe the processes in each.

d.   What technical development by LaMantia and Purves increased our understanding of brain development? What was their major finding?

e.   What is apoptosis? What type of chemical can prevent apoptosis?

f.   Who discovered nerve growth factor? What happens if a neuron in the sympathetic nervous system does not receive enough nerve growth factor?

g.   List five neurotrophins. What three functions do they serve?

2.   *Pathfinding by axons*
    a.   What did Weiss observe in his experiments on salamanders' extra limbs? What principle did he conclude directed the innervation of the extra limb? Is this principle still believed to be correct?

b.	What did Sperry observe when he damaged the optic nerve of newts? What happened when he rotated the eye by 180 degrees? How did the newt with the rotated eye see the world?

c.	What conclusion did these results suggest?

d.	What is TOP_{DV}? What is its role in directing retinal axons to the tectum?

e.	Describe the pattern of goldfish retinal connections when half the tectum was destroyed. when half the retina was destroyed. What does this suggest about the precision of connections of axons with target cells?

f.	What happens to axons that form active synapses? What happens to axons that do not form active synapses?

g.	Describe the principle of neural Darwinism. How does this relate to the initial overproduction and subsequent death of large numbers of neurons?

h.   What factors might lead a postsynaptic cell to accept certain synapses but not others?

3.   *Fine-tuning by experience*
   a.   Describe the effects of environmental "enrichment".

   b.   What physiological process appears to be correlated with song learning in mynah birds?

   c.   Describe the effects of early visual deprivation on brain development in kittens. in humans.

   d.   What is a brain correlate of absolute pitch? What evidence suggests that this may result from extensive early musical training?

   e.   What brain area is frequently larger in people who had extensive experience playing stringed instruments?

f. How does a lateral geniculate neuron "know" which axons originated near one another in the retina?

4. *The vulnerable developing brain*
   a. What are the effects of thyroid deficiency in adulthood? Compare these with the effects of thyroid deficiency in infancy.

   b. Describe fetal alcohol syndrome. How are dendrites affected? How much alcohol is necessary to produce the syndrome?

The evolution of the brain and its capacities
1. *Inferring the evolution of the brain and behavior*
   a. What kinds of evidence can we use to make inferences about the evolution of the brain?

   The skull size & shape since there are v. few brain fossils

2. *What makes the human brain special?*
   a. Besides body mass, what is a good predictor of the brain mass at birth?

   The mothers Basal Metabolic Rate

   b. In what way do the brains of primates differ from predictions based on body mass or mother's metabolic rate?

   Body mass & Brain size direct correltn. differs. from prev. pred. b/c if body mass is already a determng factr. than the mothrs. BMR. will have little or no effect if all were placed on 7 plain and were to determn. size But w/in same grp. BMR. would be primary factr. outsd. of grp. body mass. would weigh a heavier factr.
   77

c. Describe some of the differences among mammalian brains.

singl and *organization*
↓   *of cortex & obr.*
                 brain organs
compard.to   *including. the*
B.M.   *absence or prcs.*

d. What disadvantage is encountered by larger brains, compared to smaller brains? How might a larger brain solve this problem?

Longer time for signals & comm.
b/c of Incrsd. space
        Prac/study/know your stuff

e. What can we say about monkeys' and rats' relative abilities to acquire the concept of oddity?

Rats R less discr-minant of oddity than monkeys
Monkeys process of learning & registrng. odd things is long.
prob. w/ deciphrng. old from newly learnd matrls.

f. Describe the findings of the MRI study of college students with higher and lower IQ scores.

        Inclusv. b/c Sampl. study too small
students. w/ hér scores suppsdly. had largr. brains/heavier

g. What factors, other than genetics, have contributed to the increase in brain size in the past 200 to 300 years?

        Nutrition, Envirmntl. factrs

h. What are several distinctive features of the human brain?

More Axons. & closr.
Organization of Organs
Size
Ability to Expand

78

POSTTEST

Multiple-Choice Questions

1. The neural tube
   a. arises from a pair of long thin lips that merge around a fluid-filled cavity.
   b. develops into the spinal cord; the brain arises from a separate structure.
   c. eventually merges to form a solid structure, squeezing out the primitive cerebrospinal fluid.
   d. none of the above.

2. The four major stages in the development of neurons, in order, are
   a. proliferation, differentiation, migration, myelination.
   b. proliferation, growth, myelination, migration.
   c. proliferation, migration, myelination, growth.
   d. proliferation, migration, differentiation, myelination.

3. The cerebral cortex develops
   a. from cells whose characteristics are fully programmed genetically.
   b. from cells proliferating on the outermost layer of the brain.
   c. from the inside out, with new cells migrating beyond previous cells.
   d. from the outside in, with new cells remaining nearer their site of formation in the ventricles.

4. Which of the following is true?
   a. Myelination is complete by the end of the first year in humans.
   b. Neurons experimentally transplanted from one site to another at an intermediate stage of development keep some properties of cells in the old location and develop some that are characteristic of their new location.
   c. Dendrites usually form before axons, and are usually fully formed before migration begins.
   d. Neurons are incapable of conducting action potentials until they are fully myelinated.

5. As the olfactory bulbs grow
   a. the number of glomeruli stays the same, but the size of each glomerulus increases.
   b. the glomeruli that were characteristic of the infant brain merge to form one continuous functional unit in the adult.
   c. the size of each glomerulus increases considerably, but the number of glomeruli actually decreases.
   d. the number of glomeruli increases, and the average size of each glomerulus also increases.

6. Apoptosis
   a. is the cell's "suicide program".
   b. occurs in only a few areas of the brain.
   c. is caused by an excess of neurotrophin.
   d. was the first neurotrophin to be discovered.

7. Nerve growth factor
   a. is important for the health of all neurons throughout life.
   b. is important for the survival and growth of sympathetic neurons.
   c. is important for the survival of all sensory neurons, but not motor neurons.
   d. is important for the initial survival of all neurons but becomes less important after synapses are formed.

8. When Paul Weiss grafted an extra leg onto a salamander
   a. the extra leg received no neurons and therefore could not move.
   b. the extra leg moved in the opposite direction from the normal adjacent leg.
   c. the extra leg moved in synchrony with the normal adjacent leg.
   d. the leg degenerated because the immune system rejected it.

9. Sperry's work with the eyes of newts and goldfish led him to conclude that
   a. neurons attach to postsynaptic cells randomly, and the postsynaptic cell confers specificity of function.
   b. axons follow a chemical trail that places them in the general vicinity of their target.
   c. innervation in the sensory system is guided by specific genetic information, whereas that in the motor system is random.
   d. neurons follow specific genetic information that directs each of them to precisely the right postsynaptic cell.

10. TOP_{DV}
   a. is a trophic factor necessary for the survival of neurons of the sympathetic nervous system.
   b. is a protein that is more concentrated in neurons of the dorsal retina and the ventral tectum than in the ventral retina and dorsal tectum.
   c. is a protein that guides axons to the developing legs of newts.
   d. is a protein that causes a group of neurons that possess it to fire together, thereby increasing their chance of survival.

11. If the caudal half of the goldfish tectum is removed and the optic nerve is cut, the retinal axons that would have made contact with the removed part
   a. form synapses with the most caudal part of the remaining tectum.
   b. die, because their target is missing.
   c. make random connections throughout the remaining tectum, because their chemical "map" is missing.
   d. grow back toward the retina and make synapses with other retinal neurons.

12. Massive cell death early in development
   a. would be so maladaptive that it hardly ever occurs.
   b. occurs only when the sensory environment has been highly restricted or when the fetus has been exposed to toxins.
   c. occurs as a result of genetic mistakes, which fail to direct the cells to their genetically programmed target. As a result the neurons wander aimlessly until they die.
   d. is a normal result of unsuccessful competition for synapses and growth factors.

13. Which of the following is true?
   a. A postsynaptic cell is more likely to form synapses with groups of axons whose activity is uncorrelated with one another than with those that are simultaneously active, because that provides the postsynaptic cell with a greater range of information.
   b. If a postsynaptic cell finds an axon unacceptable, it sends out a rejection chemical that causes the axon to degenerate.
   c. Excess neurons enable the nervous system to compensate for variations in body size.
   d. All of the above are true.

14. Neural Darwinism
    a. was formulated by Roger Sperry.
    b. proposes that synapses form somewhat randomly at first; those that work best are kept, while the others degenerate.
    c. has recently been shown to be false.
    d. all of the above.

15. Environmental enrichment
    a. produces greater dendritic branching.
    b. produces changes in the structure of neurons, but no changes in their function.
    c. produces changes in the function of neurons, but no changes in their structure.
    d. has beneficial effects only in primates.

16. During their first year, mynah birds
    a. have decreasing numbers of dendritic spines in the song control areas of the brain.
    b. have an increase in size of the surviving dendritic spines.
    c. learn many songs, but, by the end of the year, have decreased ability to learn additional songs.
    d. all of the above.

17. Mental retardation
    a. can be caused by thyroid deficiency during adulthood.
    b. results directly from excessively high levels of thyroid hormones during infancy.
    c. can be caused by thyroid deficiency in infancy.
    d. almost never results from genetic mutations.

18. Fetal alcohol syndrome
    a. results in decreased alertness, hyperactivity, varying degrees of mental retardation, motor problems, heart defects, and facial abnormalities.
    b. is observed only in children whose mothers drank very large quantities of alcohol throughout pregnancy.
    c. results from excessively long, heavily branched dendrites.
    d. all of the above.

19. Which of the following is a factor correlated with brain mass?
    a. the mother's basal metabolic rate
    b. body mass
    c. health and nutrition
    d. all of the above

20. Which of the following is true concerning brain size and intelligence?
    a. MRI results have shown a correlation between IQ and brain size in college students.
    b. Animals with small brains, such as rats, are unable to grasp the concept of oddity.
    c. The increased intelligence of humans, compared with other primates, is due entirely to our larger brains, since the organization of our brains is essentially identical to that of other primates.
    d. Examination of Einstein's brain revealed that his great intelligence was due primarily to his greatly enlarged frontal lobes.

Answers to Multiple-Choice Questions

1. a	6. a	11. a	16. d
2. d	7. b	12. d	17. c
3. c	8. c	13. c	18. a
4. b	9. b	14. b	19. d
5. d	10. b	15. a	20. a

BRAIN PARTS AND DEVELOPMENT

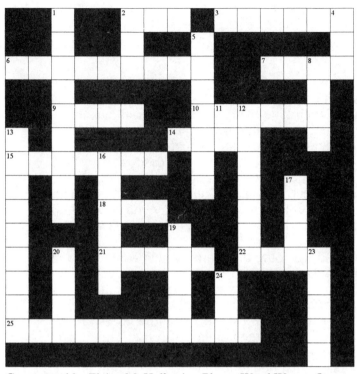

Constructed by Elaine M. Hull using Plexus Word Weaver®

Across

2 Master gland (abbr.)

3 Distruction or disruption of an area of the brain

6 Device for cutting the brain into thin slices

7 Acronym for a method of estimating brain activity using radioactive substances injected into the circulatory system

9 Hindbrain structure anterior or dorsal to the medulla

10 An interconnected set of subcortical forebrain structures

14 ____-knockout, method of producing a specific mutation

15 Structure in the basal ganglia

18 Method of measuring the brain's magnetic fields (abbr.)

21 Group of neurons in pons and medulla whose axons extend throughout the forebrain

22 Limbic system structure in the temporal lobe (abbr.)

25 Division of the autonomic nervous system responsible for "fight or flight"

Down

1 Lobe containing visual cortex

2 Acronym for a method of mapping brain activity by recording radioactivity from injected chemicals

4 A neurotrophin that prevents apoptosis in the sympathetic nervous system (abbr.)

5 Result of lesions to parietal lobe

8 Kluver-____ syndrome, the result of temporal lobe lesions

11 Opposite of 'out'

12 Most posterior or ventral part of hindbrain

13 Programmed cell death

16 Function for which hippocampus is important

17 Color of brain containing cell bodies

19 Color of brain containing myelinated axons

20 Control procedure for lesion experiments

23 protuberance of the cerebral cortex

24 Acronym for a method of brain imaging using a magnetic field and a radiofrequency field to align atoms, then removing the fields and measuring released energy

6

VISION

INTRODUCTION

Sensory systems, including vision, are concerned with reception (absorption of physical energy) and transduction of that energy into neural activity that encodes some aspect of the stimulus. The structure of each kind of sensory receptor allows it to be stimulated maximally by one kind of energy, and little or not at all by other forms of energy. The brain interprets any information sent by nerves that synapse with those receptors as being about that form of energy. This principle was described by Müller as the law of specific nerve energies. This principle has been updated with three additional stipulations: (1) increases and decreases from a spontaneous rate of firing may signal different stimuli; (2) the timing of action potentials may code certain kinds of sensory information; and (3) perception is determined by activity of the whole system.

Light is focused by the cornea and lens onto the retina, which contains two kinds of receptors. Cones are most densely packed in the fovea, an area in the center of the retina with the most acute (detailed) vision. This acuity is largely the result of the small number of cones that synapse with each bipolar cell. Rods are located more peripherally in the retina than are cones and are more sensitive to low levels of light. Furthermore, each bipolar receives input from a large number of rods. This improves sensitivity to dim light but sacrifices acuity.

All photopigments contain 11-cis-retinal bound to one of several opsins. Light converts 11-cis-retinal to all-trans-retinal, which in turn activates second-messenger molecules. This results in the closing of sodium channels, which hyperpolarizes the receptor. In the dark the receptor steadily discharges an inhibitory transmitter; light decreases the output of that transmitter.

Cones mediate color vision because three different photopigments are found in three types of cones. Each photopigment is maximally sensitive to one wavelength of light but responds less readily to other wavelengths. Thus, each wavelength produces a certain ratio of responses from the three receptors; the ratio remains essentially constant regardless of brightness. Rods, in contrast to cones, contain only one photopigment and therefore do not contribute directly to our perception of colors. Processing of color vision beyond the receptor level depends on an opponent-process mechanism, in which a given cell responds to one color with increased firing and to another color with a decrease below its spontaneous rate of firing.

Visual input is processed neurally in order to provide an organized, useful representation of the environment. A visual receptor is able not only to stimulate its own bipolar(s) but also to inhibit activity in neighboring bipolars. It accomplishes this feat through the cooperation of horizontal cells, which receive input from a number of receptors and synapse with a number of bipolars. Electrical activity can flow in all directions in horizontal cells. The advantage of this arrangement is that borders are enhanced at the expense of redundant input. The process is called lateral inhibition.

A receptive field of a neuron in the visual system is that area of the retina in which the presence or absence of light affects that neuron's activity. Most receptive fields contain both excitatory and inhibitory regions. The receptive fields of bipolar, ganglion, and geniculate cells are concentric circles. For some cells light in the center is excitatory, and for other cells it is inhibitory; light in the surround has the opposite effect. Cells in the visual cortex (occipital lobe) have bar shaped receptive fields as a result of summing the receptive fields of their lateral geniculate cell inputs.

84

Ganglion cells have been divided into two major types. Parvocellular neurons are relatively small cells, located in or near the fovea, that respond differentially to colors. Because they have small receptive fields, they are highly sensitive to details. Magnocellular neurons are larger, are spread evenly across the retina, and respond best to moving stimuli; they respond only briefly to a sustained stimulus. Because their receptive fields are large, they are not sensitive to small details; they also do not respond differentially to colors. A smaller group of cells, koniocellular neurons, respond weakly to light and are poorly understood. At the lateral geniculate nucleus of the thalamus, most parvocellular ganglion cell axons synapse with parvocellular geniculate neurons, and most magnocellular ganglion cell axons synapse with magnocellular geniculate neurons.

Most of the input from the lateral geniculate goes to the primary visual cortex (area V1), which in turn projects to secondary visual cortex (area V2). From area V2, information branches out to numerous additional areas. At the cortex, the parvocellular and magnocellular systems split into three pathways. One pathway processes shape information from the parvocellular system. Another processes movement information from the magnocellular system. The third pathway processes brightness input from the magnocellular system and color information from the parvocellular system.

David Hubel and Torsten Wiesel received the Nobel Prize for their pioneering work on feature detectors in the visual cortex. They distinguished three categories of neurons: simple, complex, and end-stopped, or hypercomplex. Simple cells respond maximally to a bar oriented in a particular direction and in a particular location on the retina. Their receptive fields can be mapped into fixed excitatory and inhibitory areas. Complex cells, on the other hand, have larger receptive fields, respond to correctly oriented bars located anywhere within the field (i.e., they do not have fixed excitatory and inhibitory areas), and respond best to stimuli moving perpendicular to the receptive field axis. End-stopped, or hypercomplex, cells are like complex cells, except for an area of strong inhibition at one end of the field. Cortical cells with similar properties are grouped in columns perpendicular to the surface.

Additional processing of shape information is accomplished by the inferior temporal cortex, which responds preferentially to highly complex shapes such as hands or faces. Cells in this area ignore changes in size and perspective; they may contribute to our capacity for shape constancy. Damage to the pattern pathway results in visual agnosia, the inability to recognize visual objects. Some people have difficulty identifying almost all objects; others experience agnosia for only one or a few classes of stimuli. Although each cell in inferior temporal cortex is more responsive to some stimuli than to others, it does respond fairly strongly to a range of similar objects. Therefore, no one cell is the only detector for a given object.

Area V4, or a nearby area, is especially important for color constancy. Animals with damage to this area retain some color vision, but lose the ability to recognize the color of an object across lighting conditions. Area V4 receives input from the "blobs" of area V1, which in turn receive input from parvocellular color processing cells and magnocellular brightness cells. Area V4 also contributes to visual attention.

Some cells in the magnocellular system are specialized for depth perception. They are sensitive to the amount of discrepancy between the images from the two eyes. Another branch of the magnocellular system detects motion. It projects to area V5 (middle temporal cortex, or MT) and an adjacent area (medial superior temporal cortex, MST). Neurons in these areas respond preferentially to different speeds and directions of movement, without analyzing the object that is moving. Many cells in MT respond best to moving borders of single objects, while cells in the dorsal part of MST prefer expanding, contracting, or rotating large scenes. These two types of cells send their output to the ventral part of MST, which allows us to perceive the motion of an object against a stationary field. There appears to be no single area of the brain that puts together all the information about a given object; perhaps the simultaneous processing of all the aspects of the object is sufficient.

Cells in the mammalian visual cortex are endowed at the individual's birth with certain adultlike characteristics. However, normal sensory experience is necessary to develop these characteristics fully and to prevent them from degenerating. If only one eye is deprived of vision during an early sensitive period, the brain becomes unresponsive to that eye. Input from the active eye displaces the early connections made by the inactive eye. It is likely that axons from the active eye compete successfully for nerve growth factor or some other neurotrophin provided by the postsynaptic cells. If both eyes are kept shut, cortical cells remain at least somewhat responsive to both eyes, though their responses are sluggish. Visual experience after the sensitive, or critical, period does not restore responsiveness to the previously inactive eye, unless the previously active eye is covered for a prolonged time. Other aspects of vision that require early experience for proper development are stereoscopic depth perception, ability to see lines of a given direction, and motion perception.

KEY TERMS AND CONCEPTS

Visual coding and the retinal receptors
1.   Reception, transduction, and coding
      From neuronal activity to perception
            Generator potential
            Shape of object not duplicated in brain
      General principles of sensory coding
            Law of specific nerve energies
            Spontaneous rate of firing
            Timing of action potentials

2.   The eye and its connections to the brain
      Cornea
      Pupil
      Lens
      Retina
      Fovea (pit)
      Visual streak
      Receptors
      Bipolar cells
      Ganglion cells
      Optic nerve
            Blind spot

3.   Visual receptors: Rods and cones
      Acuity
            Best in fovea
            Few receptors send input to each bipolar cell
      Sensitivity to dim light
            Best in periphery
            Many rods send input to each bipolar cell
      The chemical basis for receptor excitation
            Photopigments
            11-cis-retinal
            All-trans-retinal
            Opsins

86

Transduction
    Conversion of 11-cis-retinal to all-trans-retinal
    Second messenger molecules
    Hyperpolarization

4. Color vision
    Trichromatic (Young-Helmholtz) theory
        Psychophysical color matching
        Three different opsins bound to 11-cis-retinal in three types of cones
    Opponent-process (Hering) theory
        Negative afterimage
    Color blindness: sex linked

The neural basis of visual perception
1. An overview of the mammalian visual system
    Retina
        Receptors (rods and cones)
        Horizontal cells
        Bipolar cells
        Amacrine cells
        Ganglion cells
            Axons form optic nerve
            Optic chiasm
    Lateral geniculate nucleus
    Cerebral cortex

2. Mechanisms of processing in the visual system
    Receptive fields
    Lateral inhibition
        Horizontal cells
        Bipolar cells
    How receptive fields are built
        Concentric circles in retina and lateral geniculate
        Bars and edges in cortex

3. Concurrent pathways in the visual system
    In the retina and lateral geniculate
        Parvocellular: small cell bodies, small receptive fields, in fovea, good acuity,
            color discrimination
        Magnocellular: larger cell bodies, larger receptive fields, even distribution,
            best response to moving stimuli, no color discrimination
        Koniocellular: least responsive, least understood
        Lateral geniculate
            Parvocellular geniculate cells: input from parvocellular ganglion cells
            Magnocellular geniculate cells: input from magnocellular ganglion cells
    In the cerebral cortex
        Primary visual cortex, striate cortex (V1)
        Secondary visual cortex (V2)
        Thirty or more brain areas receiving visual input
        Three pathways
            Details of shape (parvocellular)
            Movement (magnocellular)
            Brightness (magnocellular) and color (parvocellular)

4.   The cerebral cortex: The shape pathway
      Hubel and Wiesel's cell types in primary visual cortex
            Binocular receptive fields, bar- or edge-shaped receptive fields
            Simple cells (V1)
                  Fixed excitatory and inhibitory zones in receptive fields
            Complex cells (V1 and V2)
                  Larger receptive fields
                  Cannot be mapped into excitatory and inhibitory zones
                  Response to moving bar of light
            End-stopped or hypercomplex cells
                  Strong inhibitory area at one end of bar-shaped receptive field
      The columnar organization of the visual cortex
            Columns perpendicular to surface
            Similar response properties within a column
      Are visual cortex cells feature detectors?
            Prolonged exposure: decreased sensitivity to feature
            Ambiguity of response of a single cell
            Spatial frequencies, sine-wave gratings
      Shape analysis beyond areas V1 and V2
            Inferior temporal cortex
                  Advanced pattern analysis
                  Shape constancy
                  Huge receptive fields, always include fovea
      Disorders of object recognition
            Visual agnosia
                  Prosopagnosia
                  Inferior temporal cortex and other cortical areas
                  Distinctive pattern across a population of neurons

5.   The cerebral cortex: The color pathway
      Area V1 "blobs"
            Input from parvocellular (color) and magnocellular (brightness) pathways
            Output to V2, V4, and posterior inferior temporal cortex
      Area V4
            Color constancy
            Visual attention

6.   The cerebral cortex: The motion and depth pathways
      Stereoscopic depth perception
            Magnocellular pathway
      Structures important for motion perception
            Area V5 (middle temporal cortex, MT)
            Medial superior temporal cortex (MST)
      Motion blindness

7.   Coordinating separate visual pathways
      Current hypothesis: No single part of the brain puts together information from
            different pathways
            Simultaneous processing of different aspects

The development of the visual system
1.   Infant vision
      More time looking at patterns
      Difficulty shifting attention

2. Effects of experience on visual development
    Effects of early lack of stimulation of one eye
        Blindness in deprived eye
    Effects of early lack of stimulation of both eyes
        Cortical cells: sluggish response to both eyes
        Difficulty identifying objects visually
        Sensitive, or critical, period
    Restoration of response after early deprivation of vision
        Lazy eye, or amblyopia ex anopsia
    Uncorrelated stimulation in both eyes
        Stereoscopic depth perception
        Retinal disparity
        Strabismus
        Synchronous messages
        Nerve growth factor (NGF) and other neurotrophins, including NT-4
    Effects of early exposure to a limited array of patterns
        Astigmatism
    Effects of not seeing objects in motion
        Stroboscopic illumination
        Motion blindness

SHORT-ANSWER QUESTIONS

Visual coding and the retinal receptors
1. *Reception, transduction and coding*
    a. Distinguish between reception, transduction, and coding.

    b. What is a generator potential?

    c. State the law of specific nerve energies. Who formulated it?

d.   How does this law apply to neurons with spontaneous firing rates?

e.   What two additional modifications of this principle seem necessary in light of current knowledge?

2.   *The eye and its connections to the brain*
     a.   What is the fovea? How did it get its name?

     b.   How have many bird species solved the problem of getting detailed information from two different directions?

     c.   Trace the path of visual information from a receptor to the optic nerve. What is the blind spot?

3.   *Visual receptors: Rods and cones*
     a.   Compare peripheral and foveal vision with regard to acuity, sensitivity to dim light, and color vision.

b. What is the specific role of light in the initiation of a response in a receptor?

c. What is the relationship of 11-cis-retinal to all-trans-retinal?

d. What kind of electrical response is produced in the receptor, and how does this affect the bipolars with which it synapses?

4. *Color vision*
    a. Why does the presence of cones in the retina of a given species not guarantee color vision? Why does color vision necessarily depend on the pattern of responses of a number of different neurons?

    b. How did Young and Helmholtz propose to account for color vision? On what kind of data was their theory based?

    c. What kind of theory did Hering propose? What observations supported his theory?

d.   What is an opsin? What is its role in a photopigment?

e.   What is the current relationship between the three-receptor and the opponent-process theories?

f.   What is the genetic basis for the most common form of color blindness? Why are more males than females color blind?

The neural basis of visual perception
1.   *An overview of the mammalian visual system*
     a.   Draw a diagram showing the relationships among the rods and cones, the bipolar and horizontal cells, and the ganglion and amacrine cells.

     b.   Axons of which kind of cell form the optic nerve? What is the name of the site where the right and left optic nerves meet? What percentage of axons cross to the opposite side of the brain in humans? in species with eyes far to the sides of their heads?

c.   Where do most axons in the optic nerve synapse? Where do some other optic nerve axons synapse?

d.   What is the destination of axons from the lateral geniculate nucleus?

2.   *Mechanisms of processing in the visual system*
    a.   What is the definition of the receptive field of a neuron in the visual system?

    b.   What is lateral inhibition? How does it enhance contrast?

    c.   How is lateral inhibition accomplished in the vertebrate retina?

    d.   If several bipolar cells provide input to a certain ganglion cell, what can be said about the location of their receptive fields relative to that of the ganglion cell?

e. How do receptive fields of ganglion cells and lateral geniculate cells differ from those of visual cortical cells?

f. Describe the set of synaptic connections that might produce a bar-shaped receptive field characteristic of cortical cells.

3. *Concurrent pathways in the visual system*
    a. Describe the characteristics of parvocellular ganglion cells.

    b. How do they differ from magnocellular ganglion cells?

    c. Which ganglion cells provide input to parvocellular geniculate neurons? to magnocellular geniculate neurons?

    d. What happens to the parvocellular and magnocellular pathways in the cortex? What type of information does each of the three main concurrent visual pathways process?

4. *The cerebral cortex: The shape pathway*
   a. For what accomplishment did David Hubel and Torsten Wiesel share the
       Nobel Prize?

   b. Describe the receptive fields of simple cells.

   c. What is the major difference between responses of simple and complex
       visual cortical cells?

   d. Describe the receptive field of an end-stopped, or hypercomplex, cell?

   e. What can be said about the receptive fields of neurons in a column in the
       visual cortex?

   f. What is a feature detector?

g.   What evidence suggests that neurons in areas V1 and V2 are feature detectors?

h.   What are the problems with that interpretation?

i.   Which area, beyond V1 and V2, is important for shape analysis? What is its major contribution?

j.   Describe the symptoms of visual agnosia. What is prosopagnosia?

5.   *The cerebral cortex: The color pathway*
   a.   What are the sources of input to the "blobs" of area V1? Where do the "blobs" send their output?

   b.   What appears to be the special function of area V4?

c.   What might the magnocellular pathway, which does not analyze color information directly, contribute to color constancy?

d.   To what other function does area V4 contribute?

6.   *The cerebral cortex: The motion and depth pathways*
   a.   Cells of which pathway are specialized for stereoscopic depth perception? To what aspect of the visual stimulus are they highly sensitive?

   b.   Which two areas of the cortex are specialized for motion perception? How "picky" are cells in these areas to the specific characteristics of the stimulus that is moving?

   c.   Describe the response characteristics of some cells in area V5.

   d.   Describe the preferred stimuli for many cells in the dosal part of area MST.

e. What is the role of cells in the ventral part of MST?

f. Describe the symptoms of motion blindness.

The development of the visual system
1. *Infant vision*
    a. What is the evidence that newborn infants can perceive complex stimuli? Do they see better in the periphery or in the center of their visual field?

    b. How easy is it for infants to shift their attention to other visual stimuli?

2. *Effects of experience on visual development*
    a. What is the effect of depriving only one eye of pattern vision during the critical period?

    b. For what human condition does this principle have relevance? What is the usual treatment for this condition? Why is it important to begin treatment as early as possible?

c. What happens if both eyes are kept shut early in life?

d. What is a sensitive or critical period?

e. Define retinal disparity. How does the brain use this information to produce stereoscopic depth perception?

f. What is strabismus? Does surgical correction in adulthood improve depth perception in people with this disorder?

g. What chemicals may normally promote survival of synapses from the most active eye?

h. What is the effect of supplying excess neurotrophins during the time when one eye is closed?

i. What happens to the response characteristics of visual cortical cells in a kitten exposed to only horizontal lines early in life?

j. What is astigmatism? What happens if a child has severe, uncorrected astigmatism during the first few years of life?

k. What was the effect of rearing kittens in an environment illuminated only by a strobe light?

POSTTEST

Multiple-Choice Questions

1. The one-to-one correspondence between some aspect of the physical stimulus and some aspect of the nervous system activity is known as
    a. reception
    b. transduction
    c. coding
    d. a generator potential

2. The law of specific nerve energies
    a. implies that if the visual receptors were connected to the auditory nerve, and the auditory receptors were connected to the optic nerve, we would "see" sounds and "hear" lights.
    b. states that the kind of message a nerve carries depends only on the kind of stimulus that initiated it; that is, light can give rise only to visual messages, and so on.
    c. is true as it was originally stated; therefore, both increases and decreases in firing rates of cells with spontaneous firing rates must signal the same thing.
    d. is no longer thought to be true, and is now only of historical interest.

3. The fovea
   a. is completely blind because axons from ganglion cells exit from the retina there.
   b. covers approximately half the retina.
   c. contains no rods and is bypassed by most blood vessels and axons of more distant ganglion cells.
   d. is color blind because it contains no cones but has good sensitivity to dim light.

4. Which of the following is true?
   a. The fovea is more sensitive to dim light than is the periphery.
   b. The fovea has more detailed vision because relatively few receptors synapse with each bipolar.
   c. Cones mediate more detailed vision because of their shape.
   d. Cones are situated peripherally in the retina, rods more centrally, though there is some overlap.

5. A photopigment molecule absorbs a photon of light whose energy converts
   a. all-trans-retinal to 11-cis-retinal. Somehow this leads to hyperpolarization of the receptor.
   b. opsin to all-trans-retinal. Somehow this leads to depolarization of the receptor.
   c. 11-cis-retinal to all-trans-retinal. Somehow this leads to depolarization of the receptor.
   d. 11-cis-retinal to all-trans-retinal. Somehow this leads to hyperpolarization of the receptor.

6. The opponent-process theory
   a. is now thought to describe color processing by neurons after the receptor level, whereas the Young-Helmholtz theory describes activity at the receptor level.
   b. is now thought to describe color processing at the receptor level, whereas the Young-Helmholtz theory describes processing at higher levels.
   c. states that each receptor is sensitive only to a narrow band of wavelengths of light and that wavelength bands of different receptor groups do not overlap.
   d. is true only for rods, not cones.

7. The most common form of color blindness
   a. is more common in women than in in men.
   b. has been well known since the earliest civilizations.
   c. is characterized by difficulty distinguishing blue from yellow.
   d. is characterized by difficulty distinguishing red from green.

8. Which of the following best describes the main route of visual information in the retina?
   a. receptor--> ganglion cell--> bipolar cell
   b. receptor--> bipolar cell--> ganglion cell
   c. receptor--> ganglion cell--> amacrine cell
   d. receptor--> horizontal cell--> amacrine cell

101

9. Which of the following is true concerning receptive fields?
   a. They are always defined as an area surrounding "their" neuron; the receptive field for a simple cortical cell is itself in the cortex.
   b. The presence of both excitatory and inhibitory areas in the same receptive field is maladaptive and is a holdover from an earlier, inefficient way of processing information.
   c. Receptive fields of simple cortical cells are circular.
   d. For mammalian ganglion and lateral geniculate cells, they are generally circular, with the center being either excitatory or inhibitory and the surround being the opposite.

10. Lateral inhibition
   a. increases sensitivity to dim light.
   b. ordinarily decreases contrast at borders.
   c. ordinarily heightens contrast at borders.
   d. interferes with processing of color information.

11. Horizontal cells
   a. send axons out of the retina through the blind spot.
   b. send graded inhibitory responses to neighboring bipolar cells.
   c. are located behind the receptors so that they are out of the way of incoming light bound for receptors.
   d. all of the above.

12. Parvocellular ganglion cells
   a. are highly sensitive to both detail and color.
   b. are located primarily in the periphery of the retina.
   c. are among the largest ganglion cells in the retina.
   d. respond only weakly to visual stimuli.

13. Parvocellular lateral geniculate neurons
   a. receive input primarily from parvocellular ganglion cells.
   b. receive input primarily from koniocellular ganglion cells.
   c. receive input primarily from magnocellular ganglion cells.
   d. receive more or less equal input from all types of ganglion cells.

14. The parvocellular and magnocellular systems
   a. merge in area V1 and remain one system for subsequent analysis.
   b. remain as two systems throughout visual processing.
   c. divide into three systems, with much of the parvocellular system continuing to analyze details of shape, most of the magnocellular system analyzing movement, and the third system containing parvocellular cells that analyze color and magnocellular cells that analyze brightness.
   d. divide into many concurrent pathways, each analyzing a different color, direction of movement, or shape, but then converge in one master area, where all of these aspects are put together into a unified perception.

15. Simple cells in the visual cortex
   a. respond maximally to bars of light oriented in one direction but not to bars of light oriented in another direction.
   b. respond to "correctly" oriented bars of light only when they are in the "correct" part of the retina.
   c. were first described by Hubel and Wiesel.
   d. all of the above.

16. Simple and complex cells differ in that
   a. the receptive field of a simple cell is larger than that of a complex cell.
   b. the receptive field of a complex cell cannot be mapped into fixed excitatory and inhibitory zones, but that of a simple cell can.
   c. a simple cell does not respond at all to small spots of light, whereas complex cells respond best to small spots of light.
   d. all of the above.

17. Simple and complex cells are similar in that
   a. most of them receive input from both eyes.
   b. most respond maximally to bars of light oriented in a particular direction.
   c. both may be found in the striate cortex.
   d. all of the above.

18. End-stopped, or hypercomplex, cells
   a. have extremely small receptive fields.
   b. are similar to complex cells, except that there is a strong inhibitory area at one end of the receptive field.
   c. respond only to very complex stimuli, such as faces.
   d. respond best to small spots of light.

19. Neurons along the track of an electrode inserted perpendicular to the surface of visual cortex
   a. have response characteristics that vary widely, but systematically, from the top to the bottom.
   b. have a random distribution of response characteristics.
   c. have certain response characteristics in common.
   d. cannot have their responses recorded, since the electrode damages them severely.

20. The hypothesis that neurons in the visual cortex are feature detectors
   a. is supported by the observation that prolonged exposure to a given feature seems to fatigue the relevant detectors.
   b. is supported by the finding that each cell in the primary visual cortex responds only to one very precise stimulus, so its response is not at all ambiguous.
   c. is disproved by the observation that visual cortical cells respond only to sine-wave gratings, and not at all to bars and edges.
   d. is now known to be true for cells in area V1, but not for any other visual processing area.

21. The inferior temporal cortex
   a. has receptive fields that always include the fovea.
   b. is concerned with advanced pattern analysis and complex shapes.
   c. may provide our sense of shape constancy.
   d. all of the above.

22. A person with visual agnosia
   a. may have lost recognition only for a few kinds of stimuli, such as faces, as in prosopagnosia.
   b. has lost the ability to read.
   c. is blind.
   d. has had damage limited to the primary visual cortex (area V1).

23. Area V4
    a. seems to be especially important for face recognition.
    b. seems to be especially important for color constancy.
    c. seems to be especially important for shape constancy.
    d. receives input only from the parvocellular system.

24. Occipital area V5 (MT, middle-temporal cortex) and area MST (medial superior temporal cortex)
    a. analyze complex shapes.
    b. analyze colors.
    c. analyze speed and direction of movement.
    d. analyze stereoscopic depth cues.

25. Cells in the dorsal part of MST that respond to expansion, contraction, or rotation of a large visual scene
    a. probably help to record the movement of the head with respect to the world.
    b. probably help to keep track of a single object.
    c. are very particular about the specific objects in their receptive field.
    d. receive input primarily from the parvocellular system.

26. Cells in the ventral part of MST
    a. receive input from cells in MT that respond best to moving borders.
    b. receive input from cells in MST that respond best to expansion, contraction, or rotation of a large visual scene.
    c. respond whenever an object moves relative to its background.
    d. all of the above.

27. Human infants
    a. are unable to see patterns for at least several weeks.
    b. see better in their central field of vision because their fovea develops before the periphery of the retina.
    c. have trouble shifting their attention before about 6 months of age.
    d. all of the above.

28. If a kitten's eyelid is sutured shut for the first 6 weeks of life, and the sutures are then removed, the kitten
    a. is totally blind in the inactive eye only if the other eye had normal visual input.
    b. is totally blind in the inactive eye regardless of the other eye's visual experience.
    c. is able to see horizontal and vertical lines, but not diagonal lines or curves.
    d. sees normally out of the eye, since all of its connections were formed before birth.

29. Children with lazy eye (amblyopia ex anopsia)
    a. should have the active eye covered continuously until adulthood.
    b. should have the active eye covered as early as possible, but only until the lazy eye becomes functional.
    c. should have the active eye covered only after they have reached normal adult size, in order to avoid reorganization of connections.
    d. should not be treated at all, since they will eventually outgrow the condition.

30. Retinal disparity
    a. is an abnormal condition that should be treated as early as possible.
    b. is a cue for depth perception only in people with strabismus.
    c. can be used as a cue for depth perception no matter what the organism's early experience was.
    d. can normally be used for stereoscopic depth perception because cortical cells respond differentially to the degree of retinal disparity.
31. Nerve growth factor (NGF), if injected in large amounts into the brains of infant rats with strabismus,
    a. allowed cortical cells to maintain a strong response to both eyes.
    b. destroyed the ability to detect movement.
    c. made the animals blind.
    d. resulted in inability to use the fovea.

32. Neurotrophin NT-4, if injected in large amounts into the brains of infant rats while one eye was surgically closed,
    a. decreased responsiveness to the closed eye, so that even extensive visual experience while the previously active eye was covered could not restore vision to the previously closed eye.
    b. cortical cells that received the NT-4 remained responsive to both eyes.
    c. cortical cells that received the NT-4 became unresponsive to either eye.
    d. resulted in astigmatism in the previously closed eye.

33. Experiments on abnormal sensory environments have shown that
    a. if kittens are reared in an environment in which they see only horizontal lines, at maturity all cells are completely normal, because receptive field characteristics are fully determined at birth.
    b. if kittens are reared with only horizontal lines, they will become so habituated to that stimulus that they soon lose their ability to see horizontal lines.
    c. if kittens are reared with only horizontal lines, they will lose the ability to see vertical lines.
    d. if the environment is illuminated only with a strobe light during development, kittens lose their ability to see either horizontal or vertical lines.

34. Astigmatism
    a. is caused by too much retinal disparity and results in loss of depth perception.
    b. is caused by strabismus and results in color blindness.
    c. is caused by amblyopia and results in loss of binocular cells in the cortex.
    d. is caused by asymmetric curvature of the eyes and results in blurring of vision for lines in one direction.

Answers to Multiple-Choice Questions

1. c	10. c	19. c	28. a
2. a	11. b	20. a	29. b
3. c	12. a	21. d	30. d
4. b	13. a	22. a	31. a
5. d	14. c	23. b	32. b
6. a	15. d	24. c	33. c
7. d	16. b	25. a	34. d
8. b	17. d	26. d	
9. d	18. b	27. c	

Helpful Hint

Here is an analogy of the selective absorption of different wavelengths by the three types of cones. Think of three tennis nets with different sized holes. The one with the largest holes will easily "catch" a red foam-rubber ball about the same size as its holes. Larger or smaller balls will tend to either bounce back off the net or to go through it, though if they are hit just right, they may be caught in the net. A net with medium-sized holes will easily catch a yellow tennis ball, and a net with even smaller holes will catch a blue golf ball.

Diagrams

1. Label the following components of the vision pathways on this horizontal section of the brain: optic nerve, optic chiasm, lateral geniculate nucleus, primary visual cortex, superior colliculus.

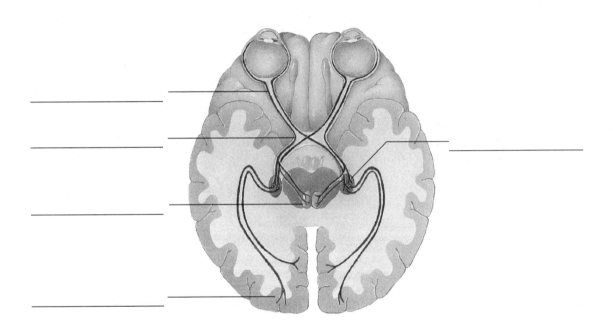

2. Does the following diagram represent the response characteristics of a retinal ganglion cell, a lateral geniculate cell, a "simple" cortical cell, or a "complex" cortical cell?

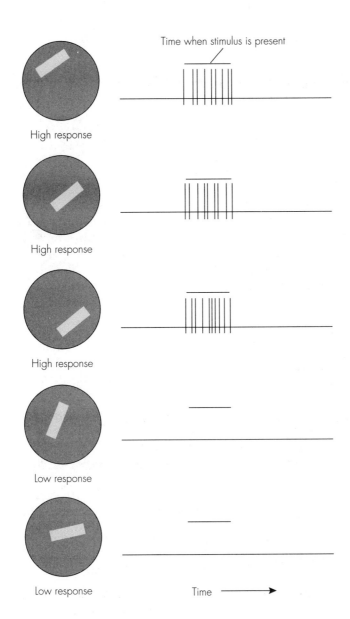

107

7

THE NONVISUAL SENSORY SYSTEMS

INTRODUCTION

Sensory systems have evolved to provide information most useful for each species. Although humans can perceive a relatively wide range of stimuli, our sensory systems also show certain specializations.

The sense of hearing uses air vibrations to move the tympanic membrane and three middle ear bones (the hammer, anvil, and stirrup), which focus the force of the vibrations so that they can move the heavier fluid inside the cochlea. The basilar membrane forms the floor of a tunnel, the scala media. Receptor cells are embedded in the basilar membrane; hairs in the top of the receptors are in contact with the overlying tectorial membrane. Inward pressure of the stirrup on the oval window increases pressure in scala vestibuli, which presses down on scala media, which in turn bulges downward into scala tympani and pushes the round window outward. The opposite happens when the stirrup moves outward. The movement of the basilar membrane (the floor of scala media) relative to the tectorial membrane produces a shearing action that bends the hair cells, thereby generating a potential.

Pitch perception depends on a combination of three mechanisms. At low frequencies, neurons can fire with each vibration. At medium frequencies, neurons split into volleys, one volley firing with one vibration, another with the next, and so on. At higher frequencies the area of the basilar membrane with greatest displacement is used as a place code. The characteristics of the basilar membrane vary along the length of the cochlea. At the basal end a bony shelf occupies most of the floor of scala media, and the basilar membrane, which attaches to the shelf, is thin and stiff. At the apex, there is almost no bony shelf, and the basilar membrane is larger and floppier, even though the cochlea as a whole is smaller. The size and stiffness of the basilar membrane determine which part of the basilar membrane will respond to various frequencies of sound with the greatest-amplitude traveling wave. High-pitched tones cause maximal displacement near the base, and low-pitched tones cause maximal displacement closer to the apex. There is considerable overlap of pitches coded by frequency of firing and by place.

After passing through several subcortical structures, auditory information reaches the primary auditory cortex in the temporal lobes. Neurons with similar preferred tones cluster together there. Damage to the primary auditory cortex does not impair responses to simple sounds but does impair responses to combinations or sequences of sounds. Neurons in the secondary auditory cortex respond best to complex combinations of sounds, such as speech.

There are two categories of hearing impairment. Nerve, or inner ear, deafness is caused by damage to the cochlea, the hair cells, or the auditory nerve. Prenatal infections or toxins, inadequate oxygen during birth, diseases, reactions to drugs, and exposure to loud noises are frequent causes of nerve deafness. Conductive, or middle ear, deafness results from failure of the middle ear bones to transmit sound waves to the cochlea. It can be caused by diseases, infections, or tumorous growths in the middle ear.

Sound localization is accomplished by two methods. The difference in loudness between the two ears is used for high-frequency sounds, while the phase difference for sound waves arriving at the two ears is used for low-frequency sounds. However, for animals with small heads, there is little phase difference in the sound waves reaching the two ears. Therefore, it is difficult for them to localize low-frequency tones.

Furthermore, they can use loudness differences only for higher frequencies than humans can. These animals have evolved the ability to perceive sounds that they can localize easily.

Vestibular sensation, based on the otolith organs and the semicircular canals in the inner ear, contributes to our sense of balance and guidance of our eye movements. Our auditory system, and perhaps other mechanical systems, including the vestibular system, may have evolved from the lateral line system of primitive fish.

The sense of touch is composed of several modalities, some of which are fairly well correlated with activity in specific receptor types. For example, free nerve endings are involved in sensations of pain, warmth, and cold. Hair-follicle receptors respond to movement of hairs; Meissner's corpuscles and Pacinian corpuscles signal sudden displacement of skin. Merkel's disks produce a prolonged response to steady indentation of the skin, while Ruffini endings respond to skin stretching.

Sensory nerves enter and motor nerves exit the spinal cord through each of 31 openings in the vertebral canal. These nerves innervate overlapping segments of the body (dermatomes). Several well defined pathways ascend from the spinal cord to separate areas of the thalamus, and thence to appropriate areas of somatosensory cortex in the parietal lobe. Thus, the various aspects of somatosensation are at least partially separated from the receptor level to the cerebral cortex. Since bodily sensations depend on activity in the cerebral cortex, some people may experience a "phantom limb" after a part of the body has been amputated. In other patients damage to the somatosensory cortex may result in impairment of body perception.

Pain information is transmitted to the spinal cord by axons with little or no myelin, using substance P as their transmitter. From the spinal cord, pain information is sent to certain thalamic nuclei, and then to three cortical areas: the insula, cingulate cortex (which is linked to emotional responses), and somatosensory cortex. Capsaicin, derived from hot peppers, elicits the release of substance P and thereby produces a sensation of pain or heat. However, following application of capsaicin, there is a prolonged decrease in pain sensations. According to the gate theory, various kinds of nonpain stimuli can modify pain sensations. Pain sensations can be counteracted by release of the brain's endogenous opiates (endorphins), including leu- and met-enkephalin, dynorphin, beta-endorphin, and alpha-neoendorphin. In contrast, nociceptin actually increases pain. Endorphins are concentrated in the periaqueductal gray area of the midbrain. These neurons and others in the medulla block the release of substance P in the spinal cord and brainstem. Several stimuli can elicit the release of endorphins; these include pain, stress, acupuncture, and transcutaneous electrical nerve stimulation. However, some types of analgesia are dependent, not on endorphins, but on activity at certain glutamate synapses. Morphine administered for serious pain is almost never addictive. Furthermore, although opiates inhibit the immune system temporarily, prolonged pain or stress weakens the immune system for a much longer time. The body sometimes increases the sensitivity to pain. Tissue damage results in the release of histamine, nerve growth factor, and other chemicals that help repair the damage. However, they also increase the number of sodium gates in receptors and axons, and may thereby enhance pain sensitivity.

Our understanding of the senses of taste and olfaction is plagued with many unresolved issues. There is lack of agreement as to whether there are a fixed number of primary stimuli, which send information to the brain via "labeled lines," or whether the brain analyzes patterns of firing across whole populations of neurons, with sensations varying along continuous dimensions. Compromises between the two positions will probably be required for both senses, but the exact nature of the compromises has not been specified. Studies of cross-adaptation suggest that we have at least four types of taste receptor: sweet, sour, salty, and bitter. There may also be a receptor for monosodium glutamate and additional receptors for bitter and sweet. The mechanisms of activation of some taste receptors have been discovered. Sodium ions activate salty receptors; acids close potassium channels in sour receptors; and

109

sweetness and bitterness receptors respond to molecules that activate G proteins, which then release a second messenger within the cell. The anterior two-thirds of the tongue sends information via the chorda tympani, a branch of the seventh cranial nerve (facial nerve) to the nucleus of the tractus solitarius in the medulla. The posterior third of the tongue and the throat send input via branches of the ninth and tenth cranial nerves to different parts of the nucleus solitarius. From there the information is sent to numerous areas, including the pons, lateral hypothalamus, amygdala, ventral-posterior thalamus, and two areas of the cerebral cortex. The nucleus of the tractus solitarius in rats and the cerebral cortex in monkeys can respond differentially according to the acceptability of a taste.

Olfactory cells have cilia that extend into the mucous lining of the nasal passages. Odorant molecules must diffuse through a mucous fluid in order to reach the receptor sites on the cilia. There may be 1000 or more olfactory receptor proteins, which operate on the same principles as some neurotransmitter receptors. When activated by an odorant molecule, the receptor triggers a change in a G protein, which in turn elicits chemical activities within the cell. People with specific anosmias lack one or more of these receptors. Because there are so many types of receptor, olfaction has more of a labeled-line system of coding than does, for example, color vision, which has only three types of cones. However, even in olfaction, each receptor responds to other odorants that are similar to its preferred stimulus. Therefore, a single receptor can provide an approximate classification of an odorant, but related receptors provide more exact information. A population of varied receptors can provide information about complex mixtures of odors.

KEY TERMS AND CONCEPTS

Audition
1. Sound
    Amplitude
        Loudness
    Frequency
        Pitch

2. Structures of the ear
    Outer ear
        Pinna
    Middle ear
        Tympanic membrane (eardrum)
        Middle ear bones
            Hammer (malleus)
            Anvil (incus)
            Stirrup (stapes)
    Inner ear
        Oval window
        Cochlea
            Scala vestibuli
            Scala tympani
            Scala media
                Basilar membrane
                Hair cells
                Tectorial membrane
        Auditory nerve (part of eighth cranial nerve)

3. Pitch perception
   Frequency theory
      Volley principle
   Place theory
      Base: thin, stiff basilar membrane
      Apex: larger, floppier basilar membrane
      Traveling wave
   Pitch perception in the cerebral cortex
      Primary auditory cortex (temporal lobes)
         Important for combinations or sequences of sounds
      Secondary auditory cortex
         Complex combination of sounds, such as speech

4. Deafness
   Nerve deafness
      Inner-ear deafness
      Prenatal exposure to rubella, syphilis, or other contagious diseases or to toxins
      Inadequate oxygen to brain during birth
      Inadequate thyroid activity
      Diseases, including multiple sclerosis and meningitis
      Childhood reactions to drugs, including aspirin
      Prolonged exposure to loud noises
   Conductive deafness
      Middle-ear deafness
      Certain diseases or infections
      Tumorous bone growth in middle ear
      Can hear sounds that bypass middle ear, including own voice

5. Localization of sounds
   Difference in intensity
      Sound shadow
      High frequencies
   Difference in time of arrival
      Phase difference
      Low frequencies

The mechanical senses
1. Lateral line system

2. Vestibular sensation
   Vestibular organ (adjacent to cochlea)
      Otolith organs
         Saccule
         Utricle
      Semicircular canals (three planes)
   Eighth cranial nerve, vestibular component
   Brain stem and cerebellum

3. Somatosensation
   Somatosensory receptors
      Free nerve endings
      Hair-follicle receptors
      Meissner's corpuscles
      Pacinian corpuscles

Merkel's disks
Ruffini endings
Krause end bulbs
Input to the spinal cord and the brain
31 sets of spinal nerves
Dermatome
Somatosensory thalamus
Somatosensory cortex
Parietal lobe
Four parallel strips
Two for touch
Two for deep pressure and joint and muscle movement
Input primarily from contralateral side, but also via corpus callosum
from opposite hemisphere
Impaired perception of body (damage to cortex)
Phantom limbs (intact cortex, peripheral damage)

4. Pain
Pain neurons and their neurotransmitters
Substance P (unmyelinated and thinly myelinated fibers)
Capsaicin (induces releae of substance P)
Spinal cord -- > thalamic nuclei -- > cerebral cortex (insula, cingulate and
somatosensory cortex)
Events that limit pain
Gate theory
Opioid systems
Endorphins
Enkephalins (met-enkephalin and leu-enkephalin)
Dynorphin
Beta-endorphin
Alpha-neoendorphin
Nociceptin (increases pain, unlike other endorphins)
Analgesia
Periaqueductal gray area

Stimuli that produce analgesia
Pain or stress
Naloxone
Glutamate (nonendorphin) analgesia
Acupuncture
Transcutaneous electrical nerve stimulation (TENS)
The pros and cons of morphine analgesia
Rarely addicitve
Less inhibition of immune system than pain
The sensitization of pain
Tissue damage -- >
Release of histamine, nerve growth factor -- >
Repair tissue and increase sodium gates in receptors and axons -- >
Enhance pain sensitivity

The chemical senses
1. General issues about chemical coding
Labeled-line principle
Across-fiber pattern principle

2.	Taste
	Taste receptors
		Taste buds
		Papillae
	How many kinds of taste receptors?
		Adaptation and cross adaptation
		Four main types: sweet, sour, salty, bitter
		Other possibilities
			Monosodium glutamate
			Multiple bitter and sweet receptors
	Mechanisms of taste receptors
		Salty: sodium influx
			Amiloride: blocks sodium entry --> decreases salty taste
		Sour: acid closes potassium channels --> depolarize membrane
		Sweet: G protein and second messenger
		Bitter: G protein and second messenger
	The coding of taste information
		Labeled-line theory
		Across-fiber pattern theory
	Taste coding in the brain
		Information from anterior two-thirds of tongue
			Chorda tympani: branch of seventh cranial nerve (facial nerve)
		Information from posterior third of tongue and throat
			Ninth and tenth cranial nerves
		Nucleus of the tractus solitarius (NTS, in medulla)
		Pons, lateral hypothalamus, amygdala, ventral-posterior thalamus, two
			areas of cerebral cortex (taste and touch)
		Acceptability of a taste: altered by changes in response in NTS or cortex

3.	Olfaction
	Olfactory receptors
		Olfactory cells: replaceable
		Olfactory epithelium
		Cilia
		Mucous fluid
		Olfactory bulb
		Cerebral cortex, hippocampus, amygdala, hypothalamus
	Behavioral methods of identifying olfactory receptors
		Specific anosmias
			Isobutyric acid
			Musky, fishy, urinous, spermous, malty
			Up to 26 others
	Biochemical identification of receptor types
		Similar to neurotransmitter receptors
			Seven transmembrane sections
			G proteins
		Possibly 1000 or more receptor proteins
		Arranged in nonrandom order
	Implications for coding
		Each receptor: identify approximate nature of molecule
		Receptor population: more precise; identify complex mixture
		Space for many receptors not a problem
		Mostly labeled-line
		Some across-fiber pattern
	Pheromone

SHORT-ANSWER QUESTIONS

Audition
1. *Sound*
   a. What is the relationship between amplitude and loudness? between frequency and pitch?

2. *Structures of the ear*
   a. What is the role of the tympanic membrane and the hammer, anvil, and stirrup?

   b. Where are the auditory receptors located? How are they stimulated?

3. *Pitch perception*
   a. What led to the downfall of the frequency theory of pitch discrimination in its simple form?

   b. What is the volley theory?

c. What observation led to the downfall of the place theory as originally stated?

d. What is the current compromise between the place and frequency theories of pitch discrimination?

e. At which end of the cochlea is the basilar membrane stiffest?

f. How does the traveling wave along the basilar membrane lead to place coding?

g. Describe the location and function of the primary auditory cortex.

h. What are the preferred stimuli for cells in secondary auditory cortex?

4. *Deafness*
   a. For what type of deafness is hearing impaired for a limited range of frequencies?

   b. For which type of deafness can one hear one's own voice, though external sounds are heard poorly?

   c. What are some causes of nerve deafness? of conductive deafness?

5. *Localization of sounds*
   a. For which frequencies is the "sound shadow" method of localization best? Why?

   b. What is the other major method of sound localization? For which frequencies is it most effective?

   c. Which method of sound localization is best for a species with a small head? Why?

The mechanical senses
1. *The lateral line system*
   a. Describe the lateral line system of fish. To what type of stimuli do its receptors respond? Which of our senses probably evolved from the lateral line system?

2. *Vestibular sensation*
   a. What are the main parts of the vestibular organ? What are otoliths? What is their function?

   b. What are the semicircular canals? How do they differ from the otolith organs?

3. *Somatosensation*
   a. List the somatosensory receptors and their probable functions.

   b. How many sets of spinal nerves do we have?

   c. What is a dermatome?

d. Describe briefly the cortical projections of the somatosensory system.

e. Why do some people feel phantom limbs after loss of a limb?

f. Describe the loss of body sense that may accompany Alzheimer's disease.

4. *Pain*
   a. What is substance P? What sensation would be produced by an injection of substance P into the spinal cord?

   b. What is capsaicin? How does it work? What food contains capsaicin?

   c. What theory did Melzack and Wall propose to account for the variations in pain responsiveness? What is its main principle?

118

d.   What are endorphins? How was the term derived?

e.   List the endorphins. Which one increases pain, unlike the rest?

f.   Where are endorphin synapses concentrated? What is their function there?

g.   List four kinds of stimuli that can reduce pain.

h.   What is naloxone? How is it used experimentally?

i.   What neurotransmitter may mediate nonendorphin analgesia?

j.   What are the pros and cons of morphine analgesia in cases of serious pain?

k. Describe the process by which tissue damage results in pain sensitization.

The chemical senses
1. *General issues about chemical coding*
   a. Describe the labeled-line type of coding. Give an example.

   b. Describe the across-fiber pattern type of coding. Give an example.

2. *Taste*
   a. Where are the taste receptors located? What is the relationship between taste buds and papillae?

   b. How can cross adaptation be used to help determine the number of taste receptors?

   c. What are the four major kinds of taste receptor? What additional kinds may we have?

d.   What are the mechanisms of activation of salty, sour, sweet, and bitter receptors? How does amiloride affect salty tastes?

e.   What evidence favors the labeled-line theory of taste? the across-fiber pattern theory?

f.   Which structures in the brain process taste information?

g.   What property, other than the physical identity of tastes, is classified by the nucleus of the tractus solitarius of rats? Which area performs this function in monkeys?

3.   *Olfaction*
   a.   Describe the olfactory receptors. Why is there a delay between inhaling a substance and smelling it?

   b.   What is a specific anosmia? What can we conclude about the number of olfactory receptors, based on information about specific anosmias?

c.   How are olfactory receptors similar to neurotransmitter receptors? How many olfactory receptor proteins are estimated to exist, based on isolation of these proteins?

d.   What can we say about the labeled-line theory vs. the across-fiber pattern theory for smell?

POSTTEST

Multiple-Choice Questions

1.   Which of the following is true of auditory perception?
      a.   Loudness is the same thing as amplitude.
      b.   Pitch is the perception of intensity.
      c.   Perception of low frequencies decreases with age.
      d.   Perception of high frequencies decreases with age.

2.   The function of the tympanic membrane and middle-ear bones is to
      a.   directly stimulate the auditory receptors.
      b.   move the tectorial membrane to which the stirrup is connected.
      c.   focus the vibrations on a small area, so that there is sufficient force to produce pressure waves in the fluid-filled cochlea.
      d.   none of the above.

3.   The auditory receptors
      a.   are called hair cells.
      b.   are embedded in the basilar membrane below and the tectorial membrane above.
      c.   are stimulated when the basilar membrane moves relative to the tectorial membrane; displacement of the hair cells by about the diameter of one atom opens ion channels in the membrane of the neuron.
      d.   all of the above.

4.   The frequency theory
      a.   cannot describe coding of very high-frequency tones because the refractory periods of neurons limit their firing rates.
      b.   can be modified by the volley principle to account for pitch discrimination of all frequencies.
      c.   is now thought to be valid for high-frequency tones, whereas the place theory describes pitch coding of lower tones.
      d.   is a form of labeled-line theory.

5. The place theory
   a. received experimental support from demonstrations that the basilar membrane was composed of a series of separate strings.
   b. has been modified so that a traveling wave produces a greater displacement at one area of the basilar membrane than at others.
   c. cannot be true at all, because the basilar membrane is the same throughout its length and therefore cannot localize vibrations.
   d. cannot be true at all, because the basilar membrane is too loose and floppy to show any localization.

6. The basilar membrane
   a. is smallest and stiffest at the apex (farthest, small end) of the cochlea.
   b. is smallest and stiffest at the base (large end) of the cochlea.
   c. has the same dimensions and consistency throughout its length.
   d. shows maximum displacement for low tones near its base.

7. Pitch discrimination
   a. depends on a combination of mechanisms: frequency coding for low pitches, place coding for high pitches, and both mechanisms for intermediate pitches.
   b. depends on a combination of mechanisms: frequency coding for high pitches, place coding for low pitches, and both mechanisms for intermediate pitches.
   c. cannot be satisfactorily explained by any theory.
   d. is accomplished only by place coding.

8. Inner-ear deafness
   a. is frequently temporary; if it persists, it can usually be corrected by surgery.
   b. is characterized by total deafness to all sounds.
   c. may result from exposure of one's mother to rubella or other contagious diseases during pregnancy.
   d. is characterized by being able to hear one's own voice but not external sounds.

9. A "sound shadow"
   a. is useful for sound localization only for low-pitched sounds.
   b. is useful for sound localization only for wavelengths shorter than the width of the head (that is, higher pitches).
   c. is a means of sound localization that uses differences in time of arrival between the two ears.
   d. cannot be used at all by small-headed species such as rodents.

10. The lateral line organ of fish
    a. is a row of receptors on each side of the body that detect the fish's own movement.
    b. is probably the evolutionary precursor to our olfactory cells.
    c. is a row of receptors in the inner ear of fish that detect sounds in the water.
    d. is a row of touch receptors on each side of the body that detect vibrations in the water.

11. Vestibular sensation
    a. arises from free nerve endings in the inner ear.
    b. is produced by a traveling wave along a membrane in the otolith organs.
    c. arises from hair cells in the otolith organs and the semicircular canals.
    d. plays only a minor role in balance and coordination.

12. Which of the following pairs of receptors and sensations is most correct?
    a. free nerve endings: pain, warmth, cold
    b. Merkel's disks: sudden movement across skin
    c. Pacinian corpuscles: steady indentation of skin
    d. Ruffini endings: movement of hairs

13. Dermatomes
    a. are sharply defined, nonoverlapping areas innervated by single sensory spinal nerves.
    b. are overlapping areas innervated by single sensory spinal nerves.
    c. are symptoms of a skin disorder, much like acne.
    d. are found only on the trunk of the body, not the arms, legs, or head.

14. Somatosensory information
    a. travels up a single pathway to one thalamic nucleus, which projects to one strip in the parietal lobe.
    b. travels up different pathways to separate thalamic areas, which project to four parallel strips in the parietal lobe.
    c. travels directly from the spinal cord to the parietal lobe, without any synapses on the way.
    d. travels to separate thalamic areas, which project to four parallel strips in the temporal lobe.

15. Phantom limbs
    a. result from activity in the cerebral cortex that used to be associated with the lost body part.
    b. are rarely experienced for more than a day or two after loss of the body part.
    c. result from the subconscious desire to regain the body part.
    d. are felt only if there is no reorganization of the cerebral cortex.

16. Substance P
    a. is an endogenous opiate.
    b. activates receptors that are normally blocked by capsaicin.
    c. is released in the spinal cord by unmyelinated and thinly myelinated axons carrying pain information.
    d. none of the above.

17. The gate theory of pain
    a. was proposed by Melzack and Wall.
    b. states that nonpain input can close the "gates" for pain messages.
    c. may explain why athletes and soldiers may report little pain from a serious injury.
    d. all of the above.

18. Leu- and met-enkephalin
    a. have chemical structures virtually identical to morphine.
    b. are two nociceptins in the brain.
    c. are peptide neurotransmitters, consisting of five amino acids each, that have opiate-like effects.
    d. all of the above.

19. Which of the following is true of the periaqueductal gray area?
    a. It is an area in the spinal cord where substance P is released to cause pain.
    b. Stimulation of enkephalin receptors there blocks release of substance P in pain pathways.
    c. Stimulation of it reduces sharp pain, but not slow, dull pain.
    d. It is a major site for the induction of pain sensitization.

20. Naloxone
    a. blocks opiate receptors.
    b. is one of the enkephalins.
    c. is released by transcutaneous nerve stimulation (TENS).
    d. depletes substance P.

21. Which of the following is true of analgesia?
    a. All forms are blocked by naloxone.
    b. Morphine administered for serious pain is especially addictive, and should be avoided.
    c. Certain glutamate synapses inhibit some kinds of pain.
    d. Morphine seriously weakens the immune system for as long as it is administered.

22. Which of the following is true?
    a. Sensitization of pain results when damaged tissue becomes inflamed and triggers the release of histamine and other chemicals that help repair damage; those chemicals increase the number of sodium gates in nearby receptors and axons.
    b. Transcutaneous electrical nerve stimulation (TENS) works by releasing capsaicin in the spinal cord.
    c. Because pain is an evolutionarily old sense, it is very simple in its mechanisms.
    d. Even low doses of morphine can suppress breathing, so it is better for a patient to suffer the pain of an injury rather than risk loss of the control of breathing.

23. The labeled-line principle
    a. states that each receptor responds to a wide range of stimuli and contributes to the perception of each of them.
    b. states that each receptor responds to a narrow range of stimuli and sends a direct line to the brain.
    c. describes color coding better than does the across-fiber pattern principle.
    d. describes most sensory systems in vertebrates.

24. Which of the following is true concerning taste receptors and neurons?
    a. Each receptor has its own taste bud and its own neuronal fiber.
    b. There are about two to three receptors in each taste bud, and each receptor has its own neuronal fiber.
    c. There are about 50 receptors in each taste bud, and each neuron receives synaptic contacts from a number of receptors.
    d. There is only one receptor per taste bud, but each receptor on the tongue makes contact with numerous neurons.

25. Cross-adaptation studies have suggested that
    a. there are at least four kinds of taste receptors.
    b. there may be a separate receptor for monosodium glutamate.
    c. there may be more than one kind of receptor for both bitter and sweet tastes.
    d. all of the above.

26. Which of the following is an appropriate pairing of receptor type with its method of activation?
    a. salty: sodium inflow
    b. sweet: closing potassium channels
    c. sour: activation of G protein
    d. bitter: sodium outflow

27. Amiloride
    a. facilitates sodium flow across the membrane and intensifies salty tastes.
    b. blocks sodium flow across the membrane and intensifies salty tastes.
    c. blocks sodium flow across the membrane and reduces the intensity of salty tastes
    d. facilitates potassium flow across the membrane and intensifies sweet tastes

28. The across-fiber pattern principle of taste
    a. assumes that there are seven basic taste qualities.
    b. holds that taste is coded in terms of a pattern of neural activity across a great many neurons.
    c. has been disproven by the finding that every receptor responds only to one taste.
    d. none of the above.

29. The nucleus of the tractus solitarius (NTS)
    a. is located in the cerebral cortex and projects to the medulla.
    b. is located in the medulla and projects to the pons, lateral hypothalamus, amygdala, thalamus, and cerebral cortex.
    c. is located in the medulla and sends its output primarily to cranial nerves.
    d. is responsible only for information about the physical identity of substances; acceptability of tastes is classified only at the level of the cerebral cortex, even in rats.

30. Olfactory receptors
    a. are not replaceable, once they die.
    b. each respond to only one specific odor.
    c. respond equally well to a great many odors.
    d. have cilia that extend into the mucous surface of the nasal passage; odorant molecules must pass through a mucous fluid to reach the receptor site.

31. Specific anosmias
    a. are usually very debilitating.
    b. have shown that there are only 4 kinds of olfactory receptors.
    c. suggest that there are probably a fairly large number of kinds of olfactory receptors.
    d. suggest that identification of odors depends entirely on an across-fiber pattern code.

32.   Isolation of olfactory receptor molecules has shown that
   a.   olfactory receptors are similar to neurotransmitter receptors in that they have seven transmembrane sections and trigger changes in a G protein, which then provokes chemical activities inside the cell.
   b.   there are at least 18, and perhaps as many as 1000, olfactory receptor proteins.
   c.   olfactory receptors are arranged in a nonrandom order in the olfactory epithelium.
   d.   all of the above are true.

Answers to Multiple-Choice Questions

1. d	7. a	13. b	19. b	25. d	31. c
2. c	8. c	14. b	20. a	26. a	32. d
3. d	9. b	15. a	21. c	27. c	
4. a	10. d	16. c	22. a	28. b	
5. b	11. c	17. d	23. b	29. b	
6. b	12. a	18. c	24. c	30. d	

Diagram

Label the following structures of the inner ear: basilar membrane, hair cell, cochlear neuron.

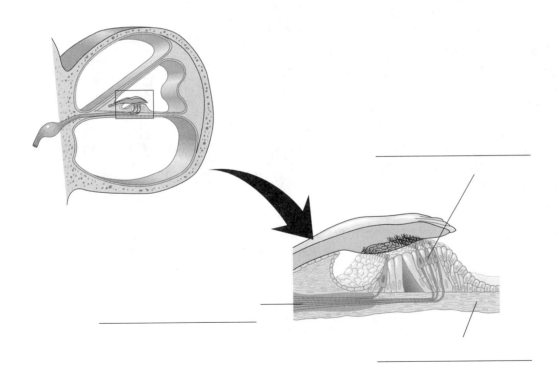

SENSE AND NONSENSE

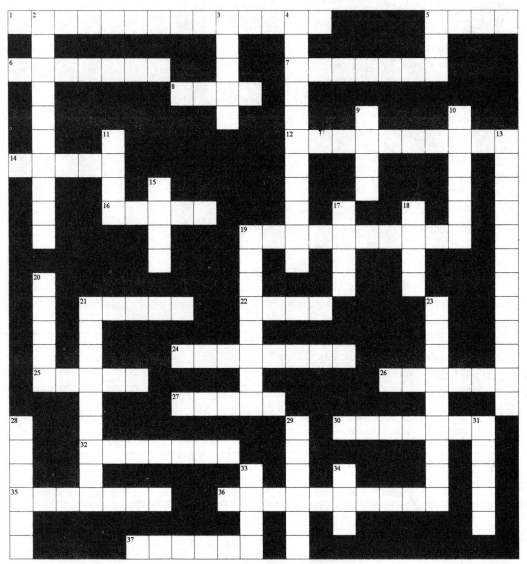

Constructed by Elaine M. Hull using Plexus Word Weaver®

Across

1 Area on the retina that affects
   the firing of a certain neuron
   (2 words)

5 Part of the cochlea where the
   basilar membrane is smallest,
   though the cochlea is largest

6 Retinal neurons that receive

input directly from receptors

7 Membrane that forms the
   floor of scala media, and
   contains auditory receptors

8 The end of the cochlea where
   the basilar membrane is
   largest, though the cochlea
   itself is smallest

12 Chemicals of the brain that

activate opiate receptors

14 Theory of pitch perception,
   which holds that the location
   of greatest activation on the
   basilar membrane determines
   pitch

16 Taste receptor that operates
   like a metabotropic synapse,
   by activating a G protein

19 Lateral _____ nucleus, visual relay nucleus in the thalamus

21 Aspect of vision coded by cones

22 _____ theory, assumption that stimulation of nonpain axons inhibits pain messages

24 Lobe of cerebral cortex that processes somatosensory information

25 Protein part of photopigment

26 Eye part that contains receptors, etc.

27 _____ spot, site in the retina where ganglion cell axons exit

30 One of the three middle ear bones

32 Structure in the inner ear containing auditory receptors

35 _____ limb, a sensation that feels like a body part after that part has been amputated

36 A neuron in the retina responsible for lateral inhibition

37 Taste receptor that operates like a metabotropic synapse, by activating a G protein

Down

2 Tissue containing olfactory receptors

3 Area of the retina containing only cones

4 Theory that each receptor responds to a limited range of stimuli and has a direct line to the brain (2 words)

5 Shape of receptive fields in primary visual cortex

9 Visual receptor primarily active in bright light, responsible for color vision

10 Threadlike dendrites that extend from olfactory receptors into the mucous surface of the nasal passage (Latin: plural)

11 Acronym for method of relieving pain by applying mild electrical shock

13 Canal lined with hair cells, sensitive to direction of tilt of the head

15 Structure that focuses light rays on the retina

17 Substance that stimulates sour receptors

18 _____ eye, otherwise known as "amblyopia"

19 Retinal neurons that send input to the lateral geniculate nucleus

20 _____ cellular neuron, large celled neuron of the visual system, sensitive to movement and brightness

21 Chemical that causes release of substance P

23 Membrane in scala media in which tops of hair cells are embedded

28 Neuron in primary visual cortex that can be excited by a point of light anywhere in the excitatory part of its receptive field

29 Visual sensitivity to detail

31 _____ cellular neuron, small celled neuron of the visual system, sensitive to color and detail

33 Taste sensation coded by closing of potassium channels

34 Visual receptor primarily active in dim light

8

MOVEMENT

INTRODUCTION

All movements of the body result from muscle contractions. Acetylcholine is the neurotransmitter released at the neuromuscular junction; it always results in contraction of the recipient muscle. We manage to move our limbs in two opposite directions by alternately contracting antagonistic muscles, such as flexors and extensors. There are three categories of muscle: smooth, skeletal (or striated), and cardiac. Skeletal muscles may be either fast or slow. Fish have three types of muscle: red, slow, fatigue-resistant; pink, intermediate-speed, moderately fatigue-resistant; and white, fast, easily fatigued. Birds have dark and light muscles that correspond to the red and white muscles of fish. Mammals have muscles composed of mixed fast-twitch and slow-twitch fibers. Muscles consist of many fibers, each of which is innervated by one axon; however, each axon can innervate more than one fiber. Greater precision of movement can be achieved if each axon innervates few muscle fibers.

Two kinds of receptors signal change in the state of muscle contraction. The muscle spindle is a stretch receptor located in fibers parallel to the main muscle. Whenever the main muscle and spindle are stretched, the spindle sends impulses to the spinal cord that excite the motor neurons innervating the main muscle. This results in contraction of the main muscle, opposing the original stretch. The Golgi tendon organ is located at both ends of the main muscle and responds to increased tension in the muscle, as when the muscle is contracting or being actively stretched by an external stimulus. Its impulses to the spinal cord inhibit the motor neuron, leading to relaxation of the muscle. Combinations of activity in these two receptors allow one to maintain steady positions, to resist external forces, and to monitor voluntary movement.

Most behaviors are complex mixtures of voluntary and involuntary, or reflexive, components. Some movements are ballistic, which means that they proceed automatically once triggered. Other movements require constant sensory feedback. Central pattern generators control rhythmic movements, such as wing flapping and scratching. Motor programs are fixed sequences of movements; they may be learned or innate, rhythmic or not.

The spinal cord receives sensory nerves entering dorsally and projects motor axons from its ventral side. In addition, it contains motor programs that direct the specific muscle movements for common behaviors such as walking, running, and scratching. The cerebellum is important for learning, planning and coordinating complex movements, especially rapid ballistic sequences that require accurate timing and aiming. It also contributes to sensory and cognitive processes, especially those that guide movement and integrate several problem-solving steps into a smooth sequence. Damage to the cerebellum impairs rapid alternating movements, saccades, and the ability to touch one's nose with one's finger. Parallel fibers in the cerebellar cortex activate Purkinje cells, which in turn inhibit the cerebellar and vestibular nuclei. Inhibiting these nuclei for shorter or longer times determines the duration and distance of a movement. Information from these nuclei is then sent to the midbrain and thalamus.

The basal ganglia are a group of subcortical structures that contribute to the planning and organization of movements, the control of muscle force, and memory and problem solving. They consist of the caudate nucleus, putamen, globus pallidus, substantia nigra, and subthalamic nucleus. They receive input from, and send output to, the thalamus and cerebral cortex. They may synchronize outputs from the cortex by activating certain movements and inhibiting others.

The cerebral cortex coordinates complex plans of movement. The primary motor cortex sends axons to the medulla and spinal cord, which in turn innervate the muscles. It has overlapping areas that control different parts of the body. The posterior parietal cortex responds to visual and somatosensory input and to future or current movements; it is important for converting perception into action. The primary somatosensory cortex provides the primary motor cortex with sensory information and also sends axons directly to the spinal cord. Several other cortical areas guide the preparation for movement. Prefrontal cortex responds mostly to sensory stimuli that lead to movement; premotor cortex is active before a movement; supplementary motor cortex is active before a rapid series of movements. Neurons in primary motor cortex respond differentially to movements in different directions; a movement vector is a representation of the relative activity of a group of neurons, each of which has a preferred direction of movement.

Output from the cortex to the spinal cord can be divided into two tracts. The dorsolateral tract controls movements in the periphery of the opposite side of the body. It includes axons from the primary motor cortex and adjacent areas and from the red nucleus, all of which cross from one side to the other in bulges in the medulla called the pyramids. These axons extend without synapsing to motor neurons or interneurons in the medulla and spinal cord. The ventromedial tract controls movements near the midline of the body that require bilateral control. It consists of some axons from primary and supplementary motor cortex, others from widespread areas of cortex, and those from the midbrain tectum, reticular formation, and vestibular nucleus. None of them cross within the brain, although some axons branch to both sides of the cord. They control muscles of the neck, shoulders, and trunk.

Myasthenia gravis is a disease characterized by weakness and fatigue. It results from autoimmune destruction of acetylcholine receptors on muscle fibers. It may be treated either with immune-suppressant drugs or with drugs that inhibit the enzyme acetylcholinesterase, which breaks down acetylcholine. The symptoms of Parkinson's disease include muscle rigidity and tremor, slow movement, inaccurate aim, difficulty initiating physical or mental activity, spatial disorientation, and depression. Parkinson's disease results from degeneration of dopamine neurons ascending from the substantia nigra in the midbrain to the caudate nucleus and putamen, which are part of the basal ganglia. There is also degeneration in the amygdala. Loss of dopamine stimulation of D_1 and D_2 receptors in the basal ganglia results in increased inhibition from globus pallidus to the thalamus, which then leads to less excitation from the thalamus to the cortex. Therefore, the cortex is less able to initiate movements. The symptoms of Parkinson's disease can be lessened with L-DOPA, the precursor of dopamine, although such treatment frequently results in undesirable side effects. One possible cause of this disease is MPTP in the environment, possibly in the form of herbicides and pesticides, including paraquat. In order for MPTP to destroy the dopaminergic neurons, it must first be converted to MPP+ by the enzyme monoamine oxidase B. This enzyme can be inhibited by deprenyl; treatment with deprenyl has been shown to slow the progress of Parkinson's disease. Other possible treatments include low doses of dopamine agonists, nicotine, and brain grafts.

Whereas Parkinson's disease results from degeneration of the dopaminergic input to the basal ganglia, Huntington's disease results from degeneration of the postsynaptic neurons there and in the cortex. Many of those cells use GABA as their neurotransmitter; however, since many types of cells are lost, no single therapy is very successful. Symptoms begin with a facial twitch and progressively lead to tremors in other parts of the body and to writhing movements and psychological disorders. An autosomal dominant gene on chromosome 4 has been identified as the ultimate cause of the disease. In people with Huntington's disease this gene contains extra

131

repetitions of a sequence of bases in the genetic code for a protein called huntingtin. Huntingtin binds with another protein and together they somehow interfere with the brain's ability to use glucose.

KEY TERMS AND CONCEPTS

The control of movement
1. Muscles and their movements
    Categories of muscle
        Smooth
        Skeletal or striated
        Cardiac
    Neuromuscular junction
        Acetylcholine
        Muscle contraction
    Antagonistic muscles
        Flexor
        Extensor
    Relation of sensory and motor nerves to spinal cord
        Sensory nerves enter dorsally
        Motor nerves exit ventrally
    Fast and slow muscles
        Fish
            Red, slow, resistant to fatigue
            Pink, intermediate speed, moderately resistant to fatigue
            White, fast, forceful, fatigue quickly
        Birds: white and dark muscles
        Humans and other mammals: mixed fibers in each muscle
            Fast-twitch fibers
            Slow-twitch fibers
    Muscle control by proprioceptors
        Stretch reflex
        Muscle spindle
            Stretch receptor parallel to muscle
            Causes muscle to contract: decreases stretch
        Golgi tendon organ
            In tendons at opposite ends of muscle
            Inhibits muscle: brake against too vigorous contraction
        Location of body parts

2. Units of movement
    Voluntary and involuntary movements
        Reflexes
    Movements with different sensitivity to feedback
        Ballistic movement
        High sensitivity to feedback
            Threading needle
            Singing
                Delayed auditory feedback
    Sequences of behaviors
        Central pattern generators
            Rhythmic movements
        Motor program: learned or built in

Brain mechanisms of movement
1. The role of the spinal cord
    Motor programs for walking and scratching
    Rhythm generator

2. The role of the cerebellum
    Learned motor responses
    Rapid ballistic movements
    Effects of damage to the cerebellum
        Inability to link motions rapidly and smoothly
    Tests of cerebellar functioning
        Saccades
        Finger-to-nose test
            Move function: cerebellar cortex
            Hold function: cerebellar nuclei
    Evidence of a broad role
        Response to signals that direct movement
        Cognitive programs for problem solving
        Careful timing of brief intervals
    Cellular organization
        Cerebellar cortex
            Parallel fibers activate Purkinje cells
            Purkinje cells inhibit cerebellar nuclei and vestibular nuclei of brain
                stem
        Cerebellar and vestibular nuclei
        Output to midbrain and thalamus
        Control duration of movement

3. The role of the basal ganglia
    Component structures
        Caudate nucleus
        Putamen
        Globus pallidus
        Substantia nigra
        Subthalamic nucleus
    Output from globus pallidus to thalamus, which projects to motor and prefrontal
        cortex
    Active after motor cortex, but before movement
    Functions
        Memory and problem solving, as well as movement
        Select correct movement and inhibit other movements
        Planning and organizing movements
        Control of muscle force

4. The role of the cerebral cortex
    Primary motor cortex
        General movement plans
        Overlapping areas of control
    Areas near the primary motor cortex
        Posterior parietal cortex
            Converting perception into action
        Primary somatosensory cortex
            Sensory information to motor cortex
            Direct output to spinal cord

133

Prefrontal cortex
    Response to sensory signals that lead to a movement
Premotor cortex
    Preparation for movement
Supplementary motor cortex
    Preparation for rapid series of movements
Movement coding in the primary motor cortex
    Direction of movement
        Movement vector
Connections from the brain to the spinal cord
    Dorsolateral tract of spinal cord
        Axons from primary motor cortex and surrounding areas and from red
            nucleus of midbrain
        Direct connection to spinal cord
        Cross in pyramids of medulla
        Controls peripheral movements on opposite side of body
    Ventromedial tract of spinal cord
        Uncrossed axons from cortex, tectum, reticular formation and
            vestibular nucleus
        Axons branch to both sides of spinal cord
        Controls midline movements requiring bilateral influence

Disorders of movement
1.   Myasthenia gravis
    Autoimmune destruction of acetylcholine receptors
    Progressive weakness and fatigue
    Treatments
        Suppress immune system
        Inhibit acetylcholinesterase

2.   Parkinson's disease
    Symptoms
        Rigidity
        Muscle tremors
        Slow movements
        Inaccurate aim
        Difficulty initiating physical and mental activity
        Spatial disorientation
        Depression
    Degeneration of dopamine neurons projecting from substantia nigra to caudate
        nucleus and putamen; also degeneration in amygdala
        Decreased dopamine at D_1 and D_2 receptors
        Increased inhibitory output from globus pallidus to thalamus
        Decreased excitation from thalamus to cerebral cortex
    Possible causes
        Relatively low heritability
        Interruption of blood flow to some brain areas
        Encephalitis or other viral infections
        Prolonged exposure to certain drugs or toxic substances
            MPTP, MPPP, MPP+
            Herbicides, pesticides (including paraquat)
    L-DOPA treatment
        Precursor to dopamine
        Side effects: nausea, restlessness, sleep problems, low blood pressure,
            stereotyped movements, hallucinations, delusions

Other therapies
        Deprenyl (monoamine oxidase B inhibitor)
        Low dose of dopamine receptor stimulant
        Nicotine
        Brain grafts

3.   Huntington's disease (Huntington's chorea)
      Symptoms
            Twitches and tremors
            Writhing movements
            Impaired ability to form new movement habits
            Psychological symptoms: depression, memory impairment, anxiety,
                  hallucinations and delusions, poor judgment, alcoholism, drug abuse,
                  sexual disorders
      Nature of brain damage
            Loss of neurons in basal ganglia and cortex
            Loss of GABA neurons
      Heredity and presymptomatic testing
            Gene on chromosome #4
            Extra repetitions of sequence of bases
            Protein encoded: huntingtin
                  Binds to another protein and inhibits glucose metabolism

SHORT-ANSWER QUESTIONS

The control of movement
1.   *Muscles and their movements*
      a.   List the three categories of muscle.

      b.   What is the transmitter at the neuromuscular junction? What is its effect?
            How do we move our limbs in two opposite directions?

      c.   What is the relationship of sensory and motor nerves to the spinal cord?
            Where are the cell bodies and axon terminals of the motor neurons?

d.   List the types and functions of skeletal muscle in fish and birds.

e.   How are mammalian muscles different from those of fish and birds? Contrast the muscles of sprinters and marathon runners.

f.   What is a proprioceptor? a stretch reflex?

g.   What is a muscle spindle? What is its effect on the spinal motor neuron that innervates its associated muscle?

h.   Explain the knee-jerk reflex in terms of the above mechanism.

i.   What is a Golgi tendon organ? What is its effect on the spinal motor neuron that innervates its associated muscle? What is its functional role?

2. *Units of movement*
   a. What is a reflex?

   b. Describe some of the involuntary components of "voluntary" behaviors, such as walking or talking.

   c. What is a ballistic movement?

   d. What is the effect of delayed auditory feedback on a singer's ability to hold a single note for a long time?

   e. What is a motor program? Give examples of "built-in" and learned motor programs.

   f. Do humans have any built-in motor patterns?

Brain mechanisms of movement

1. *The role of the spinal cord*
    a. Where is the rhythm generator for the cat's scratch reflex? What happens to the rhythm generator if the muscles are paralyzed?

2. *The role of the cerebellum*
    a. What kinds of movements are especiallly affected by cerebellar damage?

    b. Discuss the role of the cerebellum in controlling saccades.

    c. Describe the motor control required to touch one's finger to one's nose as quickly as possible.

    d. Why may a police officer use the finger-to-nose test to check for alcohol intoxication?

    e. What types of cognitive activity may be controlled by the cerebellum?

f.   From what sources does the cerebellum receive input? To which structures do its output fibers project?

g.   Describe the relationship between the Purkinje cells and the parallel fibers. How does this affect movement?

3.   *The role of the basal ganglia*
    a.   What structures comprise the basal ganglia?

b.   Which are the main receptive areas? the main output area? Where does the sensory input come from, and where does the output go?

c.   To what cognitive functions may the basal ganglia contribute?

d.   How does cerebellar function compare with that of the basal ganglia?

4. *The role of the cerebral cortex*
    a. Contrast the roles of the spinal cord and primary motor cortex in the control of movement.

    b. To what two processes do neurons in the posterior parietal cortex respond? What is the result of damage there?

    c. Describe the roles of the prefrontal, premotor, and supplementary motor cortex.

    d. What is a movement vector? Describe the experiment that suggested that monkeys could do a "mental rotation."

    e. Where does the dorsolateral tract begin? Where does it cross from one side to the other?

    f. From which structures does the ventromedial tract originate? What is the relationship between this tract and the two sides of the spinal cord?

g. Which movements are controlled by the dorsolateral tract, and which by the ventromedial tract?

Disorders of movement
1. *Myasthenia gravis*
    a. Describe the symptoms and cause of myasthenia gravis.

    b. What are two kinds of treatment for this disease?

2. *Parkinson's disease*
    a. Describe the symptoms of Parkinson's disease.

    b. What is its immediate cause? What is the result of loss of dopamine stimulation of D_1 and D_2 receptors in the substantia nigra?

    c. How strong is the evidence for a genetic predisposition for Parkinson's disease?

d. List the possible environmental factors in Parkinson's disease.

e. How did the experience with a heroin substitute lead to suspicion of an environmental toxin as a cause of this disease?

f. How may herbicides and pesticides be implicated?

g. Discuss the problems with the toxin-exposure hypothesis.

h. What is the rationale for treatment of Parkinson's disease with L-DOPA? What are the side effects of this treatment?

i. What is the rationale for the use of deprenyl to slow the progress of Parkinson's disease? Contrast the effects of deprenyl and of L-DOPA on Parkinson's disease.

j.   What are three other possible treatments for Parkinson's disease?

3.   *Huntington's disease*
      a.   What are the physical and psychological symptoms of Huntington's disease?

      b.   Which neurons degenerate in Huntington's disease?

      c.   Discuss the role of genetics in Huntington's disease. On which chromosome is the gene for Huntington's disease located?

      d.   What is huntingtin? What do we know about the base sequence of the gene that codes for it? What may it do inside the cell?

POSTTEST

Multiple-Choice Questions

1.   Which of the following is true of nerves and muscles?
      a.   There is a one-to-one relationship between axons and muscle fibers.
      b.   Each axon innervates several or many muscle fibers.
      c.   Each muscle fiber receives several or many axons.
      d.   Each axon innervates many muscle fibers, and each muscle fiber receives many axons.

2. Acetylcholine
   a. has only excitatory effects on skeletal muscles.
   b. has excitatory effects on some skeletal muscles and inhibitory effects on others.
   c. has only inhibitory effects on skeletal muscles; norepinephrine has only excitatory effects on those muscles.
   d. is released only onto smooth muscles, never onto skeletal muscles.

3. Which of the following is a type of skeletal muscle in fish?
   a. slow, white, fatigue-resistant
   b. fast, white, fatigue-resistant
   c. slow, pink, fatigue-prone
   d. slow, red, fatigue-resistant

4. Mammalian muscles
   a. can be classified as red, pink, and white, as in fish.
   b. contain either fast-twitch or slow-twitch fibers, but not both.
   c. contain both fast-twitch and slow-twitch fibers in the same muscles.
   d. show only genetic, and not any environmental, determination of the ratio of fast-twitch to slow-twitch fibers.

5. The muscle spindle
   a. is a stretch receptor located in parallel to the muscle.
   b. inhibits the motor neuron innervating the muscle when it is stretched; this leads to relaxation of the muscle.
   c. responds only when the muscle contracts.
   d. synapses onto the muscle to excite it directly.

6. The Golgi tendon organ
   a. is also located in the muscle spindle.
   b. affects the motor neuron in the same way as the muscle spindle, thereby enhancing its effect.
   c. responds when the muscle contracts.
   d. excites the motor neuron that innervates the muscle.

7. Ballistic movements
   a. proceed automatically once triggered.
   b. require feedback as they are being executed.
   c. are controlled largely by the basal ganglia.
   d. are required when a singer holds a note for a long time.

8. The rhythm of a dog's scratch reflex
   a. varies, though the length and strength of each scratching movement are constant.
   b. is constant at four to five scratches per second, though the length and strength of each scratch can vary.
   c. is an example of feedback control.
   d. is organized in the cerebellum.

9. Which of the following is true?
   a. Feedback control must be at the root of all movements; otherwise we would be unable to modify our behavior.
   b. Singing a single note does not require feedback, although singing several notes in a sequence does require feedback.
   c. Even ballistic movements are in reality feedback controlled.
   d. There are involuntary components of many voluntary behaviors.

10. Grooming behavior of mice
   a. is an example of a built-in motor program.
   b. is an example of feedback-guided behavior.
   c. totally disappears if the mouse has no forelimbs to execute the main movements.
   d. can be observed as disorganized random elements of behavior if the mouse has no forelimbs to execute the main movements.

11. The cerebellum
   a. is large and critical for the behavior of sloths.
   b. is especially important for planning and coordination of complex, rapid movements.
   c. is important only for innate, not learned, motor responses.
   d. more than one of the above.

12. Damage to the cerebellum produces
   a. Parkinson's disease.
   b. Huntington's disease.
   c. deficits in saccadic movements of the eyes.
   d. deficits in slow feedback-controlled movements.

13. In executing the "finger-to-nose" movement quickly
   a. the cerebellar cortex is important in the initial rapid movement.
   b. the cerebellar nuclei are important in maintaining the brief hold pattern.
   c. other structures are important in the final slow movement.
   d. all of the above.

14. Purkinje cells in the cerebellum
   a. receive input from parallel fibers.
   b. send output to parallel fibers.
   c. excite cells in the cerebellar nuclei.
   d. send output to the basal ganglia and cerebral cortex.

15. Cerebellar neurons
   a. show most activity during purely motor tasks.
   b. contribute to any behavior that requires careful timing of brief intervals.
   c. are now thought to contribute only to cognitive tasks, and not to motor tasks.
   d. are especially important for controlling muscle force.

16. The basal ganglia are important for
   a. rapid ballistic movements.
   b. planning and organizing physical and mental activity.
   c. wing flapping in birds.
   d. fine control of movement.

17. The primary motor cortex
    a. sends axons to the medulla and spinal cord.
    b. includes the somatomotor, prefrontal, premotor, and supplementary motor cortex, as well as the basal ganglia.
    c. is active before, but not during, a movement.
    d. all of the above.

18. The order of activity in preparing for and executing a movement is
    a. primary motor, premotor, prefrontal cortex.
    b. premotor, prefrontal, primary motor cortex.
    c. prefrontal, premotor, primary motor cortex.
    d. primary motor, prefrontal, premotor cortex.

19. The posterior parietal cortex
    a. is the main receiving area for somatosensory information.
    b. helps us to convert perception into action.
    c. helps us to program a series of rapid movements.
    d. is part of the primary motor cortex.

20. A movement vector
    a. is a type of neuron in the primary motor cortex.
    b. is a type of neuron in the supplementary motor cortex.
    c. is a representation of the activity of a single neuron, which may produce movement in one direction at one time, and in another direction at another time.
    d. is a representation of the relative activity of a group of neurons, each of which has a preferred direction of movement.

21. The dorsolateral tract of the spinal cord
    a. originates mostly in the primary motor cortex and adjacent areas and in the red nucleus of the midbrain.
    b. controls movements in the periphery of the body.
    c. controls movements on the side of the body opposite the brain area where the fibers originate.
    d. all of the above.

22. The ventromedial tract of the spinal cord
    a. contains crossed fibers from the primary motor cortex and adjacent areas and from the red nucleus of the midbrain.
    b. controls movements near the midline of the body that are necessarily bilateral.
    c. controls movements on the side of the body opposite the brain area where the fibers originate.
    d. works independently from the dorsolateral tract.

23. The pyramids of the medulla
    a. contain the cell bodies of the dorsolateral tract.
    b. contain the cell bodies of the ventromedial tract.
    c. are the site where axons of the dorsolateral tract cross from one side to the other.
    d. are the site where axons of the ventromedial tract cross from one side to the other.

24. Myasthenia gravis
    a. results from destruction of acetylcholine receptors at neuromuscular junctions by an autoimmune process.
    b. is helped by drugs that increase the effect of acetylcholinesterase.
    c. is helped by drugs that enhance the function of the immune system.
    d. all of the above.

25. Parkinson's disease
    a. results from too much dopamine in the basal ganglia.
    b. results from too little acetylcholine at the neuromuscular junction.
    c. results from too little dopamine in the basal ganglia.
    d. can be cured by taking dopamine pills.

26. MPTP
    a. has been used with some success in treating Parkinson's disease.
    b. may be an environmental cause of Parkinson's disease.
    c. may be an environmental cause of myasthenia gravis.
    d. has been used with some success in treating myasthenia gravis.

27. Deprenyl
    a. blocks conversion of MPTP to MPP by monoamine oxidase B.
    b. blocks conversion of paraquat to MPTP by monoamine oxidase B.
    c. decreases symptoms of Parkinson's disease but does not slow its progress.
    d. slows the progress of Huntington's disease.

28. Huntington's disease
    a. results from destruction of dopaminergic input to the basal ganglia.
    b. is characterized by great weakness.
    c. is caused by a dominant gene on human chromosome number 4.
    d. is caused by a recessive gene on human chromosome number 10.

29. Which of the following are *not* symptoms of Huntington's disease?
    a. facial twitch and tremors
    b. depression, anxiety, memory impairment, hallucinations, and delusions.
    c. memory impairment and alcohol and drug abuse
    d. weakness and difficulty initiating movements

30. The gene associated with Huntington's disease
    a. in its normal form, contains a sequence of bases repeated at least 27 times.
    b. in its normal form, does not contain any repeated sequences of bases.
    c. is now known to code for acetylcholine receptors.
    d. is now known to code for huntingtin, a protein that binds to another protein and somehow disrupts glucose metabolism.

Answers to Multiple-Choice Questions

1. b	9. d	17. a	25. c
2. a	10. a	18. c	26. b
3. d	11. b	19. b	27. a
4. c	12. c	20. d	28. c
5. a	13. d	21. d	29. d
6. c	14. a	22. b	30. d
7. a	15. b	23. c	
8. b	16. b	24. a	

Diagrams

1. Label the following components of the basal ganglia: caudate nucleus, putamen, globus pallidus (lateral part), globus pallidus (medial part), thalamus, subthalamic nucleus, substantia nigra.

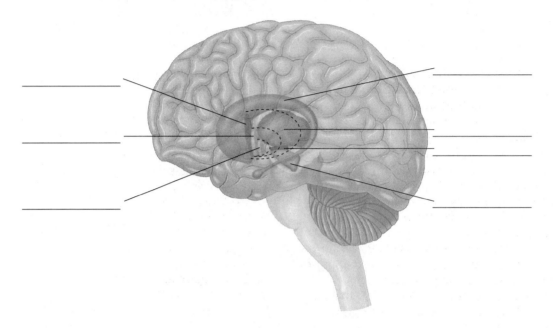

2. Label the principal areas of the motor cortex in the human brain: posterior parietal cortex, prefrontal cortex, premotor cortex, primary motor cortex, primary somatosensory cortex, supplementary motor cortex.

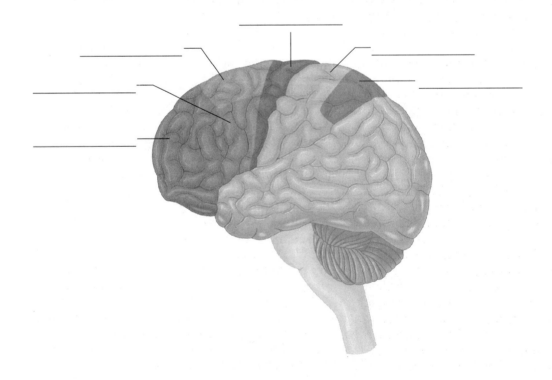

9

RHYTHMS OF WAKEFULNESS AND SLEEP

INTRODUCTION

All vertebrate species that have been studied exhibit endogenous rhythms of behavior. Circannual (approximately year-long) cycles govern hibernation, migration, and seasonal mating in some species. Virtually all vertebrates exhibit circadian (approximately 24-hour) cycles of activity and sleep as well as of other bodily functions. The "clock" governing these cycles generates the rhythm internally, although the external light cycles affect the specific settings. Light appears to act on the suprachiasmatic nucleus (SCN) of the hypothalamus. If the axons from the retina to the SCN are damaged, light can no longer reset the biological clock. Whether or not light stimuli are available to reset the clock, it will continue to generate circadian rhythms. The mechanism of the clock is not understood; however the length of the rhythm may be altered by genetic mutation. The biochemical mechanism may depend on a negative feedback cycle, in which the SCN produces a chemical for a period of hours, until the level inhibits further production. Melatonin, a hormone produced by the pineal gland, may be one means by which the SCN regulates sleeping and waking. Increased melatonin secretion begins 2 to 3 hours before the onset of sleepiness.

The basic function of sleep is ill defined. The repair and restoration theory proposes that restorative functions occur mostly during sleep, especially for the brain. The evolutionary theory proposes that sleep is basically an energy-conserving mechanism employed during times when activity would be either inefficient or dangerous. Elements of both these theories may be valid.

Relaxed wakefulness (with the eyes closed) is characterized by alpha waves at a frequency of 8 - 12 per second. Stage 1 of sleep is signaled by irregular, low-voltage waves, after which progression through stages 2, 3, and 4 is correlated with increasingly slow, large-amplitude waves. Throughout the night, there is a cyclic progression back and forth through the four stages. However, after the first period of stage 1, each return to stage 1 is correlated with rapid eye movements, relaxed muscles, and rapid and variable heart rate and breathing. Rapid eye movement (REM) sleep has also been called paradoxical sleep, because the EEG shows fast, low amplitude waves, as during wakefulness, and the heart rate and breathing are fast and variable, but the postural muscles are completely relaxed. As with sleep in general, the function of REM sleep is not well understood. REM deprivation has resulted in increased irritability, anxiety, and appetite, impaired concentration, and increased REM time on subsequent uninterrupted nights. REM may facilitate the learning of skills; non-REM (NREM) may also strengthen certain memories. In general, the percentage of sleep spent in REM correlates positively with the total amount of sleep. Dreams may result from the brain's attempt to make sense of its increased activity during REM episodes (activation-synthesis hypothesis).

Wakefulness and behavioral arousal depend, in part, on the reticular formation, a group of large, branching neurons running from the hindbrain into the forebrain. It receives input diffusely from all sensory systems and sends output equally diffusely to the cerebral cortex and other structures. It is poorly suited for processing specific sensory information but well designed to alert the whole brain to a change in the flow of sensory input. The locus coeruleus, in the hindbrain, also contributes to wakefulness; it is active in response to meaningful events and may help to form memories. The basal forebrain is the site of nuclei that send acetylcholine- or histamine-containing axons to widespread areas of the thalamus and cortex; these neurons also promote wakefulness.

Sleep does not result simply from a passive reduction of sensory input. Clusters of GABA-containing neurons in the basal forebrain promote the onset of sleep. In addition, cells in the anterior and preoptic areas of the hypothalamus excite sleep-inducing cells and inhibit arousal-related cells elsewhere in the hypothalamus and forebrain.

During REM sleep, high-amplitude potentials can be recorded in the pons, geniculate, and occipital cortex (PGO waves). Animals compensate for lost PGO waves more precisely than lost time in REM. Cells in the pons also inhibit the motor neurons that control postural muscles. Other sites that are active during REM are the amygdala and some cortical areas; other cortical areas, especially the dorsolateral prefrontal cortex, become less active during REM. Two neurotransmitters promote REM sleep. Serotonin induces the onset of REM, and acetylcholine is important for its continuation.

There are three categories of insomnia: onset, maintenance, and termination. Causes of insomnia include abnormalities of biological rhythms, withdrawal from tranquilizers, sleep apnea, and periodic limb movements in sleep. Narcolepsy refers to periods of extreme sleepiness during the day. Additional symptoms of narcolepsy are cataplexy (extreme muscle weakness while awake), sleep paralysis (inability to move during transition into or out of sleep), and hypnagogic hallucinations (dreamlike experiences that are difficult to distinguish from reality). All of these symptoms can be interpreted as intrusions of REM sleep into wakefulness. Nightmares are unpleasant dreams that occur during REM sleep; night terrors are experiences of extreme anxiety, occurring during non-REM sleep. Sleep talking occurs with similar probability in REM and non-REM sleep, whereas sleepwalking occurs mostly during stages 3 and 4 slow-wave sleep. REM behavior disorder is a condition in which people act out their dreams; this probably results from damage to the areas of the pons and midbrain that normally inhibit motor neurons during REM sleep.

KEY TERMS AND CONCEPTS

The alternation of waking and sleeping
1.   Endogenous cycles as a preparation for external changes
     Endogenous circannual and circadian rhythms
          Migratory restlessness
     Setting and resetting the cycle
          Biological clock
          Free-running rhythm
          Zeitgeber
     Attempting to alter the biological clock
          Cave experiments

2.   Resetting the biological clock
     Jet lag
          Worse going east
     Shift work
          Exposure to bright lights

3.   The mechanisms of the biological clock
     Interfering with the biological clock
          Curt Richter
          Lack of effect of most procedures

150

The suprachiasmatic nucleus (SCN)
    Axons from optic tract
    Independence from pathways for pattern vision
        Animals with little or no vision: light still resets rhythms
            Mice with genetic defect
            Blind mole rats
    Disconnected SCN still generates rhythms
    Genetic mutation that produces 20-hour rhythm
        Transplantation of mutant SCN
    Ability of retinal cells to generate rhythm
    Apparent negative feedback of some chemical produced by SCN
Melatonin
    Pineal gland
    Peak 2 to 3 hours before sleepiness
    Melatonin pill in afternoon --> phase advance
    Melatonin pill in morning --> phase delay
    Risks unknown

4.   The functions of sleep
    The repair and restoration theory of sleep
        Effects of sleep deprivation
            Human (voluntary) experiments: dizziness, impaired concentration,
                irritability, hand tremors, hallucinations
            Animal (nonvoluntary) experiments
                Few days deprivation: increased temperature,
                    metabolism, and appetite
                Longer deprivation: decreased immune and thyroid
                    function, decreased brain activity
    The evolutionary theory
        Hibernation
        Energy conservation
        Time required for food search
        Safety from predators

Sleeping and dreaming
1.   The stages of sleep
    Alpha waves (8 - 12 per second): relaxed wakefulness
    Stage 1 sleep
        Irregular, low-voltage EEG waves
    Stage 2 sleep
        Sleep spindle
        K-complex
    Stages 3 and 4 slow-wave sleep
        Synchronized EEG: slow, large amplitude waves

2.   Paradoxical or REM sleep
    Characteristics
        Irregular, low-voltage fast (desynchronized) EEG
        Rapid eye movements
        Rapid and variable heart rate and breathing
        Postural relaxation
        Penile erection or vaginal moistening
        Facial twitches
    Polysomnograph: EEG and eye movement records

Sleep cycles
    90- to 100-minute cycles
    Stages 3 and 4 predominant early in night
    REM predominant late in night
REM sleep and dreaming
    Dreams reported on 80 to 90% of awakenings from REM

3.   The functions of REM sleep
    Individual and species differences
        Percent of time in REM correlated with length of sleep
    The effects of REM sleep deprivation in humans
        Increased anxiety and irritability
        Decreased concentration
        Increased appetite
        REM rebound (increased REM in uninterrupted nights)
    The effects of paradoxical sleep deprivation in nonhumans
        Impairments in learning

4.   A biological perspective on dreaming
    Activation-synthesis hypothesis
    Paralysis of postural muscles

Brain mechanisms in sleep and its disorders
1.   Wakefulness and arousal
    Cut through midbrain: prolonged sleep
        Not due to loss of sensory input
    Reticular formation
        Interconnected network
        Multisynaptic pathways
        Diffuse input and output
        Spontaneous activity
    Locus coeruleus ("dark blue place")
        Bursts of impulses in response to meaningful events
        May aid in memory formation
    Lateral hypothalamus
    Basal forebrain nuclei (anterior and dorsal to hypothalamus)
        Transmitter: acetylcholine --> mostly excitatory effects
        Damaged in Alzheimer's disease
        Inhibited by adenosine
        Caffeine: increases arousal by inhibiting adenosine

2.   Sleep and REM sleep
    Sleep-inducing areas
        Basal forebrain nuclei
            Wide projections
            Transmitter: GABA --> inhibitory effects
            Active at sleep onset and in non-REM (NREM) sleep
        Anterior and preoptic hypothalamus
            Excite sleep-related cells and inhibit waking-related cells elsewhere
    REM inducing areas
        Increased activity in pons, thalamus and amygdala
        Increased activity in some cortical areas
        Decreased activity in other cortical areas, including dorsolateral prefrontal
            cortex

PGO (pons-geniculate-occipital) waves
        Compensation for lost PGO waves
Pons -- > spinal cord: inhibition of motor neurons
Serotonin -- > REM onset
Acetylcholine -- > REM continuation
        Carbachol

3.   Abnormalities of sleep
Insomnia
        Onset insomnia
                Possible cause: phase-delayed temperature rhythm
        Maintenance insomnia
                Possible cause: circadian rhythm irregularity
        Termination insomnia
                Possible cause: phase-advanced temperature rhythm
                Early onset of REM sleep
        Withdrawal from tranquilizers
Sleep apnea
        Sudden infant death syndrome
        Obesity
Narcolepsy
        Attacks of daytime sleepiness
        Cataplexy
        Sleep paralysis
        Hypnagogic hallucinations
        May be due to intrusion of REM into wakefulness
Periodic limb movement disorder (mostly during NREM sleep)
REM behavior disorder
        Acting out dreams
        Damage in pons and midbrain
                Motor neurons no longer inhibited
Night terrors, sleep talking, and sleepwalking
        Night terrors different from nightmares
                Occur in NREM sleep
        Sleep talking
                Occurs in REM or NREM sleep
        Sleepwalking
                Most common in children
                Mostly in Stages 3 and 4 (not during REM)

SHORT-ANSWER QUESTIONS

The alternation of waking and sleeping
1. *Endogenous cycles as a preparation for external changes*
    a.   What do we know about the factors that initiate migration in birds?

b. What are endogenous circannual rhythms? endogenous circadian rhythms? How consistent are circadian rhythms within individuals in a given environment? between individuals?

c. How can circadian rhythms be demonstrated experimentally? What are some bodily and behavioral changes that occur in circadian rhythms?

d. What is a Zeitgeber? What is the most effective Zeitgeber?

e. How easily can the biological clock be changed to a new cycle length?

2. *Resetting the biological clock*
   a. Is it easier to cross time zones going east or west? Why?

   b. What is the best way to reset the biological clock when working a night shift?

3. *The mechanisms of the biological clock*
   a.   What sorts of attempted interference with the biological clock were not effective?

   b.   What structure is the source of the circadian rhythms? What is its relationship to the visual system?

   c.   What is the evidence that the SCN generates rhythms itself?

   d.   What happened when the SCN from hamsters with a mutant gene for a 20-hour rhythm were transplanted into normal hamsters?

   e.   What is melatonin? From which gland is it secreted? When does increased secretion of melatonin occur?

4. *The functions of sleep*
   a.   Describe the repair and restoration theory of sleep.

b.   What are some effects of sleep deprivation in humans? in rats?

c.   Describe the evolutionary theory of the need for sleep. What evidence supports it?

d.   How compatible are these two theories?

Sleeping and dreaming
1.   *The stages of sleep*
    a.   Describe the usual behavioral correlate of alpha waves. What is their frequency?

    b.   Describe the EEG in stage 1 sleep.

    c.   What are the EEG characteristics of stage 2 sleep?

d.   Which stages of sleep are classed as slow-wave sleep (SWS)?

2.   *Paradoxical or REM sleep*
    a.   Why is REM sleep sometimes called paradoxical sleep? What are its characteristics?

    b.   What is a polysomnograph?

    c.   What is the typical duration of the sleep cycle? During which part of the night is REM predominant? During which part are stages 3 and 4 SWS predominant?

    d.   How good is the correlation between REM and dreaming?

3.   *The functions of REM sleep*
    a.   What is the relationship between percentage of time in REM and total sleep time?

b. What kinds of behavioral changes occur if people are selectively deprived of REM sleep? How does this compare with the effects on nonhuman animals?

c. Describe the apparent relationship between learning and paradoxical sleep. For what kind of learning is paradoxical sleep most important?

4. *A biological perspective on dreaming*
   a. What is the current view of Freud's assumptions concerning dreaming?

   b. State the activation-synthesis hypothesis. What evidence supports this hypothesis? How widely accepted is it?

Brain mechanisms in sleep and its disorders
1. *Wakefulness and arousal*
   a. What is the result of a cut through the midbrain on sleep and waking cycles? Was this result due simply to loss of sensory input or to damage to a particular brain structure?

   b. Describe the input, output, and interconnections of the reticular formation.

c.   What other areas contribute to arousal?

d.   What neurotransmitters are released by neurons in the basal forebrain that contribute to arousal?

e.   Describe the relationship between adenosine and acetylcholine. How does caffeine increase arousal?

2.   *Sleep and REM sleep*
   a.   What brain areas seem to contribute to sleep onset? What neurotransmitter is released by sleep-inducing neurons in the basal forebrain?

   b.   What are PGO waves? Where are they recorded? What happens to PGO waves after a period of REM deprivation?

   c.   Describe the mechanism for inhibiting motor activity during REM sleep.

d. Which neurotransmitter is important for REM onset? for REM continuation? What is one effect of the drug carbachol?

3. *Abnormalities of sleep*
   a. List and describe the characteristics of the three categories of insomnia. What circadian rhythm disorders may cause each category?

   b. What are the pharmacological effects of most tranquilizers that are used as sleeping pills? How may sleeping pills contribute to insomnia?

   c. Describe the symptoms of sleep apnea. What is one cause of sleep apnea?

   d. What four symptoms are commonly associated with narcolepsy? What is a likely cause of narcolepsy?

   e. Define cataplexy. What tends to trigger it? Define hypnagogic hallucinations.

f.   Describe the symptoms of periodic limb movement disorder.

g.   What are the symptoms and possible cause of REM behavior disorder?

h.   How do night terrors differ from nightmares? During which type of sleep
      are night terrors most common?

i.   During which stages does sleep talking occur? sleepwalking?

POSTTEST

Multiple-Choice Questions

1.   Curt Richter suggested the revolutionary idea that
      a.   nearly all behavior is a reaction to a stimulus.
      b.   the body generates its own cycles of activity and inactivity.
      c.   temperature fluctuations are the best zeitgeber.
      d.   animals wait till the first frost before preparing for winter so that they can
            enjoy summer longer.

2.   Migratory birds
      a.   respond only to temperature signals to begin migration.
      b.   respond only to the ratio of light to dark, especially in spring.
      c.   respond only to the availability of food.
      d.   show migratory restlessness every spring and fall, even in captivity with
            constant light/dark cycles.

3. Circadian rhythms
    a. cannot be demonstrated if lights are always on or always off.
    b. always average within a minute or two of 24 hours in length, regardless of the light cycle.
    c. include cycles of waking and sleeping, eating and drinking, temperature, hormone secretion, and urine production.
    d. are very flexible and can be changed as soon as a different light cycle is established.

4. Which of the following is true?
    a. It is easier to adjust our biological rhythms to longer cycles and to travel across time zones going west.
    b. It is easier to adjust our biological rhythms to shorter cycles and to travel across time zones going east.
    c. People on irregular shifts tend to sleep the longest when they go to sleep in the morning or early afternoon.
    d. People on night shifts that were exposed to normal levels of room lighting found it easy to adjust their cycles.

5. Which of the following can totally disrupt the biological clock?
    a. food or water deprivation
    b. anesthesia
    c. long periods of forced activity or forced inactivity
    d. none of the above

6. The suprachiasmatic nucleus
    a. is located in the brain stem.
    b. depends on the same processing as patterned vision.
    c. is concerned only with the resetting of the clock, not with generating the rhythm.
    d. if transplanted from fetal hamsters that have a mutant gene producing a 20-hour cycle, into normal hamsters, will produce 20-hour cycles in the recipients.

7. Melatonin
    a. is secreted by the pituitary gland.
    b. is secreted primarily at the time of sleep onset.
    c. is secreted 2 - 3 hours before the time of sleep onset.
    d. has been tested extensively and is known to have no side effects.

8. When people are deprived of sleep for a week or more,
    a. some report dizziness, irritability, and difficulty concentrating, but no drastic consequences.
    b. usually suffer severe consequences, including death.
    c. their immune systems and thyroid glands work overtime to compensate for the lack of sleep.
    d. they report no symptoms whatever.

9. The evolutionary theory of sleep
    a. states that species regulate their sleep time according to how much repair and restoration their bodies need.
    b. states that species evolved a mechanism to promote energy conservation at times when they are relatively inefficient.
    c. is incompatible with other theories concerning repair and restoration.
    d. is currently very well established.

10. Alpha waves are characteristic of
    a. REM sleep.
    b. alert mental activity.
    c. relaxed wakefulness.
    d. slow-wave sleep.

11. Which of the following is *not* a sign of REM sleep?
    a. tenseness in postural muscles
    b. extreme relaxation of postural muscles
    c. relatively fast, variable heart and breathing rates
    d. irregular, low-voltage, fast EEG activity

12. Paradoxical sleep is paradoxical because brain waves suggest
    a. slow-wave sleep, when one is really dreaming.
    b. dreaming, when one is really in slow-wave sleep.
    c. sleep, when one is really awake.
    d. wakefulness, when one's postural muscles are most relaxed.

13. REM sleep occurs
    a. only early in a night's sleep.
    b. cyclically, about every 90 minutes.
    c. randomly throughout the night.
    d. only after a period of physical exercise.

14. Dreams
    a. are highly correlated with sleep talking.
    b. are of greater duration and frequency during the early part of the night.
    c. are correlated highly, but not perfectly, with periods of REM sleep, even in those who claim not to dream.
    d. all of the above.

15. After about a week of REM deprivation, at least some subjects
    a. reported increased anxiety, irritability and impaired concentration.
    b. experienced increased appetite and weight gain.
    c. spent more sleep time on subsequent nights in REM sleep.
    d. all of the above.

16. Comparisons of sleep patterns across individuals and across species indicate that
    a. percentage of time spent in REM increases as total amount of sleep increases.
    b. percentage of time in REM decreases as total amount of sleep increases.
    c. percentage of time in REM remains the same, no matter how long the individual sleeps.
    d. percentage of time spent in REM is extremely variable, and shows no relationship to the total amount of sleep.

17. The activation-synthesis hypothesis proposes that dreams result from
    a. unconscious wishes struggling for expression.
    b. the ego's attempt to gain control of the id.
    c. the brain's attempt to make sense of its activity.
    d. the brain's attempt to wake up.

18. A cut through the midbrain
    a. left the animal sleeping constantly because most sensory input was cut off from the brain.
    b. produced prolonged sleep because an area that promotes wakefulness was cut off from the rest of the brain.
    c. left the animal sleeping and waking normally, since structures that control these functions are anterior to the midbrain.
    d. left the animal more wakeful than usual because much of the reticular formation was still connected to the brain, but a sleep-promoting system had been damaged.

19. The reticular formation
    a. is very discretely organized, with few interconnections.
    b. is important in generating slow-wave sleep.
    c. is primarily concerned with sensory analysis.
    d. none of the above.

20. The locus coeruleus
    a. is very active during REM sleep.
    b. is very active during slow wave sleep.
    c. is very active during meaningful events, such as reinforcements and punishments.
    d. got its name from its dark red color.

21. Sleep-inducing nuclei in the basal forebrain
    a. use GABA as their neurotransmitter.
    b. use acetylcholine as their neurotransmitter.
    c. have very restricted projections to specific cortical areas.
    d. work by inhibiting nuclei in the anterior and preoptic hypothalamus.

22. PGO waves
    a. occur during REM sleep.
    b. are recorded in the pons, lateral geniculate, and occipital cortex.
    c. are compensated more completely than total REM time, if "lost" due to REM deprivation.
    d. all of the above.

23. Neurons that are more active during REM are located in
    a. the reticular formation.
    b. the pons, thalamus, amygdala, and some cortical areas.
    c. the basal forebrain.
    d. the dorsolateral prefrontal cortex.

24. Inhibition of motor neurons during REM is induced by neurons in
    a. the dorsolateral prefrontal cortex.
    b. the reticular formation.
    c. the pons.
    d. the amygdala.

25. Which of the following is true?
    a. Acetylcholine is important for the continuation of REM sleep.
    b. Acetylcholine promotes slow-wave sleep.
    c. Carbachol inhibits REM sleep.
    d. Serotonin inhibits REM sleep.

26. People with phase-delayed temperature rhythms who try to fall asleep at the normal time may experience
   a. excess sleep.
   b. maintenance insomnia.
   c. termination insomnia.
   d. onset insomnia.

27. Which of the following is a cause of insomnia?
   a. narcolepsy
   b. cataplexy
   c. sleep apnea
   d. hypnagogic hallucinations

28. Which of the following is true of sleeping pills?
   a. They are the best treatment for jet lag.
   b. Withdrawal from previous use can lead to insomnia.
   c. They are generally harmless remedies for insomnia.
   d. They are the major cause of REM behavior disorder.

29. Which of the following is associated primarily with REM sleep?
   a. nightmares
   b. night terrors
   c. sleep talking
   d. all of the above

Answers to Multiple-Choice Questions

1. b	7. c	13. b	19. d	25. a
2. d	8. a	14. c	20. c	26. d
3. c	9. b	15. d	21. a	27. c
4. a	10. c	16. a	22. d	28. b
5. d	11. a	17. c	23. b	29. a
6. d	12. d	18. b	24. c	

DOING AND DREAMING

Constructed by Elaine M. Hull using Plexus Word Weaver®

Across

1 Midbrain area containing dopamine cell bodies (2 words)
5 Area of frontal cortex active during the planning of a movement
9 Initials of the author of your Study Guide
11 Brain neurotransmitter important for REM onset
13 Charged particle that crosses the membrane through protein channels
14 Taste sensation activated by acids
15 The direction of travel for which it is harder to reset the biological clock
16 Characteristic of muscle in fish that is white and easily fatigued
17 Part of the brain important for ballistic movements, timing of brief intervals, and response to movement signals

Down

1 Area of hypothalamus where damage disrupts the biological clock
2 Subcortical structures important for planning movements, controlling force, and problem solving (2 words)
3 Neurotransmitter at the neuromuscular junction and, in brain, promotes REM continuation
4 Speed of pink muscles in fish
6 Disease caused by damage to a dopamine pathway
7 Precursor of dopamine, used to treat disorder named in 6 down
8 Result of central pattern generator in the spinal cord
10 The neurons that exit the spinal cord on the ventral side
12 Type of insomnia that results from phase delay of body temperature

10

THE REGULATION OF
INTERNAL BODY STATES

INTRODUCTION

Homeostatic drives are drives that tend to maintain certain biological conditions within a fixed range. Temperature regulation in mammals and birds is such a drive. Constant relatively high temperatures provide conditions in which chemical reactions can be regulated precisely and, by increasing the metabolic rate, increase capacity for prolonged activity. Several physiological mechanisms, including shivering, sweating, panting, and redirection of blood flow, raise and lower temperature appropriately. These are coordinated primarily by the preoptic area, which monitors both its own temperature and that of the skin and spinal cord. Behavioral regulation of temperature is used both by animals that are poikilothermic (body temperature matches that of environment) and by those that are homeothermic (body temperature is regulated within a few degrees of a constant setting). The preoptic area, the posterior hypothalamus, and other areas are important for behavioral temperature regulation. Fever is produced when leukocytes (white blood cells) release interleukin-1, which causes production of prostaglandins E_1 and E_2, which in turn cause the preoptic area to raise body temperature. Moderate fevers are helpful in combating bacterial infections. Body temperature of infant animals may be an important influence on their behaviors, such as the tonic immobility response.

Water balance is critical, both for regulating the concentration of chemicals in our bodily fluids (and therefore the rate of chemical reactions) and for maintaining normal blood pressure. If we have ample supplies of palatable fluids to drink, we may drink a great deal of them and let the kidneys discard the excess. If there is a shortage of fluids to drink, or a large loss of water, the posterior pituitary releases vasopressin (also known as antidiuretic hormone, or ADH), which increases both blood pressure and water retention by the kidneys. There are two major types of stimuli for thirst: decreased water content inside cells and decreased blood volume. When water is lost from the body, or when there are increased solutes in the blood, the blood and extracellular fluid become more concentrated. Water tends to flow out of cells into the area of higher osmotic pressure (extracellular fluid). The resulting loss of water from cells in the OVLT (organum vasculosum laminae terminalis) elicits neural responses that are relayed to several hypothalamic nuclei, including the supraoptic and paraventricular nuclei, which produce vasopressin, the hormone that is released from the posterior pituitary and that increases blood pressure and urine concentration. The OVLT also relays information to the lateral preoptic area, which gives rise to osmotic thirst. Thus, an increase in osmotic signals results in greater water retention, increased water intake, and higher blood pressure. If large amounts of whole blood are lost, the resulting hypovolemia (low volume of blood) is detected by baroreceptors in the large veins; these receptors send information to areas in the hypothalamus that increase drinking. Baroreceptors in the kidney also detect the hypovolemia. The kidney then releases renin, which acts in the blood to produce angiotensin II. This hormone causes constriction of blood vessels to maintain blood pressure. It also stimulates neurons in the subfornical organ, which in turn relay the signal to neurons in the preoptic area, which produces hypovolemic thirst. The signals from the baroreceptors and angiotensin II are synergistic.

Loss of sodium and other solutes results in an immediate and automatic craving for sodium. This sodium hunger depends largely on two hormones, aldosterone and angiotensin II. Aldosterone, secreted by the adrenal glands, causes the kidneys, salivary glands, and sweat glands to conserve sodium; it also stimulates the OVLT and other areas around the third ventricle to increase salt intake. Angiotensin II, as noted above, stimulates sodium hunger. The effects of aldosterone and angiotensin II are strongly synergistic.

The factors regulating hunger, satiety, and the selection of specific foods are very complex. Food selection is influenced by the digestive system (including intestinal enzymes), cultural factors, taste, familiarity, and memories of the consequences of consuming a particular food. Hunger and satiety depend on stimuli from the mouth, stomach, and duodenum, as well as blood levels of glucose and other nutrients. Damage to the lateral hypothalamus results in self-starvation, unless the animal is force-fed. The intact lateral hypothalamus contributes to feeding by modifying activity in the nucleus of the tractus solitarius (NTS), which may influence taste sensations and salivation, and also by increasing the release of digestive juices and of insulin, which promotes storage of circulating glucose. Lateral hypothalamic axons also carry input to forebrain structures that facilitate ingestion. In addition, dopamine-containing fibers passing through the lateral hypothalamus contribute to arousal and reinforcement of learned behaviors. Damage to the ventromedial hypothalamus results in obesity. This results from faster emptying of the stomach and increased release of insulin, which promotes fat storage and inhibits its release for use as fuel. As a result, the animal consumes more frequent meals. Damage to the paraventricular nucleus (PVN) also results in overeating. However, rats with PVN damage eat larger meals, rather than more frequent meals.

Genes control body weight in many ways, including metabolic rate. Other genetic influences include the production of and sensitivity to peptides and other neurotransmitters that regulate feeding. Leptin is a peptide produced by fat cells that increases energy expenditure and decreases feeding. One means by which leptin decreases feeding is by inhibiting the release of neuropeptide Y (NPY), which normally increases feeding by inhibiting the PVN. Thus, the effect of NPY is similar to lesions of the PVN (failure to end meals appropriately), and leptin inhibits that effect. Another neurotransmitter that inhibits feeding is serotonin; drugs that increase serotonin activity decrease the rate of eating and meal size. Several chemicals, including CCK and glucagon (similar to GLP-1 in the brain), have central and peripheral effects that are complementary.

Anorexia nervosa is a disorder in which people eat much less than they need, sometimes starving themselves to death. They are usually perfectionistic, most frequently women, and often are depressed; however, antidepressant drugs are seldom effective in treating anorexia. People with bulimia nervosa alternate between overeating and dieting, frequently eating a huge meal and then vomiting. People with bulimia have low levels of CCK and decreased production of, or sensitivity to, serotonin. Drugs that increase serotonin are frequently effective in treating bulimia; however, it is not clear whether transmitter abnormalities precede or result from the bulimia.

KEY TERMS AND CONCEPTS

Temperature regulation
1. Homeostasis
    Set range
    Set point

2.   Mechanisms for controlling body temperature
Poikilothermic
Homeothermic
    Allows for activity in cold environments
    Trade-off between potential for activity and fuel requirements
    Optimal temperatures for enzymes
Brain mechanisms
    Hypothalamus
    Preoptic area
        Monitors own temperature
        Monitors temperature of skin and spinal cord
Behavioral mechanisms
    Preoptic area
    Posterior hypothalamus
    Other brain areas
Fever
    Leukocytes
        Interleukin-1
    Prostaglandins E_1 and E_2
    Preoptic area
    Moderate fevers helpful

3.   Temperature regulation and behavior
The development of animal behavior
    Improved behavioral capacities in warm environment
The tonic immobility response
    Terminated by increased temperature

Thirst
1.   Mechanisms of water regulation
Increasing intake
Decreasing output
    Vasopressin or antidiuretic hormone (ADH)

2.   Osmotic thirst
Osmotic pressure
Semipermeable membrane
Increase in solute concentration
    Water leaves cells
Brain areas
    OVLT (organum vasculosum laminae terminalis)
    Supraoptic nucleus
    Paraventricular nucleus
    Lateral preoptic area

3.   Hypovolemic thirst
Loss of blood volume
Satisfied best by salt water
Mechanisms
    Baroreceptors
    Hormones from kidneys
        Renin
        Angiotensinogen in blood
        Angiotensin II
    Subfornical organ

Preoptic area
Synergistic effects
Sodium-specific cravings
Automatic preference (not learned)
Aldosterone
Increased sodium retention by kidney, salivary glands, and sweat glands
Increased salt craving
Angiotensin II

Hunger
1. How the digestive system influences food selection
Mouth
Saliva: carbohydrate digestion
Stomach
Hydrochloric acid
Enzymes for protein digestion
Small intestine
Protein, fat, and carbohydrate digestion
Absorption
Large intestine
Water and mineral absorption
Lubrication
Enzymes and consumption of dairy products
Lactose, milk sugar
Lactase enzyme
Other influences on food selection
Carnivore, herbivore, omnivore
Culture, taste, familiarity, learning

2. How taste and digestion control hunger
Oral factors
Desire to taste or chew
Fifth cranial nerve (trigeminal)
Sham feeding
The stomach and intestines
Vagus nerve (cranial nerve X)
Information about stretching of stomach
Splanchnic nerves
Information about nutrient contents
The duodenum and the hormone CCK (cholecystokinin)
Inhibits stomach emptying
CCK also released in brain
Blood glucose
Availability of all types of nutrients
Insulin: facilitates glucose entry into cells
Glucagon: liver releases glucose

3. The hypothalamus and feeding regulation
The lateral hypothalamus
Lesions: starvation or weight loss
Electrical stimulation: eating
Neurons vs. dopamine axons passing through
Damage to dopamine axons with 6-OHDA: loss of arousal
Damage to cell bodies: loss of feeding
Mechanisms

NTS (nucleus of the tractus solitarius in medulla): taste, salivation
Dopamine-containing cells: initiation and reinforcement of learned
    behaviors
Forebrain structures: facilitate ingestion
Stimulation of secretion of insulin and digestive juices
Medial areas of the hypothalamus
    Lesions: weight gain
    Ventromedial hypothalamic syndrome
        Ventral noradrenergic bundle
        Finickiness
        More meals per day
        Increased stomach motility and secretions
        Faster stomach emptying
        Increased insulin and fat storage
    Paraventricular nucleus
        Critical for ending meals

4.   Genetics, neurotransmitters, and feeding regulation
Eating and storing vs. speed of running
Genetics, metabolic rate, and body weight
    Heat production vs. fat storage
Leptin
    Produced by fat cells
    Decreases hunger, increases energy expenditure in mice
    Obese people: more leptin than lean people; insensitive to it
Neuropeptide Y (NPY)
    Inhibits paraventricular nucleus (PVN), which would otherwise end the
        meal
    Inhibited by leptin
Other neurotransmitters and hormones
    Microdialysis
    Similarity of function across species
        CCK -- > satiety in humans and snails
    Similarity of function in brain and periphery
        Glucagon and GLP-1 decrease feeding
        CCK in intestines and brain inhibits feeding
    Numerous chemicals affect feeding
        Serotonin
Anorexia and bulimia
    Anorexia nervosa
        Hardworking perfectionists (obsessive-compulsive)
        Depression
        Elevated cortisol
    Bulimia nervosa
        Eat enormous meal, then purge
        High levels of peptide YY (PYY)
        Low levels of CCK
        Decreased serotonin levels or receptor sensitivity

SHORT-ANSWER QUESTIONS

Temperature regulation
1. *Homeostasis*
   a. What is a homeostatic process?

   b. What are some of the physiological processes that are controlled near a set point? What are some homeostatic processes that anticipate future needs?

   c. Why does the scrotum of most male mammals hang outside the body? Why should pregnant women avoid hot baths?

2. *Mechanisms for controlling body temperature*
   a. Define the terms poikilothermic and homeothermic.

   b. What is a major advantage of a constant body temperature? What is the cost to the animal for maintaining homeothermy?

   c. What two kinds of stimuli does the preoptic area monitor for temperature control?

d. What prevents the temperature of fish, amphibians, and reptiles from fluctuating wildly?

e. Describe the temperature regulation of infant rats and of mammals with damage to the preoptic area? What brain area, besides the preoptic area, is important for behavioral temperature regulation?

f. What are prostaglandins E$_1$ and E$_2$, and what are their roles in producing a fever?

g. Of what benefit is a fever?

3. *Temperature regulation and behavior*
   a. What was the key to eliciting behaviors such as odor conditioning and female sexual behavior in baby rats?

   b. Describe the tonic immobility response of baby birds. What is a major stimulus governing the duration of immobility?

Thirst
1. *Mechanisms of water regulation*
    a. Describe the different mechanisms of maintaining water balance that have been developed by desert animals and by animals with an abundant water supply.

    b. What are the two functions of vasopressin when body fluids are low? What is its other name?

2. *Osmotic thirst*
    a. What is osmotic pressure?

    b. How does the body "know" when its osmotic pressure is low?

    c.   What are the roles of the OVLT, the supraoptic and paraventricular nuclei of the hypothalamus, and the lateral preoptic area?

3. *Hypovolemic thirst*
    a. Why is hypovolemia dangerous?

b. Under what circumstances does hypovolemic thirst occur?

c. Will an animal with hypovolemic thirst drink more pure water or more salt water with the same concentration as blood? Why?

d. What is the role of baroreceptors in hypovolemic thirst?

e. Describe the steps leading to the production of antiotensin II. What are its two main effects?

f. Which brain structures seem to mediate hypovolemic thirst?

g. How may the effects of angiotensin II be enhanced?

h. What two effects of aldosterone are beneficial in cases of sodium deficiency? What other hormone contributes to salt hunger?

Hunger
1. *How the digestive system influences food selection*
    a. Enzymes for the digestion of what type of nutrient(s) are present in saliva? in the stomach? in the small intestine?

    b. From which structure is digested food absorbed?

    c. Why do newborn mammals stop nursing as they grow older?

    d. Discuss the evidence that humans are a partial exception to the principle of lactose intolerance in adults.

    e. List the factors that may influence food selection.

2. *How taste and digestion control hunger*

a. Summarize the evidence for the importance of oral factors in hunger and satiety. What is the evidence that these factors are not sufficient to end a meal normally?

b. How did Deutsch et al. demonstrate the importance of stomach distention in regulating meal size?

c. Which two nerves convey the stomach's satiety signals?

d. What is CCK? In what two places is it produced? What is one likely mechanism by which it induces satiety?

e. Summarize the evidence for and against the importance of blood glucose in the regulation of appetite.

f. What is the effect of insulin on blood glucose? How does this affect hunger? Compare the effects of glucagon with those of insulin.

g. Why do people with untreated diabetes eat a lot but gain little weight? How is this similar to, and how is it different from, the effects of high levels of insulin?

3. *The hypothalamus and feeding regulation*
   a. Describe the evidence that the lateral hypothalamus is important for hunger.

   b. What is 6-hydroxydopamine? What kind of neuronal damage does it inflict when injected into the lateral hypothalamus? What are the behavioral results of such damage?

   c. What is the result of damage to lateral hypothalamic cell bodies?

   d. By what four mechanisms may the lateral hypothalamus contribute to feeding?

e.   Describe the various behavioral changes produced by lesions of the ventromedial hypothalamus, ventral noradrenergic bundle, and surrounding areas. Can we say that animals with such lesions show an overall increase in hunger or a lack of satiety?

f.   To what factors can we attribute the obesity induced by ventromedial hypothalamus lesions?

g.   What are the effects of damage to the paraventricular nucleus (PVN)? How are these effects different from those of ventromedial hypothalamus damage?

4.   *Genetics, neurotransmitters, and feeding regulation*
   a.   Discuss the role of basal metabolic rate in weight regulation. Why is it difficult to lose more than a few pounds?

   b.   What type of cells produce leptin? What message does leptin convey? Is there any evidence that overweight humans produce too little leptin?

c. What brain area is inhibited by neuropeptide Y (NPY)? What are the effects of NPY on feeding? What chemical inhibits the release of NPY?

d. What is microdialysis?

e. What are two means by which CCK inhibits feeding? What are the effects of glucagon and GLP-1?

f. What is the influence of serotonin on feeding? What types of drugs decrease the rate of eating and the size of meals?

g. Compare the symptoms of anorexia nervosa with those of bulimia nervosa.

h. What chemical differences are seen in bulimics, compared to other people. What drug treatments are often effective in treating bulimia?

POSTTEST

Multiple-Choice Questions

1. Temperature regulation
   a. is an example of a homeostatic mechanism.
   b. is important in mammals and birds for increasing resting metabolic rate and, thereby, capacity for prolonged activity.
   c. maintains body temperature at levels that maximize the enzymatic properties of proteins.
   d. all of the above.

2. The preoptic area monitors
   a. only its own temperature.
   b. only skin and spinal cord temperature.
   c. both its own and skin and spinal cord temperature.
   d. the temperature of internal organs via nerve input from those organs.

3. Behavioral means of temperature regulation
   a. are the only means of temperature regulation in poikilotherms.
   b. are the only means of temperature regulation in homeotherms.
   c. do not become functional until adulthood.
   d. are regulated entirely by the preoptic area.

4. Fever
   a. is harmful and should always be reduced with aspirin.
   b. is produced primarily by prostaglandins E_1 and E_2 acting on cells in the preoptic area.
   c. is produced directly by bacteria acting on the preoptic area.
   d. is especially high in baby rabbits, in response to infections.

5. Which of the following is true?
   a. Infant rats, in the first week of life, can exhibit odor conditioning and female sexual behavior, but only if tested at normal room temperature (20_o-23_oC).
   b. Infant rats, in the first week of life, can exhibit odor conditioning and female sexual behavior, but only if tested at room temperatures above 30_oC.
   c. Chicks, when grabbed by a predator, will feign death for many hours, because the predator's warmth keeps the chick warm enough so that it does not have to move around.
   d. Chicks, when grabbed by a predator, will feign death because they know that this decreases the probability of being attacked.

6. Vasopressin
   a. raises blood pressure by constricting blood vessels.
   b. is also known as antidiuretic hormone, because it promotes water retention by the kidney.
   c. is secreted from the posterior pituitary, as a result of control by the supraoptic and paraventricular nuclei of the hypothalamus.
   d. all of the above.

7. The main reason that a salty meal makes us thirsty is that
   a. excess salt in extracellular fluid produces cellular dehydration; such dehydration of cells in the OVLT results in osmotic thirst.
   b. increased salt in extracellular fluid causes the fluid to enter OVLT cells, thus distending them and producing osmotic thirst.
   c. increased salt in the blood causes the liquid portion of the blood to enter cells throughout the body, thus producing hypovolemia.
   d. the salt enters cells in the OVLT and stimulates them directly.

8. The lateral preoptic area
   a. controls hypovolemic, but not osmotic, thirst.
   b. is the site of receptors for osmotic thirst.
   c. receives input from the OVLT and controls drinking.
   d. primarily responds to signals concerning dryness of the throat.

9. After its blood volume has been reduced, an animal
   a. will drink more pure water than salt water of the same concentration as blood.
   b. will drink more salt water of the same concentration as blood than pure water.
   c. will not drink any more than usual, since both liquid and solute have been removed.
   d. will drink only highly concentrated salt water.

10. Angiotensin II
    a. is secreted by the kidney.
    b. causes water to leave cells in the preoptic area and thereby stimulates osmotic thirst.
    c. stimulates the subfornical organ, which relays the information to the preoptic area, which in turn can induce drinking.
    d. all of the above.

11. Which of the following is *not* likely to induce drinking?
    a. application of angiotensin II to the OVLT
    b. application of angiotensin II to the subfornical organ
    c. low blood pressure signals from baroreceptors in the large veins
    d. a salty meal

12. Salt craving
    a. occurs automatically, without learning, when sodium is low.
    b. depends largely on aldosterone secreted by the adrenal glands.
    c. is enhanced by angiotensin II.
    d. all of the above.

13. In the stomach
    a. food is mixed with hydrochloric acid and enzymes for the digestion of protein.
    b. food is mixed with hydrochloric acid and enzymes for the digestion of carbohydrates.
    c. food is mixed with enzymes that aid the digestion of fats.
    d. absorption of food through the walls of the stomach occurs.

14. Lactase
    a. is the sugar in milk.
    b. is an intestinal enzyme for the digestion of milk.
    c. is abundant in almost all adult humans, but is lacking in adults of other mammalian species.
    d. is abundant in birds and reptiles, but is lacking in mammals.

15. Oral factors
    a. contribute to satiety but are not sufficient to determine the amount of food consumed.
    b. are irrelevant to satiety.
    c. are the single most important factor in inducing satiety.
    d. include only the taste of food.

16. If a cuff closes the outlet from the stomach to the small intestine
    a. the animal will not eat because of the trauma of the cuff.
    b. the animal will continue eating indefinitely, since food must pass beyond the stomach to trigger satiety.
    c. the animal will eat a normal-sized meal and stop.
    d. the animal will eat a normal meal, wait for it to be absorbed through the walls of the stomach, and then eat again.

17. Splanchnic nerves
    a. carry information about the nutrient contents of the stomach.
    b. carry information about the stretching of the stomach walls.
    c. are stimulated directly by cholecystokinin (CCK).
    d. secrete CCK into the circulatory system.

18. CCK
    a. is produced by the duodenum in response to the presence of food there.
    b. works, in part, by closing the sphincter muscle between the stomach and duodenum, thus allowing the stomach to fill faster.
    c. is also produced in the brain, where it tends to decrease eating.
    d. all of the above.

19. Glucose levels in the blood
    a. are the primary signal for hunger.
    b. may be a contributing factor in hunger motivation, but not the only one.
    c. are irrelevant as hunger signals.
    d. are elevated by insulin.

20. Insulin
    a. promotes entry of glucose into cells.
    b. is released by the liver.
    c. is no longer secreted after VMH lesions.
    d. is secreted in response to low blood sugar.

21. People with untreated diabetes eat more food because
    a. the vagus and splanchnic nerves are damaged.
    b. they store too much of their glucose, so it is unavailable for use.
    c. they excrete most of their glucose unused.
    d. their basal metabolic rate is too high.

22. Glucagon
    a. is high in the late autumn in migratory and hibernating species.
    b. is produced by the small intestine.
    c. stimulates the liver to convert glucose to glycogen for storage.
    d. stimulates the liver to convert stored glycogen to glucose for release into the blood.

23. Which of the following is true of lateral hypothalamic damage?
    a. It results in inactivity and decreased responsiveness to stimuli.
    b. At least some of the results are due to damage to axons passing through the area, rather than to cell bodies located there.
    c. At least some of the effects on eating are due to low levels of insulin and digestive juices.
    d. All of the above are true.

24. Obesity resulting from damage to the ventromedial hypothalamus and ventral noradrenergic bundle
    a. can be prevented by allowing the animals to eat only the same amount that they ate before the lesion.
    b. occurs because the stomach empties faster than normal and because insulin secretion is increased.
    c. results from a dramatic increase in the palatability of all foods, resulting in overeating even of bitter or untasty food.
    d. results from eating much larger meals than usual, because of lack of satiety.

25. Which of the following is true of the paraventricular nucleus (PVN)?
    a. It is important for ending a meal.
    b. It is important for beginning a meal.
    c. NPY excites neurons in the PVN.
    d. Leptin increases eating by increasing NPY release in the PVN.

26. Basal metabolic rate
    a. is increased when people diet, in order to generate more heat.
    b. is decreased when people diet, in order to conserve energy.
    c. is influenced almost exclusively by what we eat; genetic influence is minimal.
    d. is virtually identical in all people.

27. Leptin
    a. increases feeding.
    b. is a neurotransmitter produced by the brain.
    c. is produced by fat cells.
    d. is reduced in quantity in overweight people.

28. Neuropeptide Y (NPY)
    a. is produced by fat cells and decreases feeding.
    b. directly increases metabolic rate.
    c. decreases fat storage by decreasing the production of leptin.
    d. inhibits activity in the PVN, similarly to a lesion, thereby increasing meal size.

29. Microdialysis
    a. is a technique used primarily for damaging axons while leaving cell bodies intact.
    b. is a technique used primarily for damaging cell bodies while leaving axons intact.
    c. is a means of detecting the release of neurotransmitters.
    d. has been used to demonstrate that serotonin is an important hunger signal.

30. Which of the following is true?
    a. Drugs that increase serotonin activity have been used successfully to treat bulimia.
    b. Bulimics have higher than normal levels of peptide YY (PYY).
    c. Bulimics have lower than normal levels of CCK and serotonin (or decreased sensitivity to serotonin).
    d. All of the above are true.

Answers to Multiple-Choice Questions

1. d	7. a	13. a	19. b	25. a
2. c	8. c	14. b	20. a	26. b
3. a	9. b	15. a	21. c	27. c
4. b	10. c	16. c	22. d	28. d
5. b	11. a	17. a	23. d	29. c
6. d	12. d	18. d	24. b	30. d

Diagram

Label the following areas: preoptic area, posterior hypothalamus, lateral hypothalamus, ventromedial hypothalamus, paraventricular nucleus of the hypothalamus.

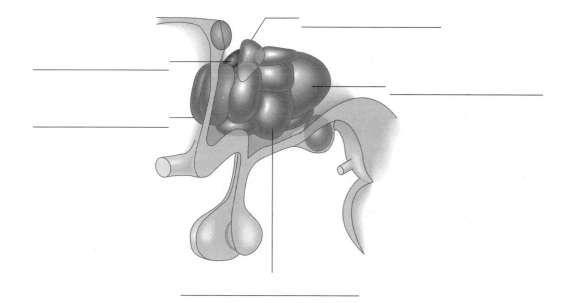

Based on *The Human Central Nervous System: A Synopsis and Atlas*, by R. Nieuwenhuys, J. Voogd, and C. van Huijzen Springer-Verlag, 1988.

11

HORMONES AND SEXUAL BEHAVIOR

INTRODUCTION

Hormones are released from various organs into the blood, which carries them throughout the body. They help to organize various organs and brain areas for a single function. There are several types of hormones. Protein and peptide hormones attach to receptors on the surface of cells, where they activate a second messenger, which in turn activates a series of enzymes. Steroid hormones attach to cytoplasmic receptors and move to the nucleus to alter gene expression. They may also have rapid effects on receptors on the cell membrane. Cortisol and corticosterone, from the adrenal cortex, elevate blood sugar and metabolism. The "sex hormones" include estrogens, progesterone, and androgens. Sex-limited genes are activated by hormones that are more abundant in one sex than in the other. High levels of steroids used by some athletes exert negative feedback effects on hormone production and may produce unwanted side effects. Additional classes of hormones include thyroid hormones, monoamines, and others that are difficult to classify.

Most endocrine glands are regulated by the pituitary, which in turn is controlled by the hypothalamus. The anterior pituitary is controlled by releasing hormones that are carried in the blood from the hypothalamus. The posterior pituitary is a neural extension of the hypothalamus.

Sex hormones have two distinct kinds of effects, depending on the stage of development at which they are present. The absence of androgens during an early critical period results in female-typical appearance and behavior, and androgens administered to a genetic female masculinize her genitals and behavior. A gene on the Y chromosome causes the primitive gonads to develop as testes and to secrete testosterone, which increases growth of the testes and Wolffian ducts (seminal vesicles and vas deferens) and also secretes Müllerian inhibiting hormone, which causes the female reproductive tract to regress. In rodents androgen appears to exert its masculinizing effects on behavior by being converted, intracellularly, to estrogen. A female is not masculinized by her own estrogen because it is bound to alpha-fetoprotein. Hormones may also have organizing effects on the hypothalamus, on nerves and muscles that control the penis, and on nonsexual characteristics, such as body size, life expectancy, play patterns, and aggressiveness.

When sex hormones are administered during adulthood, they tend to activate whatever behavior patterns were organized during development. Estrogens enhance sensory responsiveness of the pubic area of female rats. The ventromedial nucleus and the medial preoptic area (MPOA) of the hypothalamus are important brain areas for the activational effects of hormones. Stimulation of the MPOA enhances female-typical behavior in female rats and male-typical behavior in males. Both norepinephrine and dopamine in the MPOA facilitate masculine sexual behavior. Dopamine is released in the MPOA of male rats before and during copulation; dopamine is not released in males that fail to copulate. Castrated males produce dopamine in the MPOA but fail to release it. Moderate levels of dopamine stimulate D_1 or D_5 receptors, which promote erection in males and receptivity in females; higher levels stimulate D_2 receptors and promote orgasm and ejaculation. Testosterone also increases men's sexual interest, and oxytocin may enhance sexual pleasure, especially at orgasm. Although decreases in testosterone generally decrease sexual activity, low testosterone is not always the source of impotence. Treatments that reduce testosterone production or block its receptors have been used to treat sex offenders.

In women and certain other female primates, menstrual cycles result from interaction between the hypothalamus, pituitary, and ovaries. Follicle-stimulating hormone (FSH) from the anterior pituitary stimulates the growth of ovarian follicles and the secretion of estrogen from the follicles. Increasing estrogen at first decreases the release of FSH, but near the middle of the cycle, it somehow causes a sudden surge of luteinizing hormone (LH) and FSH. These hormones cause an ovum to be released and cause the uterine lining to proliferate. They also cause the remnant of the follicle (the corpus luteum) to release progesterone, which further prepares the uterus for implantation of a fertilized ovum. Progesterone inhibits release of LH; therefore, near the end of the cycle, all hormones are low, resulting in menstruation if fertilization does not occur. If the ovum is fertilized, estradiol and progesterone increase throughout the pregnancy. Combination birth-control pills contain estrogen, which suppresses the release of FSH early in the cycle, and progesterone, which inhibits the secretion of LH. Women's sexual interest is somewhat higher during the periovulatory period, but hormones are less important for women's sexual response than for females of other species.

Hormones also have activational effects on nonsexual behaviors. Testosterone enhances aggression in many species. Estrogen increases the number of certain dopamine and serotonin receptors in the nucleus accumbens and several cortical areas; these areas are thought to control reinforcement and emotion. Times of decreasing estrogen, such as before menstruation, after childbirth, and after menopause, may be associated with depression and irritability in some women. Premenstrual syndrome may also be related to increased cortisol, decreased vasopressin, or decreased activity of several neurotransmitters. Estrogen also enhances memory and fine motor skills, and testosterone given to older men improved their spatial skills.

Puberty is influenced by body weight and other factors. The hypothalamus begins to release bursts of luteinizing hormone releasing hormone (LHRH), which stimulates the pituitary to secrete LH and FSH, which in turn stimulate the gonads to release estradiol or testosterone.

Parental behavior in rodents can be rapidly induced by hormonal patterns characteristic of the time of delivery. This suggests that the immediate maternal behavior that occurs with delivery may be under hormonal control. Oxytocin and prolactin appear to be especially important. However, repeated exposure to pups can induce parental behavior after about 6 days, even in males and in females without ovaries. The MPOA is important for both the early hormone-dependent and the later experience-dependent phase of parental behavior. However, brain areas that respond to pheromones from the young animals initially suppress parental behavior; their activity is inhibited in the later phase.

Early fetal gonadal structures differentiate in either a male or a female direction, depending on the presence or absence of androgen. If a female is exposed to excess androgen during the critical period for sex differentiation, she may develop structures intermediate between those of a normal female and a normal male. Such an individual is called an intersex or pseudohermaphrodite. Most intersexes have been reared as females, since they are usually infertile, and it is easier to feminize the genitals surgically than to masculinize them. However, the surgery frequently impairs genital sensation. A genetic male may develop a relatively normal female appearance and gender identity because of androgen insensitivity (testicular feminization), due to a lack of androgen receptors. In the Dominican Republic some genetic males lack an enzyme that converts testosterone to DHT (5-alpha-dihydrotestosterone). Because DHT is more effective than testosterone for masculinizing the genitals, these boys appeared to be girls early in life; however, they became masculinized by high levels of testosterone at puberty. They then developed male gender identity, which was consistent with their prenatal testosterone. It was more difficult for a genetic male, whose penis was accidentally removed at birth, to develop a female identity. These

187

cases suggest that prenatal hormones play an important role in determining gender identity, although environmental factors may have some influence.

Genetic factors may promote homosexual orientation in both men and women. A gene that contributes to male homosexuality appears to be on the X chromosome, and therefore is inherited from the mother. A gene that increases homosexuality, and therefore decreases reproductive success, would be expected to be selected against in the course of evolution. However, it may be perpetuated through kin selection or by increasing the reproductive ability of the women who carry the gene. Homosexuality is not well correlated with hormone levels in adulthood. However, there is some evidence that low levels of prenatal testosterone, sometimes caused by stress, may predispose males to homosexuality in adulthood. These stress effects may be mediated by endorphins and may be influenced by social experiences after birth. Some women whose mothers took diethylstilbestrol (DES) to prevent miscarriage may have increased bisexual or homosexual responsiveness. Some brain structures show sex differences in size. For some of these structures, including the anterior commissure, the suprachiasmatic nucleus, and the interstitial nucleus 3 of the hypothalamus, homosexual men have structures more similar in size to those of women than to those of heterosexual men. We do not know whether these differences are a cause or an effect of homosexuality, or indeed, if they are relevant at all.

KEY TERMS AND CONCEPTS

Hormones and behavior
    Endocrine glands

1.   Mechanisms of hormone action
    Types of hormones
        Protein and peptide hormones
            Glycoproteins
            Induction of membrane changes
                Second messenger
                Cyclic AMP
        Steroid hormones: four carbon rings
            Cytoplasmic receptors
            Gene expression
            Some rapid membrane effects
            Adrenal cortex: cortisol and corticosterone
            Sex hormones: estrogens, progesterone, androgens
            Sex-limited genes
            Negative feedback by high levels
        Thyroid hormones
        Monoamines: epinephrine, norepinephrine, and dopamine
        Miscellaneous other hormones
    Control of hormone release
        Hypothalamus
        Posterior pituitary
            Neural extension of hypothalamus
            Oxytocin
            Vasopressin (antidiuretic hormone)
        Anterior pituitary
            Hypothalamic releasing hormones
            Adrenocorticotropic hormone (ACTH)
            Thyroid-stimulating hormone (TSH)
            Follicle-stimulating hormone (FSH)

188

Luteinizing hormone (LH)
Prolactin
Somatotropin (growth hormone, GH)

2. Organizing effects of sex hormones
    Organizing effects
        Permanent change of anatomy
        Sensitive stage
    Activating effects
    Sex differences in the gonads and hypothalamus
        Gonads
            Ovaries
            Testes
            Müllerian ducts
            Wolffian ducts
        Hypothalamus
            Cyclic pattern of hormone release in females
        Medial preoptic area: one portion larger in males
        Testosterone
            Masculinization of female rats by testosterone injections
            Little or no sex hormones: female development
            Aromatization of testosterone to estradiol
            Alpha-fetoprotein
            Survival of muscles and nerves of penis
    Sex differences in nonreproductive characteristics
        Body size
        Life expectancy
        Infant care
        Rough and tumble play
        Aggressiveness
        Excessive adrenal androgens in girls: "boy's toys"

3. Activating effects of sex hormones
    Sexual behavior
        Effects on rats
            Pudendal nerve
            Ventromedial nucleus
            Medial preoptic area
                Sexually dimorphic nucleus
                Stimulation: increase in male-typical behavior in males
                    and in female-typical behavior in females
                Increase in activity during copulation
                Damage
                    Male rats: decrease in all sexual behaviors
                    Male ferrets: respond to males, not females
            Norepinephrine
            Dopamine
                Released in presence of female
                Facilitates copulation
                Castration: impairs release of MPOA dopamine
                Moderate levels: D_1 and D_5 receptors
                    Erection in male
                    Receptivity in female
                    Higher levels: D_2 receptors
                    Ejaculation and orgasm

Nucleus accumbens: dopamine released during copulation
    Important for reinforcement
Effects on men
    Correlation of testosterone levels and sexual excitement
    Oxytocin release during orgasm
    Impotence not always due to low testosterone
    Sex offenders
        Cyproterone: blocks testosterone receptors
        Medroxyprogesterone: decreases production, enhances
            metabolism of testosterone
        Hypothalamic releasing hormone analog: blocks
            secretion of testosterone
Effects on women
    Menstrual cycle
    FSH
        Promotes growth of follicle, which nurtures ovum
        Increases secretion of estradiol by follicle
    Estradiol
        Decreases FSH, then causes surge of LH and FSH
    LH and FSH
        Release ovum
        Increase secretion of progesterone by corpus luteum
            (remnant of follicle)
    Progesterone
        Prepares lining of uterus
        Inhibits LH release
    Menstruation: due to decreased hormone levels
    If pregnancy: estrogen and progesterone increase
    Birth-control pills
        Combination pill: suppresses FSH and LH release
    Periovulatory period: maximum fertility and sexual interest
Nonsexual behavior
    Testosterone: increases aggression
    Estrogen: increases D_2 and $5HT_{2A}$ receptors in nucleus accumbens and
        cortex --> affects reinforcement, mood
    Premenstrual syndrome
        Decreased estrogen
        Increased cortisol
        Decreased vasopressin
        Decreased neurotransmitter activity
    Estrogen: improved memory and motor skills
        Menopause
    Testosterone: improved memory in older men

4.   Puberty
    Menarche
        Influence of body weight and male or female odors
    Luteinizing hormone releasing hormone

5.   Parental behavior
    Hormone-dependent early phase
        Oxytocin
        Prolactin
    Experience-dependent later phase
        Decreased response to pheromones

Vomeronasal organ
Medial preoptic area: important for both phases

Variations in sexual development and sexual orientation
1. Determinants of gender identity
    True hermaphrodites: some testicular and some ovarian tissue
    Intersexes or pseudohermaphrodites: intermediate appearance
        Usually reared as girls
        Surgery destructive of sexual sensation
    Testicular feminization or androgen insensitivity
        XY genotype
        Lack of androgen receptors
        Female gender identity
    Discrepancies of sexual appearance
        Penis development delayed until puberty
            Decreased enzymes that convert testosterone to DHT
                DHT more effective in masculinizing genitals
            Puberty: enough testosterone to masculinize penis
        Accidental removal of the penis

2. Possible biological bases of sexual orientation
    Genetics
        Greater similarity of orientation in identical twins
        Gene on X chromosome: increased male homosexuality
            Possible indirect effects
            Evolutionary selection
                May increase reproductive success of women
                May be perpetuated by kin selection
    Hormones
        No consistent differences in adult hormone levels
        Decreased testosterone during early development of males
        Prenatal stress or alcohol
            Endorphins: antitestosterone effects
            Social experiences
        Diethylstilbestrol (DES) in females
    Brain anatomy
        Anterior commissure
            Larger in women and homosexual men
        Suprachiasmatic nucleus (SCN)
            Larger in homosexual than heterosexual men
        Interstitial nucleus 3 of anterior hypothalamus
            Larger in heterosexual men than in women and homosexual men
            Differences not due to AIDS
            Cause vs. effect
            Functions unclear

SHORT-ANSWER QUESTIONS

Hormones and behavior
1. *Mechanisms of hormone action*
   a. Define "hormone." How clear is the distinction between hormones and neurotransmitters?

   b. What are the two major classes of hormones? What are some additional classes of hormones?

   c. By what two major mechanisms do hormones act on the nervous system?

   d. What are the major differences between control mechanisms for the anterior and posterior pituitary?

   e. List the hormones released from the posterior pituitary. the anterior pituitary.

   f. What are releasing hormones? Where are they produced?

2. *Organizing effects of sex hormones*
    a. Distinguish between organizing effects and activating effects of hormones.

    b. What are Müllerian ducts? What are Wolffian ducts?

    c. Describe the effects of testosterone injections during the first 10 days after birth on female rats.

    d. What happens if a developing mammal is exposed to neither androgens nor estrogens during early development?

    e. When is the critical period for testosterone's effects on rats? on humans?

    f. By what mechanism does testosterone exert its effects on the hypothalamus in rodents?

g. Describe the effects of injections of large amounts of estrogen on female rats during the critical period.

h. What is the role of alpha-fetoprotein?

i. Describe the organizing effects of testosterone on the nerves and muscles that control the penis.

j. What are some nonreproductive characteristics that may be influenced by prenatal hormones?

3. *Activating effects of sex hormones*
   a. Which hormones can restore male-typical sexual behavior following castration? What is the most effective hormone treatment for restoring female-typical behavior?

   b. What is the pudendal nerve? What are estrogen's effects on its function?

c.   What brain area may facilitate female-typical behavior in females and male-typical behavior in males? Describe the different effects of lesions of this area in male rats, compared to male ferrets.

d.   What two transmitters in the MPOA stimulate male sexual activity? Which other brain area is important for sexual behavior, as well as most other kinds of reinforcement?

e.   How does castration affect dopamine release in the MPOA?

f.   What may be its role in the progression from the early stages of copulation, which require erection, to the ejaculatory stage?

g.   Describe the relationship between testosterone levels and sexual activity in men. Which other hormone contributes to sexual pleasure?

h.   Which two drugs have been used to treat sex offenders? What type of drug has more recently been used? What are the effects of these drugs?

i.   List the chain of hormonal processes in the menstrual cycle.

j.   What are the two effects of follicle-stimulating hormone (FSH)?

k.   Rising levels of which hormone cause a sudden surge of LH and FSH near the middle of the cycle? What are the effects of the LH and FSH?

l.   What is the corpus luteum, and what hormone does it release?

m.   What are the effects of progesterone? Describe the levels of the major hormones shortly before menstruation.

n.   How do combination birth-control pills work?

o. The decline in which hormone may be associated with premenstrual syndrome? What are some neural effects of this hormone? What other hormones and neurotransmitters may be involved in premenstrual syndrome?

p. What cognitive effects have been demonstrated for estrogen and testosterone? How strong are these effects?

4. *Puberty*
   a. What is the role of weight in the age at which menarche occurs?

   b. What is the first sign of the onset of puberty?

5. *Parental behavior*
   a. Describe the roles of hormones and experience in parental behavior of rodents.

   b. Which two hormones have been shown to promote maternal behavior?

c.   Under what conditions do male rodents engage in parental behavior?

Variations in sexual development and sexual orientation
1.   *Determinants of gender identity*
     a.   What is an intersex or pseudohermaphrodite? What is the difference between a true hermaphrodite and a pseudohermaphrodite?

     b.   What are some developmental influences that may produce an intersex individual?

     c.   Why have most intersexes been reared as females?

     d.   How successful is the surgical treatment of intersexes?

     e.   Describe the chromosomal pattern and the genital appearance of individuals with androgen insensitivity, or testicular feminization. What causes the unresponsiveness to androgen? What two abnormalities appear at puberty?

f.   Describe two situations in which children were exposed to the prenatal hormonal pattern of one sex and then reared as the opposite sex. Can we infer from these situations that early rearing experiences are the sole (or even the major) determinants of gender identity?

2.   *Possible biological bases of sexual orientation*
    a.   Describe the evidence for a genetic predisposition towards homosexuality.

    b.   What was the likely explanation for the increased incidence of homosexuality among maternal relatives of homosexual men?

    c.   Can we conclude that there is a single gene that directly determines sexual orientation?

    d.   Discuss the problems concerning evolutionary selection of any genes predisposing toward homosexuality.

    e.   What are two possible explanations for the continued existence of those genes?

f.   Describe the experiments on the effects of stress on sex differentiation of rats. What were their results?

g.   How may endorphins be implicated in the effects of stress? What other factors may influence the effects of prenatal stress?

h.   Summarize the evidence regarding possible prenatal stress effects on homosexual men.

i.   How strong is the influence of prenatal diethylstilbestrol (DES) on homosexuality in women?

j.   What are three brain structures that show a sex difference in size? In which direction is the size difference for each? How do homosexual men compare with heterosexual men and with women regarding the size of these structures?

k.   Describe LeVay's evidence implicating the interstitial nucleus 3 of the hypothalamus in homosexuality?

l. If there is a consistent difference between homosexual and heterosexual men in the size of various brain nuclei, what can we conclude about the role of these nuclei in determining sexual orientation?

POSTTEST

Multiple-Choice Questions

1. Concerning hormones, which of the following is true?
   a. All hormones bind to membrane receptors and activate second messenger systems.
   b. Peptide hormones enter the cell and bind to receptors that carry them into the nucleus, where they alter gene expression.
   c. Steroid hormones enter the cell and bind to receptors that carry them into the nucleus, where they alter gene expression. They may also have rapid membrane effects.
   d. Cortisol and corticosterone are peptide hormones that help to conserve energy.

2. Cyclic AMP
   a. is a glycoprotein.
   b. is a steroid hormone.
   c. is a peptide hormone.
   d. is a second messenger.

3. Androgens
   a. are present only in males; estrogens are present only in females.
   b. are present in both males and females but are produced in greater quantities in males.
   c. elevate blood sugar and enhance metabolism as their main effects.
   d. more than one of the above.

4. Sex-limited genes
   a. are present on the Y chromosome and therefore are lacking in females.
   b. are present on the X chromosome and therefore are unopposed and dominant in males.
   c. are present in both sexes but are activated preferentially by androgens or estrogens.
   d. are the genes that code for the production of androgens and estrogens.

5. Which of the following is true?
   a. Hormone production by the anterior pituitary is controlled by releasing hormones secreted by the hypothalamus.
   b. Hormone production by the posterior pituitary is controlled by releasing hormones from the hypothalamus.
   c. FSH is a hypothalamic releasing hormone that causes the pituitary to release LH.
   d. Estrogen is secreted by the anterior pituitary.

6. Oxytocin
   a. is also known as antidiuretic hormone.
   b. is synthesized in the hypothalamus and released from the posterior pituitary, as is vasopressin.
   c. is synthesized in and released from the anterior hypothalamus, in response to releasing hormones from the hypothalamus.
   d. controls secretions of the adrenal cortex.

7. Wolffian ducts
   a. are the precursors of the oviducts, uterus, and upper vagina.
   b. are the precursors of the male reproductive structures.
   c. are the precursors of the external genitals.
   d. none of the above.

8. If a female rat receives testosterone injections during the last few days before birth or the first few postnatal days, then in adulthood
   a. her pituitary and ovary will produce steady levels of hormones rather than cycling in the normal manner.
   b. she will exhibit neither masculine nor feminine sexual behavior.
   c. she will exhibit normal feminine sexual behavior in spite of the full masculinization of her genitals.
   d. she will exhibit normal feminine sexual behavior, and her genitals will appear fully feminine.

9. A female pattern of development
   a. can be produced by giving a female mammal large amounts of estrogen during the sensitive period.
   b. can be produced in normal males by giving them estrogen in adolescence.
   c. can be produced in mammals of either sex by depriving the animal of testosterone during the sensitive period.
   d. all of the above.

10. Which of the following is true?
    a. Testosterone's organizing effects occur throughout the entire period of gestation.
    b. Alpha-fetoprotein is the enzyme that converts testosterone to estradiol.
    c. Estradiol masculinizes the hypothalamus by being aromatized to testosterone.
    d. Testosterone masculinizes the hypothalamus of rodents largely by being aromatized to estradiol.

11. High levels of testosterone during prenatal development
    a. cause female monkeys to display more rough and tumble play.
    b. may contribute to the shorter life spans of males.
    c. may contribute to the greater aggressiveness of males.
    d. all of the above.

12. Stimulation of the MPOA
    a. increases both male-typical behavior in males and female-typical behavior in females.
    b. decreases male-typical behavior in males and increases female-typical behavior in females.
    c. increases male-typical behavior in males and decreases female-typical behavior in females.
    d. produces homosexual behavior in both sexes.

202

13. Activation of female sex behavior by hormones
    a. is most easily elicited by injections first of progesterone and then dihydrotestosterone in females whose ovaries were removed.
    b. may be mediated in part by increasing the area of skin that activates the pudendal nerve.
    c. is mediated by a decrease in stimulation of D_1 and D_5 dopamine receptors in the MPOA.
    d. all of the above.

14. Dopamine in the MPOA of male rats
    a. is released when the male is exposed to a receptive female, but only for those males that do copulate when they are allowed to.
    b. is not released in normal amounts by castrated males.
    c. may act through different receptors to promote erection first and then ejaculation.
    d. all of the above.

15. Cyproterone, medroxyprogesterone, and a newer drug related to a hypothalamic releasing hormone
    a. are common treatments for impotence.
    b. are common treatments for premenstrual syndrome.
    c. are sometimes used to decrease sexual fantasies and offensive sexual behaviors of sex offenders.
    d. are sometimes used to elicit the maturation and release of an ovum in infertile women.

16. The corpus luteum
    a. is the remnant of the follicle, which releases progesterone.
    b. releases estrogen during the early part of the cycle, which causes the pituitary to release a surge of progesterone at midcycle.
    c. is the primary source of FSH.
    d. is the primary source of LH.

17. FSH
    a. is secreted from the uterus.
    b. is secreted from the follicle.
    c. stimulates the follicle to grow, nurture the ovum, and produce estrogen.
    d. stimulates the follicle to grow and produce LH.

18. Combination birth control pills
    a. contain both estrogen and progesterone.
    b. suppress the release of FSH.
    c. suppress the release of LH.
    d. all of the above.

19. Which of the following is true?
    a. The effects of "sex hormones" are limited to the control of reproductive behavior and the endocrine system.
    b. Declines in estrogen may result in decreased activity at D_2 and $5HT_{2A}$ receptors in the nucleus accumbens and cortex, which have been implicated in mood and reinforcement.
    c. Estrogen produces major enhancements in spatial performance.
    d. Testosterone treatments in older men impaired their spatial performance.

20. Puberty
    a. begins when the hypothalamus begins to secrete luteinizing hormone releasing hormone in hourly bursts.
    b. is influenced by weight, among other factors.
    c. may be retarded in female rodents by the odor of other females and hastened by the odor of males.
    d. all of the above.

21. Which is true concerning rodent parental behavior?
    a. Hormones are important in eliciting parental behavior soon after giving birth for the first time.
    b. Hormones continue to be the most important factor in eliciting parental behavior throughout the entire period of care of the young.
    c. Male rats do not show any parental behavior unless they are given high doses of progesterone during prenatal development.
    d. Parental behavior is enhanced by lesions of the MPOA, since that area is concerned only with male sexual behavior, which would interfere with parental behavior.

22. Intersexes, or pseudohermaphrodites,
    a. usually can be made fertile with appropriate surgery.
    b. have complete sets of both male and female structures.
    c. are frequently genetic females who have been exposed to elevated levels of androgens during fetal development.
    d. are usually genetic males who have been exposed to estrogens during fetal development.

23. Intersexes reared as females
    a. are almost never happy with the sex to which they were assigned at birth, because their brains were completely masculinized.
    b. are sometimes resentful that surgical "correction" of their genitals destroyed sexual sensation and makes them feel violated.
    c. provide clear evidence that prenatal hormones are the only determinant of gender identity.
    d. provide clear evidence that prenatal hormones are unimportant in gender identity.

24. Androgen insensitivity (testicular feminization)
    a. is characterized by normal amounts of testosterone but a lack of receptors to carry it to the nucleus.
    b. results in an individual who appears to be completely female but fails to menstruate at puberty and has no pubic hair.
    c. cannot be alleviated by giving injections of testosterone.
    d. all of the above.

25. Certain genetic males in the Dominican Republic
    a. lack the enzyme that converts testosterone to estradiol.
    b. lack the enzyme that converts testosterone to DHT (5-alpha-dihydrotestosterone)
    c. are usually reared as boys, but adapt easily to a feminine sexual identity when they begin to produce high levels of estrogen at puberty.
    d. are usually reared as girls, but are completely unable to adapt to their new male gender identity when high levels of testosterone at puberty cause growth of a penis.

26. A genetic contribution to homosexuality
    a. may be carried by a gene on the X chromosome that promotes homosexuality in males.
    b. may be carried by a gene on the Y chromosome that promotes homosexuality in males.
    c. is now known to be controlled by the same genes in male and female homosexuals.
    d. has been disproven, since evolution strongly selects against any genes that would interfere with reproduction.

27. Male homosexuality
    a. is highly correlated with low levels of testosterone in adulthood.
    b. is highly correlated with high levels of estrogen in adulthood.
    c. may be associated with increased stress during prenatal development.
    d. may be redirected to heterosexuality by injections of testosterone in adulthood.

28. Diethylstilbestrol (DES)
    a. can be used in adulthood to change the sexual orientation of homosexual men.
    b. can be used in adulthood to change the sexual orientation of homosexual women.
    c. administered to mothers during pregnancy may slightly increase the likelihood of bisexuality or homosexuality in their sons.
    d. administered to mothers during pregnancy may slightly increase the likelihood of bisexuality or homosexuality in their daughters.

29. The interstitial nucleus 3 of the anterior hypothalamus
    a. is smaller in women and homosexual men than in heterosexual men.
    b. is larger in women and homosexual men than in heterosexual men.
    c. is smaller in homosexual men than in either women or heterosexual men, primarily because the AIDS virus is known to kill neurons in that site more than in the rest of the brain.
    d. is now known to be the primary brain center that determines sexual orientation.

Answers to Multiple-Choice Questions

1. c	6. b	11. d	16. a	21. a	26. a
2. d	7. b	12. a	17. c	22. c	27. c
3. b	8. a	13. b	18. d	23. b	28. d
4. c	9. c	14. d	19. b	24. d	29. a
5. a	10. d	15. c	20. d	25. b	

Diagram

Label the following structures of the endocrine system: hypothalamus, pituitary, pineal gland, adrenal gland, ovary, placenta, testis, pancreatic islets, parathyroid, thyroid, thymus.

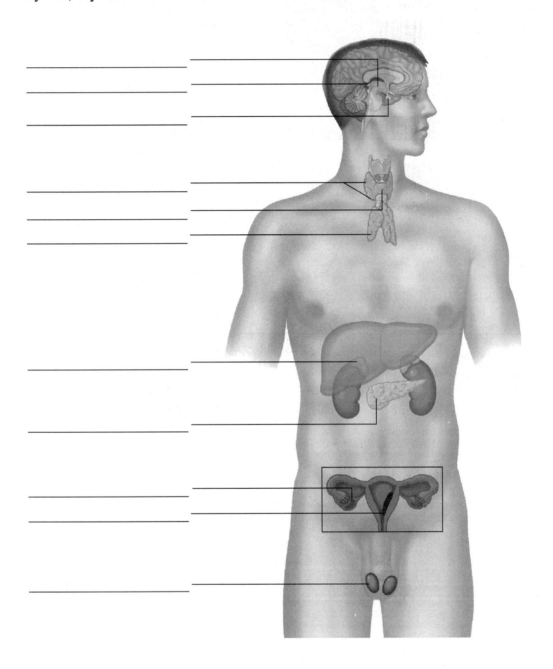

SEX, HEAT, AND GLUTTONY

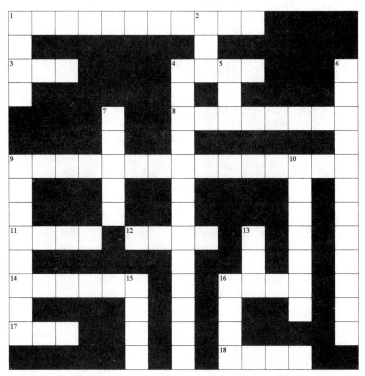

Constructed by Elaine M. Hull using Plexus Word Weaver®

Across

1 Hormone that constricts blood vessels and increases hypovolemic thirst
3 Acronym for anterior pituitary hormone that increases release of thyroid hormones
4 Part of the hindbrain dorsal or anterior to the medulla
8 Posterior pituitary hormone, also a brain transmitter, important for sexual and parental behavior
9 Hypothalamic nucleus important for ending a meal
11 Acronym for brain structure next to third ventricle, sensitive to osmotic pressure
12 Form of birth control

medication combining estrogen and progestin
14 Male gonads
16 6-____, toxin that destroys dopamine and norepinephrine neurons (abbr.)
17 Intestinal hormone and brain transmitter that promotes satiety (abbr.)
18 ____amine, a type of chemical that can serve as either a hormone or a neurotransmitter

Down

1 Acronym for anterior pituitary hormone that stimulates the adrenal cortex
2 Acronym for the brain

structure next to third ventricle that monitors blood volume information
4 Brain chemical that causes the preoptic area to raise body temperature
5 Peptide that inhibits PVN and increases eating (abbr.)
6 A region of the hypothalamus in which damage increases eating and body weight
7 An adaptive increase in temperature in response to an infection
9 Hypothalamic area important for sexual and parental behavior, thirst, and temperature regulation
10 Hypothalamic area in which damage impairs eating and drinking
13 Acronym for a pituitary chemical that stimulates the ovary
15 Preoptic area monitors the temperature of this part of the body, in addition to its own temperature
16 Gamete produced by females

207

12

EMOTIONAL BEHAVIORS AND STRESS

INTRODUCTION

Emotional feelings and behaviors are controlled and integrated largely by the limbic system, which includes the hypothalamus, amygdala, hippocampus, olfactory bulb, septum, and parts of the thalamus and cortex. The right hemisphere may be more important than the left for certain aspects of emotion.

Activity of the autonomic nervous system, composed of the sympathetic and parasympathetic divisions, has been associated with certain emotional states. For example, sympathetic activity prepares for vigorous or emergency activity. The parasympathetic system promotes digestion and conserves energy. The polygraph test measures heart rate, blood pressure, breathing rate, and galvanic skin response, all of which which increase during sympathetic arousal and are thought to reflect a person's nervousness.

Vulnerability to certain diseases is affected by our behaviors and by stress and emotions. Excessive parasympathetic activity, after a period of intense stress, may cause some cases of voodoo death. Excessive sympathetic activity may contribute to heart disease, whereas social support may decrease sympathetic activity and protect against heart disease. Chronic, uncontrollable stressors may depress the functioning of the immune system and leave an individual more vulnerable to disease. During stress, the hypothalamus directs the anterior pituitary to secrete ACTH (adrenocorticotropic hormone), which in turn stimulates the adrenal gland to secrete cortisol. Cortisol shifts energy metabolism to increase blood sugar and decrease synthesis of proteins, including the proteins necessary for immune function. Two important elements of the immune system are the B cells, which produce antibodies that attach to and inactivate specific antigens, and the T cells, which attack specific "foreign" cells or stimulate responses from other immune cells. Natural killer cells kill tumor cells and cells infected with viruses; their attacks are relatively nonspecific. Endorphins, released during prolonged stressful events, decrease pain and also decrease the number of natural killer cells. The relationship between experiences and illness in humans is complex and not well understood.

Aggression is complex and difficult to study. Increased aggressiveness is related to genetic factors in both animals and humans. Testosterone increases unprovoked aggression, although its effect is relatively weak. Stimulation of the ventromedial hypothalamus or the amygdala can promote aggressive responses, whereas lesions of the amygdala usually decrease aggressiveness and also impair the interpretation of visual information. Some people with temporal-lobe epilepsy have violent outbursts as a result of seizures that involve the amygdala. Antiepileptic drugs frequently control the epilepsy and the violence; however, for extremely violent individuals who were not helped by drugs, lesions of the amygdala have sometimes reduced the violence and/or the epilepsy. Low serotonin turnover may also be associated with aggressiveness in both animals and people. Turnover is inferred from levels of 5-HIAA, a serotonin metabolite. Low serotonin turnover was observed in mice that showed isolation-induced aggression and in monkeys that were naturally aggressive. Low serotonin turnover in humans may be associated with impulsiveness, violent crimes, and suicide.

Fear is a temporary experience, whereas anxiety is longer lasting. The amygdala, especially its central nucleus, is important for learned fear responses, including enhancement of the startle reflex. Its output to the hypothalamus controls

208

autonomic responses, and its connections to the central gray in the midbrain indirectly elicit the skeletal responses of flinching and freezing. Anxiety is commonly treated with benzodiazepine tranquilizers. These drugs exert their effect at the "benzodiazepine receptor" on the $GABA_A$ receptor complex, thereby facilitating the binding of GABA to its own receptor at the complex. The binding of GABA increases the flow of chloride ions across the membrane. Barbiturates and alcohol also bind to the $GABA_A$ complex, thereby facilitating GABA binding. Diazepam-binding inhibitor (DBI) is an endozepine (endogenous *anti*benzodiazepine); it blocks the effects of diazepam and other benzodiazepines, thereby increasing anxiety.

An overresponsive sympathetic nervous system is suspected of playing a role in panic attacks. Increases in carbon dioxide or lactate, which may be caused by stress or exercise, may be misinterpreted as signals of suffocation and lead to a panic attack. Obsessive-compulsive behavior can be treated with drugs that prolong serotonin's presence in the synapse. It may be related to excessive activity in the caudate nucleus, putamen, and orbital prefrontal cortex.

KEY TERMS AND CONCEPTS

Emotion, the nervous system, and health
1. Where is emotion in the brain?
    Limbic system ("border" around brainstem)
        Includes hypothalamus, hippocampus, amygdala, olfactory bulb, septum,
            parts of thalamus and of cerebral cortex
        Epileptic focus: associated with emotional states
        Primitive functions
    Right cerebral cortex: sad or fearful emotions

2. Autonomic nervous system arousal
    Sympathetic nervous system: vigorous, emergency activity
    Parasympathetic nervous system: digestion, conservation of energy
    Interpretation of stimuli
    James-Lange theory: autonomic arousal and actions before emotions
    Cannon-Bard theory: emotions independent from autonomic arousal
    Measures of autonomic arousal
        Polygraph
        Galvanic skin response

3. Emotions, autonomic responses, and health
    Behavioral medicine
    Voodoo death and related phenomena
        Curt Richter's swimming rats
        Excessive parasympathetic activity
    Sympathetic arousal and heart disease
        Social support: decreased heart rate and blood pressure

4. Chronic stress, the immune system, and health
    Hypothalamus -- > anterior pituitary -- > adrenal cortex
        Adrenocorticotropic hormone (ACTH)
        Cortisol
            Increased blood sugar and metabolism
            Decreased protein synthesis, including immune system proteins
    The immune system
        Autoimmune disease

Leukocytes
Bone marrow, thymus, spleen, lymph nodes
Antigens
Macrophages
B cells
Antibodies
B memory cells
T cells
Directly attack intruder
Stimulate response from other immune cells
Natural killer cells
Cytokines
Effects of stress on the immune system
Psychoneuroimmunology
Endorphins: suppress natural killer cells
Stable social relationships: stronger immune responses

Attack and escape behaviors
1.   Attack behaviors
"Play": Attack, escape
Affective attack
Corticomedial amygdala
Genetics and gene-environment interactions
Genetic factors better predictors of adult than juvenile crime
Hormones
Testosterone
Male-female differences
Smaller differences in self-reported than in observed aggression
Males: more unprovoked aggression than females
Little difference in response to serious provocation
Within age groups or prison populations: modest correlation between
aggressiveness and testosterone
Brain activity
Ventromedial nucleus of hypothalamus
A site of testosterone's effects
Output to brainstem
Amygdala
Stimulation: attacks
Rabies
Removal: tameness
Klüver-Bucy syndrome
Difficulty interpreting visual stimuli
Temporal lobe epilepsy
Symptoms: hallucinations, lip smacking, repetitive acts, in some cases
aggressive behaviors
Antiepileptic drugs
Surgical destruction of amygdala
Prefrontal cortex damage: general loss of inhibitions
Serotonin synapses and aggressive behavior
Turnover
5-HIAA (5-hydroxyindoleacetic acid)
Low serotonin turnover: correlated with aggressiveness
Social isolation
Genetically aggressive mice
Lack of 5-HT$_{1B}$ receptors

Suicide
Impulsive behavior
Tryptophan

2. Escape behaviors
Fear and anxiety
Fear, enhanced fears, and the amygdala
Startle reflex
Auditory input to cochlear nucleus of medulla, then to pons: tense muscles
Modified by experience: basolateral and central nuclei of amygdala
Output to hypothalamus: autonomic responses
Output to midbrain central gray, then to pons: skeletal responses
Larger effect of right amygdala than of left
The human amygdala
Greater response to fearful expressions
Removal: loss of learned emotional response
Urbach-Wiethe disease: atrophy of amygdala, decreased fear
Anxiety-reducing drugs
Transmitters in amygdala: CCK, excitatory; GABA, inhibitory
Barbiturates: habit forming, easy to take fatal overdose
Benzodiazepines
Diazepam (Valium)
Chlordiazepoxide (Librium)
Alprazolam (Xanax)
GABA_A receptor complex
Chloride channel: hyperpolarizes
Benzodiazepines, barbiturates, and alcohol: enhance GABA binding
Diazepam-binding inhibitor (DBI), an endozepine: endogenous
*anti*benzodiazepine
Panic disorder
Overresponsive sympathetic nervous system
Exercise or stress
Increased blood levels of lactate and carbon dioxide
Similar to suffocation
Hyperventilation: lowers carbon dioxide and decreases parasympathetic
activity: more responsive to new stressors
Tranquilizers, antidepressants, and psychotherapy
Obsessive compulsive disorder
Drugs that block serotonin reuptake
Caudate nucleus, putamen, and orbital prefrontal cortex
Alcohol and tranquilizers
Cross tolerance to alcohol, benzodiazepines, and alcohol
Ro15-4513: blocks alcohol's effects on GABA_A receptors and behavior

SHORT-ANSWER QUESTIONS

Emotion, the nervous system, and health
1. *Where is emotion in the brain?*
   a. List the major components of the limbic system.

b.   How did the limbic system get its name? What was Papez's theory concerning the neural basis for emotion?

c.   What evidence did MacLean provide in support of Papez's theory?

d.   Describe the recent evidence concerning the contributions of the right hemisphere to emotions.

2.   *Autonomic Nervous System Arousal*
    a.   What are the roles of the sympathetic and parasympathetic nervous systems?

    b.   Describe the James-Lange theory of emotions.

    c.   What is the Cannon-Bard theory of emotions?

d. Describe the evidence concerning the importance of the autonomic nervous system for emotions.

e. What does the polygraph test actually measure? What is the galvanic skin response?

f. What is the theory behind the use of the polygraph? How reliably does it indicate truthfulness? Why?

3. *Emotions, autonomic responses, and health*
   a. What are the assumptions of behavioral medicine? How strong is the link between stress and cancer?

   b. What is meant by "rebound overactivity" of the parasympathetic nervous system? How might this explain why a person may faint after escaping from something frightening?

   c. Describe Richter's experiment with swimming rats?

d. What was the cause of death in Richter's rats? Were wild or domesticated rats more likely to die? What procedure averted death of the dewhiskered rats?

e. How may frequent hostility contribute to heart disease? How important is social support in maintaining health?

4. *Chronic stress, the immune system, and health*
   a. Describe the steps in the control of cortisol secretion from the adrenal cortex.

   b. What are cortisol's major effects on blood sugar and metabolism? How does this affect the immune system?

   c. What are the most important cells of the immune system? Where are these cells produced?

   d. What are antigens? How was the name "antigen" derived?

e.　What are the roles of B cells and of T cells?

f.　What is the role of macrophages? of natural killer cells?

g.　Describe the evidence suggesting that stress impairs the function of the immune system.

h.　What is another mechanism, besides increased cortisol release, by which stress affects the immune system?

Attack and escape behaviors
1.　*Attack behaviors*
　　a.　What is one explanation of a cat's "play" behavior with its prey?

　　b.　Describe the behavioral characteristics of affective attack and "cold-blooded" attacks.

c.   What are the effects of stimulation of the amygdala on aggressive behavior? Which area of the amygdala is especially important for this effect?

d.   What conclusions can be drawn from studies of adopted children and of twins concerning the relative roles of genes and environment in promoting aggressive behavior and crimes?

e.   How strong is the correlation between testosterone levels and aggressive behavior?

f.   Stimulation of which two brain areas can elicit attack?

g.   How does rabies lead to violent behavior?

h.   What are the usual effects of amygdala damage? Describe the Klüver-Bucy syndrome.

i.   What happens in the brain during an epileptic seizure?

j.   What are some behavioral symptoms of temporal lobe epilepsy?

k.   What are two forms of medical or surgical treatment for frequent unprovoked violence?

l.   What transmitter abnormality appears to be associated with aggressive behavior? How can it be measured?

m.   Describe the experimental evidence in mice for this relationship.

n.   How was serotonin turnover related to behavior in male monkeys in a natural-environment study?

o.   What evidence implicates low serotonin turnover in humans as a factor in aggressive behavior?

2.   *Escape behaviors*
     a.   Why should researchers be interested in the startle response?

     b.   What is a key brain area for learned fears? Which of its nuclei receive sensory input?

     c.   What are the main output connections of the amygdala? What does each control?

     d.   Damage to which nucleus of the amygdala abolishes the enhancement of the startle reflex?

     e.   What causes Urbach-Wiethe disease? What are its symptoms?

f.   What are one excitatory and one inhibitory transmitter in the amygdala that have been implicated in the control of anxiety?

g.   What two types of drugs have been used to reduce anxiety? What are the relative advantages and disadvantages of the two types?

h.   When a benzodiazepine molecule attaches to its binding site on the the GABA$_A$ receptor, how is the binding of GABA affected? What effect does this have on the flow of chloride ions across the cell membrane?

i.   How do alcohol and barbiturates affect this process?

j.   What is one endogenous chemical that affects the benzodiazepine receptors? Why is the term endozepine confusing?

k.   Increases in blood levels of what two molecules can trigger panic attacks? Under what conditions do these chemicals normally increase?

l.   Explain the role of hyperventilating in panic disorder.

m.   What is one likely basis for obsessive-compulsive behavior?

n.   What are the advantages and disadvantages of a drug that blocks alcohol's effects on the GABAₐ receptor? What is your opinion of the decision not to market the drug?

POSTTEST

Multiple-Choice Questions

1.   The limbic system
   a.   gets its name from the fact that it has many limbs branching in all directions.
   b.   includes the hypothalamus, hippocampus, amygdala, olfactory bulb, septum, and parts of the thalamus and cerebral cortex.
   c.   is especially important for higher cognitive functions that differentiate humans from other mammals.
   d.   all of the above.

2.   Which of the following is true?
   a.   The left hemisphere is more important than the right for processing sad or fearful information.
   b.   The James-Lange theory proposed that emotional experience and autonomic arousal are evoked independently.
   c.   The parasympathetic nervous system rebounds with overactivity when a stimulus that strongly excites the sympathetic nervous system is removed.
   d.   Sympathetic nervous system activity prepares the body for digestion and relaxation.

3. The polygraph
   a. measures heart and breathing rates and electrical conductance of the skin.
   b. measures epinephrine levels.
   c. is virtually 100 percent accurate in detecting lies.
   d. can discriminate extremely accurately among anger, fear, and intense happiness.

4. Voodoo death occurs only
   a. if a witch doctor has special powers.
   b. in very primitive societies.
   c. if the victim believes in the hex or pronouncement.
   d. in people with underactive parasympathetic nervous systems.

5. Curt Richter found that
   a. cutting off a rat's whiskers immediately before putting it into a tank of water resulted in its struggling frantically and then sinking suddenly to the bottom, dead.
   b. laboratory rats, but not the stronger wild ones, were most susceptible to the sudden death phenomenon.
   c. rats' whiskers are necessary for swimming, since removing them negated the otherwise helpful procedure of rescue training.
   d. all of the above are true.

6. Cortisol
   a. is secreted by the anterior pituitary gland.
   b. serves primarily to activate a sudden burst of "fight or flight" activity.
   c. serves primarily to decrease metabolic activity in order to save energy for later stresses.
   d. shifts energy away from synthesis of proteins, including those necessary for the immune system, and towards increasing blood sugar.

7. T cells
   a. are specialized to produce antibodies.
   b. mature in the thymus and either attack intruder cells or stimulate other immune system cells.
   c. engulf microorganisms and display antigen of the microorganism.
   d. are useless until they are activated by B cells.

8. Stress
   a. causes the release of endorphins, which suppress certain immune responses.
   b. is by far the major factor in the success of an animal's immune resonse; however, humans are not susceptible to stress effects.
   c. is an important activator of natural killer cells and therefore enhances immune function.
   d. all of the above.

9. Affective attack
   a. is described as a "cold-blooded" attack.
   b. is the type of attack in which an animal "plays" with its prey.
   c. can be elicited by stimulation of the corticomedial amygdala.
   d. is characterized by intense parasympathetic activity during the attack.

10. Which of the following is true?
    a. The correlation between testosterone and aggression in humans is real, but of modest size.
    b. Both genetics and environmental factors contribute to the predisposition to commit crimes and aggressive behaviors.
    c. Stimulation of the ventromedial hypothalamus can increase the likelihood of an attack against an intruder.
    d. All of the above are true.

11. Lesions of the amygdala
    a. usually produce difficulty in interpreting visual information as well as decreased aggressiveness.
    b. usually cause temporal lobe epilepsy.
    c. lead to a state that resembles panic disorder.
    d. usually decrease the frequency of predatory attacks, but increase affective attacks.

12. Temporal-lobe epilepsy
    a. is invariably associated with violence.
    b. is generally untreatable except by surgery.
    c. symptoms include hallucinations, lip smacking or other repetitive acts, and, in some cases, violence.
    d. can frequently be improved with antidepressant drugs.

13. Which of the following is true?
    a. Mice with low levels of serotonin turnover are abnormally placid.
    b. Serotonin turnover has been found to be lower than normal in impulsive, aggressive humans.
    c. 5-HIAA is a drug that has been used successfully to treat uncontrollable violence.
    d. All of the above are true.

14. The brain area that is especially important for learned fears is
    a. the basolateral nucleus of the thalamus.
    b. the central nucleus of the hypothalamus.
    c. the central nucleus of the amygdala.
    d. the entire hippocampus.

15. Output from the amygdala to the hypothalamus controls
    a. the intensity of sensory input to the organism.
    b. innate, rather than learned, fears.
    c. skeletal movements of the startle response.
    d. autonomic fear responses, such as increased blood pressure.

16. After damage, inactivation, or atrophy of the amygdala
    a. a person has difficulty recognizing or portraying fearful expressions.
    b. a rat no longer shows any startle reflex.
    c. a rat shows greater deficits in remembering unpleasant experiences if the left side is damaged, compared to the right.
    d. a person shows enhanced reactions to fear-provoking stimuli.

17. Librium, Valium, and Xanax
    a. are more habit-forming than barbiturates and more likely to lead to a fatal overdose.
    b. are benzodiazepines.
    c.   act exclusively on CCK synapses.
    d. all of the above.

18. The benzodiazepines
    a. directly stimulate the same receptor sites that GABA stimulates.
    b. decrease the membrane's permeability to chloride ions.
    c.   attach to binding sites on the GABA$_A$ receptor complex, thereby facilitating GABA binding.
    d. block GABA$_A$ synapses.

19. Which of the following is true?
    a. Alcohol displaces benzodiazepines from their binding sites, thereby disrupting GABA transmission.
    b. Alcohol produces its antianxiety effects by blocking chloride channels.
    c.   The most effective anti-anxiety drugs are CCK receptor blockers.
    d. Endozepines, including diazepam-binding inhibitor (DBI), are actually endogenous *anti*benzodiazepines, which inhibit GABA transmission.

20. Which of the following is true of people who are prone to panic attacks?
    a. Their brain may misinterpret increases in blood lactate and carbon dioxide as signs of suffocation.
    b. They may have an overresponsive parasympathetic nervous system.
    c.   They should hyperventilate at the first sign of panic, in order to avert a full-blown attack.
    d. They are helped only by drug therapy; psychotherapy has no added benefit.

21. People with obsessive-compulsive disorder
    a. can be treated successfully with clomipramine or fluvoxamine, which inhibit the reuptake of serotonin at the synapse.
    b. have increased metabolic rates in the caudate nucleus, putamen, and orbital prefrontal cortex.
    c.   have their symptoms reduced by drug or behavior therapy only if the treatment also decreases activity in the caudate nucleus, putamen, and orbital prefrontal cortex.
    d. all of the above.

Answers to Multiple-Choice Questions

1. b	6. d	11. a	16. a	21. d
2. c	7. b	12. c	17. b	
3. a	8. a	13. b	18. c	
4. c	9. c	14. c	19. d	
5. a	10. d	15. d	20. a	

13

THE BIOLOGY OF LEARNING AND MEMORY

INTRODUCTION

Learning depends upon changes within single cells, which then work together as a system to produce adaptive behavior. Different kinds of learning and memory may rely on different neural mechanisms. Classical conditioning establishes a learned association between a neutral (conditioned) stimulus (CS) and an unconditioned stimulus (UCS) that evokes a reflexive response (UCR). As a result, the previously neutral stimulus comes to evoke a response (CR) similar to the reflexive response. Operant conditioning is the increase or decrease in a behavior as a result of reinforcement or punishment. Other forms of learning, such as bird song learning, may fall outside the categories of classical or operant conditioning.

Ivan Pavlov hypothesized that all learning is based on simple neural connections formed between two brain areas active at the same time. Karl Lashley tested this hypothesis by making various cuts that disconnected brain areas from each other and by removing varying amounts of cerebral cortex after rats had learned mazes or discrimination tasks. To his surprise, he found that no particular connection or part of the cortex was critical for any task. Lashley assumed that all learning occurred in the cortex and that all types of learning relied on the same physiological mechanism. Recent evidence suggests that certain subcortical nuclei may be important for specific types of learning and that several different neural mechanisms underlie different types of learning. For example, one simple type of conditioning, the eye blink response, relies on the lateral interpositus nucleus of the cerebellum. The red nucleus, a midbrain motor center, is necessary for the motor expression of the eyeblink response, but not formation of the memory.

Memory can be divided into several types: short-term vs. long-term, explicit vs. implicit, and declarative vs. procedural. Some short-term memories are consolidated rapidly into long-term memory; others are consolidated more slowly; most are not consolidated at all. Highly emotional events, which activate the sympathetic nervous system, are easily remembered. A major reason is that epinephrine released from the adrenal gland facilitates consolidation in several ways. It activates the vagus nerve, which relays activation to the brain; it indirectly increases release of norepinephrine in the brain; and it increases blood glucose, the brain's major fuel. All of these processes, and probably others, increase activation of the amygdala, which enhances storage of emotional memories. Working memory is the temporary storage of information while we are using it. We may have separate neural mechanisms for storing auditory memory (a "phonological loop") and visual memory (a "visuospatial sketchpad"), as well as a "central executive" that directs attention and determines which items will be stored. The prefrontal cortex seems to be especially important for working memory.

Information about memory has been obtained from studies of three major syndromes involving amnesia in humans. The main cognitive deficit in all three syndromes is the inability to form new long-term declarative or explicit memories. Declarative memory is memory that people can state in words, whereas procedural memory consists of motor skills. Explicit memory is deliberate recall of information that one recognizes as a memory; implicit memories can be detected as indirect influences on behavior, and do not require recollection of specific information. One syndrome results from hippocampal damage and is exemplified by the patient H. M., who had bilateral removal of the hippocampus to relieve incapacitating epilepsy.

Following surgery, H. M. suffered extensive anterograde amnesia and moderate retrograde amnesia.

The second disorder, Korsakoff's syndrome, occurs almost exclusively in severe alcoholics and is characterized by apathy, confusion, and both retrograde and anterograde amnesia. It is caused by prolonged thiamine deficiency, which results in loss of neurons throughout the brain, especially in the mamillary bodies of the hypothalamus and the dorsomedial thalamus, which projects to prefrontal cortex. In addition to their deficit in explicit memory, Korsakoff's patients also have difficulty recalling the temporal order of events.

The third human memory disorder is Alzheimer's disease, which is characterized by progressive forgetfulness, leading to disorientation. The brains of Alzheimer's victims reveal widespread neural degeneration, especially in the cerebral cortex and hippocampus and in basal forebrain neurons that release acetylcholine. The most heavily damaged area is the entorhinal cortex, which communicates with the hippocampus. Plaques and tangles of dying neurons form in areas of degeneration, which appear to be caused by deposits of amyloid beta protein. A gene on chromosome 21 determines the structure of amyloid precursor protein, which is cleaved to form amyloid beta protein. A mutation at or near that gene may cause excessive production of amyloid beta protein. People with Down syndrome, who have three copies of chromosome 21, almost always get Alzheimer's disease if they survive into middle age. In addition, mutations of a gene on chromosome 14 or on chromosome 1 increase the ratio of an abnormally long form of amyloid beta protein, which may result in early-onset Alzheimer's disease. Yet another gene, on chromosome 19, may also increase the density of amyloid deposits, resulting in later-onset Alzheimer's disease. We have learned from amnesic patients that people have several kinds of memory that depend on different brain areas.

Damage to the hippocampus of animals, as in humans, disrupts declarative, explicit memory. Rats with hippocampal damage forget which arms of a radial arm maze they have already entered in search of food; they also forget the location of a platform submerged in murky water. Primates with hippocampal or prefrontal cortex damage show deficits on delayed nonmatching-to-sample tasks under certain test conditions. The hippocampus clearly is not the storage site for memories, since previously formed memories can still be retrieved. Three theories of hippocampal function suggest that it is critical for the formation of (1) declarative, explicit memories, (2) configural conditioning (in which a combination of stimuli determine the correct response), or (3) spatial memories. Among related species of birds that live in different habitats, those that are most dependent on finding previously hidden food have the largest hippocampus. Both infant amnesia and memory problems of old people are similar to cases of damage to the hippocampus and prefrontal cortex. Infant amnesia may result from the the slow rate of maturation of the hippocampus, whereas memory problems in aging people without Alzheimer's disease may result in part from decreasing numbers of dopamine receptors in the prefrontal cortex.

Many researchers have studied the cellular mechanisms of learning in invertebrates, which have simple, well-defined nervous systems. Studies using *Aplysia* have demonstrated changes in single synapses during habituation and sensitization. These result from changes in the number of quanta of transmitter released. Long-term potentiation (LTP), an increased response in cells of the mammalian hippocampus, cortex, and other areas, depends on stimulation of two types of glutamate receptors. Stimulation of non-NMDA receptors depolarizes the neuron, thereby displacing the magnesium ions that normally block the ion channels of nearby NMDA receptors. As a result, the NMDA receptors are able to respond to glutamate, allowing both sodium and calcium ions to enter the cell. The calcium, in turn, induces the expression of genes that determine the structure of proteins that either (1) alter the structure of dendrites or (2) increase responsiveness of non-NMDA receptors. The calcium may also increase production of a retrograde transmitter, probably nitric oxide

(NO), which increases presynaptic neurotransmitter release. Although stimulation of NMDA receptors is necessary for the *establishment* of LTP, activity of these receptors is not required for its *maintenance*. Near simultaneous stimulation by two or more axons increases LTP, a process called cooperativity. Associativity refers to the increased responsiveness to a weak stimulus as a result of its being paired with a strong stimulus. LTP and NMDA receptors may underlie the consolidation of memories in the intact organism. For example, LTP can be detected first in the hippocampus during training, and then 90 to 180 minutes later, it is detectable in the entorhinal cortex, the area closest and most heavily connected to the hippocampus. LTP may also be important in the development of connections during early critical periods.

KEY TERMS AND CONCEPTS

Learning, memory, amnesia, and brain functioning
1. Localized representations of memory
    Classical conditioning
        Ivan Pavlov
        Conditioned stimulus (CS)
        Unconditioned stimulus (UCS)
        Unconditioned response (UCR)
        Conditioned response (CR)
    Operant conditioning
        Reinforcement
        Punishment
    Bird-song learning
    Karl Lashley's search for the engram
        Engram
        Amount of damage, not location
        Unnecessary assumptions:
            Cerebral cortex is the site of the engram.
            All kinds of memory are the same.
    The modern search for the engram
        Richard F. Thompson
            Rabbit eye blink response
            Lateral interpositus nucleus of cerebellum: site of conditioning
            Red nucleus: motor expression
        Classical conditioning of eyeblink in humans
            PET scans: increased activity in cerebellum, red nucleus, and other
                areas
            Damage to cerebellum: impaired eyeblink conditioning

2. Types of memory and amnesia
    Short-term and long-term memory
        Donald Hebb
    Consolidation of long-term memories
        Reverberating circuit
        Epinephrine -- > vagus nerve -- > brain activation
        Epinephrine -- > corticosterone -- > brain norepinephrine
        Epinephrine -- > glycogen to glucose -- > increased brain activity, including
            acetylcholine production and release
        Amygdala: stores some emotional memories itself and enhances storage in
            other areas

226

A modified theory: Working memory
    Phonological loop: stores auditory memory
    Visuospatial sketchpad: stores visual memory
        Delayed response task
        Cells in temporal cortex: temporary visual memory storage
        Cells in prefrontal cortex: specific locations or stimuli
    Central executive: directs attention and picks items for storage
Activity in prefrontal cortex

3. Brain damage and long-term memory
Amnesia
Memory loss after hippocampal damage
    H. M.: surgery for severe epilepsy
    Moderate retrograde amnesia (events before surgery)
    Severe anterograde amnesia (events after surgery)
    Normal short-term or working memory
    Impaired declarative memory
    Intact procedural memory
    Better implicit than explicit memory
        Priming
Korsakoff's syndrome and other prefrontal damage
    Wernicke-Korsakoff syndrome
    Thiamine deficiency
    Widespread loss of neurons, especially in:
        Mamillary bodies of hypothalamus and
        Dorsomedial thalamus (projects to prefrontal cortex)
    Both anterograde and retrograde amnesia
    Better implicit than explicit memory
    Poor recall of temporal order of events
    Confabulation
Alzheimer's disease
    Memory loss, confusion, depression, restlessness, hallucinations, delusions,
        disturbances of eating and sleeping
    Better procedural than declarative memory
    Better implicit than explicit memory
    Genetic and nongenetic causes
        Relationship to Down syndrome (3 copies of chromosome 21)
        Amyloid precursor protein --> amyloid beta protein (Aß)
        Mutation on chromosome 21: increase all Aß proteins
        Mutations on chromosome 14 or chromosome 1: increases ratio of $Aß_{42}$
            (harmful) to $Aß_{40}$ (normal) --> early onset Alzheimer's disease
        Mutations on chromosome 19: increases density of amyloid deposits -->
            later-onset Alzheimer's disease
    Atrophy of cerebral cortex, hippocampus, and other areas
        Entorhinal cortex: communicates with hippocampus
    Loss of acetylcholine neurons in basal forebrain --> impaired attention
    Plaques and tangles
What amnesic patients teach us: Independent kinds of memory depend on
    different brain areas.

4. Functions of the hippocampus in memory
Damage to the hippocampus in rats
    Radial maze: forget which arms they already tried
    Morris search task: forget location of platform

Damage to the hippocampus in primates
 Delayed matching-to-sample test
 Delayed nonmatching-to-sample test
Theories of the function of the hippocampus
 Declarative, explicit memory (hard to classify some memory tasks)
 Configural conditioning: combination of stimuli
 Spatial memories
  Clark's nutcracker: most dependent on buried food
   Largest hippocampus
   Best performance on spatial tasks
  Pinyon jays: moderately dependent on buried food
   Second largest hippocampus
   Second best performance on spatial tasks
  Scrub jay and Mexican jay: least dependent on buried food
   Smallest hippocampus
   Worst performance on spatial tasks
  No correlation of hippocampal size with color memory
  European tits and American chicadees: strong link between
  hippocampal size and spatial memory

5. Brain and memory in young and old
Infant amnesia
 Hippocampus slow to mature
 Poor declarative memory
Aging people with memory problems
 Deficits similar to those due to prefrontal cortex damage
 Decreased dopamine receptors in prefrontal cortex

Storing information in the nervous system
1. Learning and the Hebbian synapse
Simultaneous pre- and postsynaptic activity

2. Single-cell mechanisms of invertebrate behavior change
Aplysia as an experimental animal
 Plasticity
Habituation in *Aplysia*
 Decreased number of quanta from sensory neuron
Sensitization in *Aplysia*
 Increased number of quanta from sensory neuron
 Facilitating interneuron
 Serotonin (5-HT)
 Cyclic AMP
 Blocking of potassium channels
 Prolonged action potential
 Protein synthesis
 Long-term sensitization

3. Long-term potentiation in mammals (LTP)
Brief but rapid series of stimuli
Increased responsiveness for minutes, days, or weeks
Cooperativity: nearly simultaneous stimuli more effective than single stimuli
Associativity: pairing weak and strong inputs --> enhanced later response to
 weaker one
Strengthen only synapses that "cooperated"
Occurs in hippocampus, cerebral cortex, and other areas

Long term depression in hippocampus and cerebellum
    Cerebellum: Nearly simultaneous activity in parallel and climbing fibers -->
        depression of (inhibitory) Purkinje cell
    Net effect: increased excitation downstream
Cellular mechanisms
    Hippocampal slice
    NMDA glutamate receptors
    Non-NMDA receptors
    Magnesium blockade of NMDA receptors
    Removal of magnesium by depolarization
    Calcium influx into postsynaptic neuron
    NMDA receptors: establish, not maintain, LTP
    Activation of gene expression
        Alter structure of dendrites
        Increase responsiveness of the active non-NMDA receptors
    Retrograde transmitter (probably nitric oxide, NO) --> increases
        presynaptic neurotransmitter release
LTP and behavior
    LTP first in hippocampus, then in entorhinal cortex
    Mutation of gene that controls NMDA receptors
        Impaired LTP and spatial memory
    Similar effects of drugs on LTP and on memory
    "Leaky" calcium channels in old age
    Modification of synapses during developmental critical period
    LTP in *Aplysia*

SHORT-ANSWER QUESTIONS

Learning, memory, amnesia, and brain functioning
1. *Localized representations of memory*
    a. Describe the relationships among the conditioned and unconditioned stimuli and the unconditioned and conditioned responses in classical conditioning.

    b. Who discovered classical conditioning? What were the conditioned and unconditioned stimuli in his experiments? What was the unconditioned, and eventually the conditioned, response?

c. What is the fundamental distinction between classical and operant conditioning? Define reinforcement and punishment in terms of operant conditioning.

d. Why is bird-song learning difficult to classify?

e. What is an engram? What did Lashley discover in his search for the engram?

f. What two assumptions did Lashley make, which investigators have later rejected?

g. What brain area was found by Richard F. Thompson to be important for classical conditioning of the eyeblink response in rabbits?

h. What area was important for the expression of the motor response, but not for the initial conditioning?

i.   Which areas showed increased activity on PET scans during eyeblink conditioning in humans?

2.   *Types of memory and amnesia*
    a.   Define short-term memory and long-term memory.

    b.   How did Donald Hebb explain consolidation?

    c.   In what three ways do exciting experiences and epinephrine enhance memory?

    d.   What is working memory? What are its three hypothesized components? What brain area seems to be especially important for working memory?

3.   *Brain damage and long-term memory*
    a.   Why was H. M.'s hippocampus removed bilaterally? How successful was this treatment at relieving epilepsy? What were the other effects of the surgery?

b.   What is the difference between retrograde and anterograde amnesia? Which is more severely impaired in H. M.?

c.   Distinguish between declarative memory and procedural memory. Which is impaired in H. M.?

d.   Distinguish between explicit memory and implicit memory.

e.   What is priming? Is it used to test explicit or implicit memory?

f.   What is the immediate cause of Korsakoff's syndrome? What are its symptoms? In what group of people does it usually occur?

g.   Which brain areas show neuronal loss in Korsakoff's syndrome?

h. Describe the symptoms of Korsakoff's syndrome in terms of anterograde vs. retrograde amnesia and explicit vs. implicit memory.

i. How are implicit and explicit memory tested?

j. What other symptom do Korsakoff's patients have, in common with patients with frontal-lobe damage?

k. Describe the symptoms of Alzheimer's disease.

l. Why are some cases of Alzheimer's disease thought to be related to a gene on chromosome 21? How does the chromosomal abnormality differ from that in Down syndrome?

m. What is the role of the gene on chromosome 21 that is implicated in Alzheimer's disease? What is amyloid precursor protein? amyloid beta protein?

n.   What does a gene on chromosome 14 do to promote early-onset Alzheimer's disease? What are the two forms of amyloid beta (Aß) protein?

o.   Which brain areas are atrophied in Alzheimer's disease? Basal forebrain neurons containing which neurotransmitter degenerate? What physical signs are present in areas of atrophy?

p.   What have we learned about memory from amnesic patients?

4.   *Functions of the hippocampus in memory*
     a.   What two kinds of errors can rats make in the radial maze. Which type of error do rats make after damage to the hippocampus?

     b.   Describe the Morris search task. What deficits on this task are seen in hippocampally damaged rats?

     c.   Describe the delayed matching-to-sample and delayed nonmatching-to-sample tasks. Which can monkeys perform most easily?

d. Under what conditions does hippocampal damage impair performance on nonmatching-to-sample tasks? What other brain area is important for this task?

e. Why can we conclude that memories are not stored in the hippocampus itself?

f. For what three types of memory is the hippocampus hypothesized to be important?

g. Describe the relationship between birds' dependence on finding previously hidden food and the size of their hippocampus.

5. *Brain and memory in young and old*
   a. What is infant amnesia? Is there greater loss of declarative or procedural memories?

   b. Give one physiological explanation for infant amnesia.

    c.   Deterioration of which brain area may impair memory in old age? What type of receptors are lost in that area?

Storing information in the nervous system
1. *Learning and the Hebbian synapse*
    a.   Define "Hebbian synapse." How is it related to classical conditioning?

2. *Single-cell mechanisms of invertebrate behavior change*
    a.   Why should anyone be interested in the cellular mechanisms of sensitization or habituation in the lowly *Aplysia*?

    b.   What possible mechanisms of habituation were ruled out experimentally? What mechanism does seem to account for habituation in *Aplysia*?

    c.   How is sensitization produced experimentally in *Aplysia*?

    d.   Describe the cellular events that explain sensitization in *Aplysia*. How does a decrease in potassium outflow increase transmitter release?

e. How does long-term sensitization differ from the short-term variety?

3. *Long-term potentiation in mammals*
    a. How is long-term potentiation (LTP) produced? How long does it last? In what brain area was it first discovered? Where else has it been observed?

    b. What is meant by cooperativity? associativity?

    c. What is long term depression (LTD)? Where has it been observed? Which type of cell is depressed? What is the effect of that depression on "downstream" cells?

    d. Which transmitter stimulates both NMDA and non-NMDA receptors? Why must non-NMDA receptors be stimulated, in addition to NMDA receptors, in order to produce LTP?

    e. What is the effect of stimulating NMDA receptors?

f.   Are NMDA receptors important for the establishment or maintenance of LTP?

g.   Compare the temporal course of LTP in hippocampus with that in the entorhinal cortex.

h.   List the three possible mechanisms of LTP.

i.   What may be the role of nitric oxide (NO) in LTP?

j.   What kinds of experiments have shown the relevance of NMDA receptors for establishing memories in intact organisms.

k.   How may "leaky" calcium channels impair memory in aged mammals?

l.   What may be the role of NMDA receptors during the critical period in early development?

POSTTEST

Multiple-Choice Questions

1. In classical conditioning
    a.   the meat used by Pavlov was the conditioned stimulus.
    b.   the learner's behavior controls the presentation of reinforcements and punishments.
    c.   a stimulus comes to elicit a response similar to the response elicited by another stimulus.
    d.   bird-song learning can be fully explained in terms of CS and UCS.

2. Ivan Pavlov believed that learning occurs when
    a.   the connection between the CS center and the UCS center is strengthened.
    b.   the connection between the CS center and the CR center is strengthened.
    c.   the CS center takes over the UCS center's ability to elicit a UCR.
    d.   cells in the UCS center degenerate and cells in the CS center branch diffusely.

3. Lashley successfully demonstrated that
    a.   the lateral interpositus nucleus is the site of all engrams.
    b.   all learning takes place in the cerebral cortex.
    c.   the same neural mechanisms underlie all types of learning.
    d.   none of the above.

4. The lateral interpositus nucleus of the cerebellum
    a.   is important for the motor expression of eyelid conditioning in rabbits, but not the actual conditioning.
    b.   is important for the actual conditioning of the eyelid response.
    c.   is more important for explicit than implicit memory formation.
    d.   is an area that shows a great deal of damage in Korsakoff's syndrome.

5. Hebb's distinction between short-term and long-term memory
    a.   is supported by data showing that damage to the hippocampus can disrupt formation of new long-term, but not short-term, memories.
    b.   is supported by data showing that short-term memories are stored in the hippocampus and long-term memories are stored in the lateral interpositus nucleus of the cerebellum.
    c.   has been rejected by researchers because short-term and long-term memory merge so gradually that they are considered to be a single type of memory.
    d.   has recently been attributed to Pavlov, instead of Hebb.

6. Experiments on consolidation have shown that
   a. the most important factor promoting consolidation is the amount of time allowed for reverberating circuits to operate.
   b. emotional stimuli stimulate the amygdala, which stores some memories itself and also enhances memories stored elsewhere.
   c. very high levels of epinephrine are even more effective than moderate levels for promoting memory storage.
   d. all of the above are true.

7. Epinephrine in the blood facilitates memory consolidation by
   a. causing circuits to reverberate.
   b. crossing the blood-brain barrier and activating epinephrine synapses in the hippocampus.
   c. stimulating the vagus nerve, increasing blood glucose, and indirectly increasing brain norepinephrine.
   d. being converted into norepinephrine and then crossing the blood-brain barrier to activate synapses.

8. Working memory consists of
   a. a phonological loop.
   b. a visuospatial sketchpad.
   c. a central executive.
   d. all of the above.

9. The delayed response task for monkeys was used to show that
   a. visual memories are stored in primary visual cortex.
   b. each location of the to-be-remembered light activated a different group of cells in the prefrontal cortex.
   c. cells in the prefrontal cortex are more important for initiating movement than for storing information about the stimulus.
   d. damage to the prefrontal cortex produced severe deficits on tasks that required eye movements without delay, as well as with delay.

10. H. M.
    a. had his hippocampus removed because of his uncontrollable violence.
    b. acquired severe epilepsy as a result of the surgery.
    c. has a terrific memory for numbers but can learn no new skills.
    d. has more severe problems with declarative than with procedural memory.

11. Which of the following statements applies to H. M.?
    a. He has more severe anterograde than retrograde amnesia.
    b. He has more trouble with implicit than with explicit memory.
    c. His deficits show conclusively that the hippocampus is the storage site for all factual memories.
    d. All of the above are true.

12. Your memory of what you had for dinner last night is an example of
    a. explicit memory.
    b. implicit memory.
    c. procedural memory.
    d. short-term memory.

13. Priming is useful for
    a. producing memory consolidation.
    b. testing short-term memory.
    c. testing implicit memory.
    d. testing explicit memory.

14. Korsakoff's syndrome
    a. occurs because alcohol dissolves proteins in the brain, thereby shrinking presynaptic endings.
    b. is caused by prolonged thiamine deficiency.
    c. results from damage primarily to the hippocampus.
    d. all of the above.

15. Patients with Korsakoff's syndrome
    a. have damage in the mamillary bodies of the hypothalamus and the dorsomedial nucleus of the thalamus, which projects to prefrontal cortex.
    b. have symptoms somewhat similar to those of patients with damage to the prefrontal cortex.
    c. have better implicit memory than explicit memory.
    d. all of the above.

16. Alzheimer's disease
    a. results from three copies of chromosome 21.
    b. results from a long history of excessive alcohol consumption.
    c. is characterized by widespread atrophy of the cerebral cortex (especially the entorhinal cortex), hippocampus, and neurons that release acetylcholine.
    d. is characterized by severe atrophy of the prefrontal cortex, amygdala, and neurons that release enkephalins, but sparing of the rest of the brain.

17. Patients with Alzheimer's disease
    a. have plaques and tangles in damaged areas of their brains.
    b. unlike H. M. and Korsakoff's patients, have more problems with implicit than explicit memory.
    c. have a nearly 100% probability of passing the disease on to their offspring.
    d. all of the above.

18. Which of the following is true of amyloid precursor protein?
    a. Fragments of it can become amyloid beta (Aß) protein, found in plaques.
    b. The gene that determines its structure is on chromosome 21.
    c. Genes on chromosomes 21, 14, 1, and 19 all affect some aspect of amyloid production and increase the risk of Alzheimer's disease.
    d. All of the above are true.

19. Damage to the hippocampus results in
    a. rats going down a never-correct arm of the radial maze.
    b. rats forgetting which arms they have already explored.
    c. inability to climb onto a platform in the Morris search task because of motor impairment.
    d. monkeys that cannot choose a nonmatching stimulus under any conditions.

20. Damage to the hippocampus produces impairment on tasks requiring
    a. declarative, explicit memory.
    b. configural conditioning.
    c. spatial memory.
    d. all of the above.

21. Which of the following is true?
    a. Clark's nutcracker birds are very dependent on previously hidden food and have a large hippocampus.
    b. Mexican jays are also dependent on previously hidden food, but have a small hippocampus.
    c. The use of color in solving problems is a better predictor of hippocampal size than is dependence on previously hidden food.
    d. Hippocampal damage impairs performance on all tasks that use spatial memory, but does not impair any other tasks.

22. Infant amnesia
    a. shows a greater loss of implicit than explicit memories.
    b. may result from low levels of blood glucose.
    c. may result from the slow development of the hippocampus.
    d. is characterized by symptoms that are essentially the opposite of those seen in old age.

23. Memory deficits in aging people without Alzheimer's disease
    a. may result primarily from loss of neurons in the amygdala.
    b. may result from loss of dopamine receptors in the prefrontal cortex.
    c. may result from loss of serotonin receptors in the amygdala.
    d. consist mostly of inability to remember experiences from their childhood.

24. *Aplysia* are studied because
    a. they are the intellectual giants of the ocean.
    b. they have simple nervous systems with large neurons that are virtually identical among individuals.
    c. they have the most complex brains of all invertebrates.
    d. we can automatically infer the principles of learning in complex vertebrates.

25. Habituation in *Aplysia* is the result of
    a. a decrease in the number of quanta of neurotransmitter released.
    b. a decrease in the firing rate of the sensory neuron.
    c. decreased size of each quantum.
    d. muscle fatigue.

26. The mechanism mediating sensitization includes
    a. the release of dopamine from the sensory neuron onto the facilitating interneuron.
    b. the release of cyclic AMP by the sensory neuron onto the motor neuron.
    c. decreased outflow of potassium in the sensory neuron, resulting in prolonged transmitter release.
    d. hypersensitivity of the motor neuron to cyclic AMP.

27. Long-term potentiation (LTP)
    a. was first discovered in *Aplysia*.
    b. results from increased inflow of magnesium through non-NMDA receptors.
    c. requires depolarization via NMDA receptors in order to allow calcium outflow through non-NMDA receptors.
    d. requires depolarization via non-NMDA receptors in order to dislodge magnesium ions from NMDA receptors.

28. LTP
   a.   is very powerful but lasts only a few seconds.
   b.   may result from decreased sensitivity of the postsynaptic cell to the inhibitory transmitter glutamate.
   c.   may involve nitric oxide (NO) being released from the postsynaptic cell and causing the presynaptic terminal to release more transmitter.
   d.   occurs only in the hippocampus.

29. Which of the following is true?
   a.   Modification of synapses during the critical period in early development may depend on NMDA receptors.
   b.   LTP occurs first in the entorhinal cortex and then in the hippocampus.
   c.   Cooperativity refers to the strengthening of all synapses throughout an area of the brain by the activity of only one or two of them.
   d.   A problem in aged mammals is the near total closing down of calcium channels, so that NMDA receptors can no longer let calcium flow in.

Answers to Multiple-Choice Questions

1. c	6. b	11. a	16. c	21. a	26. c
2. a	7. c	12. a	17. a	22. c	27. d
3. d	8. d	13. c	18. d	23. b	28. c
4. b	9. b	14. b	19. b	24. b	29. a
5. a	10. d	15. d	20. d	25. a	

FEELING AND REMEMBERING

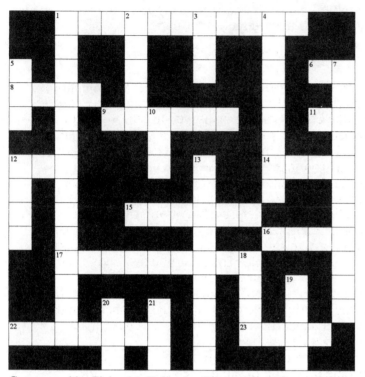

Constructed by Elaine M. Hull using Plexus Word Weaver®

Across

1 A type of chemical affecting the GABAa receptor, used as an aneshetic

6 Stimulus that evokes a particular response only after pairing with unconditioned stimulus

8 Radial ____, used to test working versus reference memory in rats

9 _____-Bucy syndrome, impairment of emotional response and visual interpretation resulting from damage to amygdala

11 Patient whose hippocampus removal led to severe anterograde amnesia

12 Acronym for a brain chemical that blocks benzodiazepine sites

14 Type of glutamate receptor that is important for forming LTP

15 Memory trace

16 The sex that is more likely to be aggressive "for the heck of it"

17 Device that measures sympathetic nervous system arousal

22 Type of conditioning in which reinforcement or punishment changes the probability of a behavior

23 ____ marrow, site of maturation of B cells

Down

1 A class of drugs that enhances GABA binding, used to treat anxiety

2 Type of leukocyte that produces antibodies

3 Stimulus that automatically evokes a response

4 A vitamin, deficiency of which results in Korsakoff's syndrome

5 Cyclic ___, second messenger that promotes sensitization in aplysia

7 Division of the autonomic nervous system that is activated in emergencies

10 Stimulus that automatically evokes a response

12 ____ Syndrome, mental retardation resulting from 3 copies of chromosome 21

13 Syndrome seen in long time alcoholics, characterized by apathy and memory impairment

18 Person who proposed that consolidation of memories resulted from reverberating circuits

19 ____ term memory, memory of an event that is not currently held in attention

20 Animal that :plays" with its prey

21 Acronym for increased responsiveness to axonal input as a result of a previous period of rapidly repeated stimulation

14

LATERALIZATION AND LANGUAGE

INTRODUCTION

Each hemisphere of the brain receives sensory input primarily from the opposite side of the body and controls motor output to that side as well. The hemispheres are connected by a large bundle of fibers, the corpus callosum, as well as several smaller bundles. In humans, the eyes are connected with the brain in such a way that the left half of each retina supplies input to the left hemisphere, and vice versa. Furthermore, the left half of each retina receives input from the right half of the visual field. Therefore, the right half of the visual field projects to the left hemisphere, and vice versa. This relationship has allowed researchers to test the roles of the two hemispheres in people whose corpus callosum had been severed in order to relieve epilepsy. Such studies have shown that the left hemisphere is specialized for language or "sequential, analytic" functions, whereas the right hemisphere is particularly adept at emotional expression, emotional perception, complex spatial problems, and "synthetic, holistic" tasks. Split-brain people sometimes seem to have two "selves" occupying the same body. In these people each half of the brain processes information and solves problems more or less independently of the other, although cooperation can be learned, thanks to enhanced function of subcortical connections. Even in intact people, evidence for hemispheric specialization can be seen.

One possible basis for the lateralization of language functions in the left hemisphere is that in 65 percent of people a portion of the left temporal lobe, the planum temporale, is larger on the left side than on the right. The size difference is apparent even shortly after birth.

The corpus callosum matures gradually, and experience determines the survival of the axons that make the best functional connections through the corpus callosum. People born without a corpus callosum are different from those who had split-brain surgery in adulthood. They can verbally describe sensory input from either hand and from either visual field. They may rely on greater development of the anterior commissure and hippocampal commissure to convey information from one hemisphere to the other.

About 10% of people are either left-handed or ambidextrous; most of them have mixed hemispheric control of speech, though the left is usually dominant. One factor promoting left-handedness may be the hormone testosterone, which may delay the maturation of the posterior left hemisphere and also of the immune system. Thus, hormonal factors may at least partially account for the correlation of left-handedness, being male, dyslexia, excellence in mathematics, and immune system disorders.

Language may have evolved as a by-product of increasing intelligence; on the other hand, the increasing intelligence may have occurred *because* of the growing importance of language for social interaction. Because new features evolve from older ones that may have served similar functions, researchers have studied the language abilities of our nearest relatives, the chimpanzees. A number of chimpanzees have been taught to communicate with their trainers, a computer, or each other using various nonspoken language systems. These animals acquire impressive vocabularies, and some have demonstrated some degree of grammatical ability. However, even after years of training, their linguistic abilities fall far short of those of young children. Pan paniscus, sometimes called pygmy chimpanzees, have shown the most impressive linguistic abilities among our primate relatives. They have learned by imitation, have used words to describe objects (as opposed to making a request) or to refer to a past event, and have created original sentences. In addition, some have learned to understand spoken English sentences. Dolphins and parrots also show some language abilities. Studies of nonhuman language abilities may provide insights about how best to teach language to brain-damaged or autistic people; they may also stimulate consideration of the unique versus shared abilities of humans and of the nature of language.

Paul Broca discovered that damage to an area of the left frontal lobe results in difficulties with pronunciation and with the use of grammatical connectives and other *closed-class* grammatical forms. However, people with such damage can usually understand both written and spoken language much better than they can produce it. Carl Wernicke, on the other hand, described a pattern of deficits almost the opposite of the pattern Broca discovered: poor language comprehension, anomia (difficulty finding the right word), but fluent (though mostly meaningless) speech. This syndrome results from destruction of an area in the left temporal lobe near the primary auditory cortex. Some patients with aphasia have symptoms that do not fall into either category. PET scans and functional MRI studies in intact adults have shown that speaking increases activity in much of the left frontal, temporal, and parietal cortex. Reading aloud increases activity in Broca's and Wernicke's areas and surrounding areas, in addition to lesser increases in corresponding areas of the right hemisphere. Naming objects activated Wernicke's area and other areas depending on the particular object.

Genetic conditions can impair language development without noticeably affecting other functions. On the other hand, people with Williams syndrome have excellent language abilities, but are impaired in nonlanguage skills; this syndrome appears to result from an unusual pattern of brain connections, rather than loss or absence of any specific area. Dyslexia, a reading disorder in otherwise normal people, may result from incomplete specialization of the hemispheress for language or from deficits in the magnocellular visual pathways. There are many kinds of dyslexia, which have different underlying causes. Some dyslexics' reading ability may be improved by focusing on one word at a time.

KEY TERMS AND CONCEPTS

Lateralization of function and the corpus callosum
    Connections
        Corpus callosum
        Anterior commissure
        Hippocampal commisure
    Lateralization
1.   Visual connections to the hemispheres
    Right visual field -- > left half of both retinas -- > left hemisphere (and vice versa)
        Optic chiasm
        Small vertical strip in center of retina -- > both hemispheres
    Both ears -- > both hemispheres
        Opposite side stronger

2.   Cutting the corpus callosum
    Epilepsy
    Left hemisphere: speech
    Split hemispheres: competition and cooperation
        Hands do competing tasks
        Learning to cooperate
            Use of subcortical connections

Verbal task: one word to each hemisphere
Right hand drew input to left hemisphere
Left hand drew two pictures, but not combined concept
The right hemisphere
Understands simple speech and some written words
Emotional content of speech, humor, and irony
Complex visual patterns
Visual imagination
Left hemisphere: sequential, analytic, time dependent
Right hemisphere: synthetic, holistic
Hemispheric specializations in intact brains
Small differences
Hemispheric differences and cognitive style: a doubtful assumption

3. Development of lateralization and handedness
Anatomical differences between the hemispheres
Planum temporale: larger in left hemisphere
Correlation with language skills
Ability of right hemisphere to acquire language after early damage to left
Sensitive period for language acquisition
Maturation of the corpus callosum
Survival of functional connections
Matures between ages 3 and 5
Development in the absence of a corpus callosum
Each hemisphere: connections to both sides of body
Anterior commissure
Hippocampal commissure
Handedness and language dominance
10% of people: left-handed or ambidextrous
99% of right-handed: left hemisphere for speech
Most left-handers: left hemisphere for speech, though some mixed control
Left-handers: thicker corpus callosum
High testosterone during development
Impairs growth of posterior left hemisphere
Left-handedness, dyslexia, stuttering
Immune disorders, allergies, migraines
Excellence in math and spatial skills

The Biological basis of language
1. The evolution of language capacities
Relationship of intelligence to language
Language ability of chimpanzees
Inability to speak
Ability to use visual symbols for words
Use of some grammatical rules
Difference from children
Few original sentences
Symbols used to request, not describe
Limited comprehension of others' communications
Pan paniscus (pygmy chimpanzees)
Understand more than they produce
Name without request
Request what they do not see
Refer to past
Creative requests

Early training by observation and imitation
Dolphins
    Respond to new combinations of words, if meaningful
Parrots
    Speak, name, count, form concepts

2. Effects of brain damage on human language
Broca's aphasia
    Nonfluent aphasia
    Difficulty in language production
        Articulation, writing, and gestures
        Omission of *closed-class* grammatical forms (prepositions, conjunctions, pronouns, helper verbs, quantifiers, tense and number endings)
        Ability to speak *open-class* forms (nouns and verbs)
    Problems comprehending grammatical words and devices
    Still use normal word order for their language
Wernicke's aphasia
    Fluent aphasia
    Articulate speech
    Anomia (difficulty finding the right word)
    Poor language comprehension
Wernicke's area: longer dendrites in more educated people
Sign language: depends on parietal lobe, not Wernicke's area
Beyond Broca and Wernicke
    Disorders
        Conduction aphasia: inability to repeat others' words; difficulty carrying on a conversation
        Alexia: inability to read
        Optic aphasia: inability to read more than one letter at a time
        Word deafness: inability to understand spoken language
        Loss of speech articulation: poor ability to speak
    PET scan and functional MRI studies of language processing
        Speaking: left frontal, temporal, and parietal cortex
        Reading aloud: Broca's and Wernicke's areas, surrounding areas; lesser increases in corresponding areas of right hemisphere
        Naming object: Wernicke's area and other areas, depending on objects
        Stating use for object: frontal cortex (motor or premotor)

3. Genetic abnormalities of language and intellect
Developmental language impairment
    Difficulties with articulation, grammar, and understanding speech
        Normal intelligence otherwise
    Williams syndrome
        Superior language skills
        Retarded in nonlanguage skills
        Smaller cortex and thalamus
        No imbalance between hemispheres
        Unusual organization of brain connections?
        Language is specialized ability, not by-product of intelligence

4. Dyslexia
No single abnormality
    Perceptual problems
        Combinations of letters
        Identifying spoken syllables

Relatively unresponsive magnocellular system
Incomplete specialization of hemispheres
Differences in attention or strategy

SHORT-ANSWER QUESTIONS

Lateralization of function and the corpus callosum

1. *Visual connections to the hemispheres*
   a. To which hemisphere(s) does the right visual field project? To which hemisphere(s) does the right half of both retinas project? To which hemisphere(s) does the right eye project?

   b. To which hemisphere(s) does the right ear project?

2. *Cutting the corpus callosum*
   a. What is the corpus callosum? Why is it sometimes severed in cases of severe epilepsy? What are the effects of such an operation on overall intelligence, motivation, and gross motor coordination?

   b. What have we learned from split-brain humans concerning specialization of the two hemispheres? Which tasks are best accomplished by the left hemisphere?

c. What is the basis for learned cooperation between the hemispheres in split-brain people?

d. What did the split-brain person draw with his right hand, when two different words were flashed to his right and left visual fields? What did he sometimes draw with his left hand? Could he combine information from his right and left visual fields to form a new concept?

e. Which tasks are best performed by the right hemisphere?

f. What kinds of tasks can show hemispheric specialization in intact people? How consistent are the results?

g. How valid is the assumption that a given individual relies consistently on one hemisphere or the other, regardless of the task?

3. *Development of lateralization and handedness*
    a. What is the planum temporale and what is its significance for language?

b.　How early is the size difference in the left vs. right planum temporale apparent?

c.　What happens to the language ability of children who suffer damage to their left hemisphere in the first 2 to 4 years of life? Is their recovery better or worse than people who have similar damage later in life?

d.　Compare the ability of 3-year-olds and of 5-year-olds to discriminate fabrics with either one hand or different hands. What can we infer from this about the development of the corpus callosum?

e.　In what ways are people who never had a corpus callosum different from split-brain people?

f.　Which other major axonal connections between the two hemispheres may compensate for the lack of a corpus callosum in people born without one?

g.　What percentage of right-handed people have left-hemisphere dominance for language? Describe the control of language in left-handed people.

h.   Is the corpus callosum thicker in right- or left-handed people? What is the functional correlate of this increased thickness?

i.   List the traits that have been proposed by Geschwind and Galaburda to be related to high levels of, or sensitivity to, testosterone during development.

j.   What effect may testosterone have on the left posterior cortex? How could this affect the development of language in boys? What may testosterone do to the immune system?

k.   How are the language areas of men and women different?

The biological basis of language
1.   *The evolution of language capacities*
   a.   Briefly discuss the proposal that our intelligence may have developed as a by-product of the selection for language.

   b.   What are some differences between the abilities of chimps and of children to use language?

c. What was unusual about the ability of some Pan paniscus to learn language? How does their understanding of language compare with their production of language?

d. In what three ways do Pan paniscus differ from common chimps in language production?

e. What are three possible explanations for why Pan paniscus have been more successful than other chimps at learning language?

f. What evidence is there that nonprimate species can learn language?

2. *Effects of brain damage on human language*
   a. Where is Broca's area located?

   b. Describe the effects of damage to Broca's area. What are closed-class words?

c.   Locate Wernicke's area.

d.   Contrast the effects of damage to Wernicke's area with those of damage to Broca's area.

e.   List five types of aphasia that do not fall into the categories of Broca's or Wernicke's aphasia.

f.   What information about language processing has been gained from PET scans and functional MRI studies?

3.   *Genetic abnormalities of language and intellect*
   a.   Compare the genetic condition resulting in severe language deficits, despite otherwise normal intelligence, with the pattern of abilities seen in Williams syndrome.

4.   *Dyslexia*
   a.   What is dyslexia? How consistent are its symptoms?

b.	What are some possible biological causes of dyslexia?

c.	What is one method of improving the ability of dyslexics to read?

POSTTEST

Multiple-Choice Questions

1.	Severing the corpus callosum
	a.	usually destroys language abilities.
	b.	usually relieves the symptoms of epilepsy.
	c.	has provided evidence that linguistic abilities reside largely in the right hemisphere.
	d.	none of the above.

2.	A person with a bisected brain
	a.	can draw pictures and arrange puzzle pieces better with the left hand than with the right.
	b.	can develop cooperation between the hemispheres because the corpus callosum grows back.
	c.	performs very poorly on intelligence tests.
	d.	more than one of the above.

3.	The only way to present visual input to only the right hemisphere of a split-brain person is to
	a.	flash it briefly to the left eye while the right eye is closed.
	b.	flash it briefly to the right eye while the left eye is closed.
	c.	flash it briefly in the left visual field while the person is looking straight ahead.
	d.	flash it briefly in the right visual field while the person is looking straight ahead.

4.	A split-brain person who hears a verbal description and feels objects with his left hand
	a.	will be able both to pick out the correct object and to name it.
	b.	will not be able to pick out the object or to name it.
	c.	will be able to pick it out, but will not be able to name it.
	d.	will be able to name it but not pick it out.

255

5. A split-brain person sees this picture flashed briefly on a screen while he is looking at a point in the middle of the screen. The person reports seeing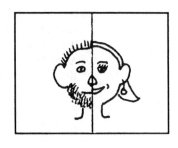
   a. a woman.
   b. a bearded man.
   c. a meaningless hodge podge of lines, since the spatial perception center has been damaged.
   d. one badly constructed face of two different people.

6. People with right-hemisphere damage
   a. have trouble producing and understanding emotional facial expressions.
   b. have trouble speaking with emotional expression and understanding others' vocal emotional expression.
   c. have trouble with some complex visual and spatial tasks.
   d. all of the above.

7. Hemispheric specialization in intact people
   a. has not been demonstrated.
   b. is consistent with that observed in split-brain people but is even more dramatic.
   c. can be shown but is small and inconsistent.
   d. is the reverse of specialization in split-brain people.

8. Which of the following is true of the planum temporale?
   a. Children with the biggest ratio of left to right planum temporale performed best on language tests.
   b. is larger in the right than in the left hemisphere for everyone.
   c. is equal in size in the two hemispheres at birth, indicating that maturation of language causes the size difference in adults.
   d. all of the above

9. What did Galin et al. discover when they asked 3-year-old and 5-year-old children to discriminate two fabrics?
   a. The 3-year-olds were better than the 5-year-olds.
   b. All children made fewer errors with their right hands than with their left.
   c. All children made 90 percent more errors using different hands than when using the same hand.
   d. Three-year-olds made 90 percent more errors using different hands than using the same hand, but 5-year-olds did equally well with one hand or two.

10. People who never had a corpus callosum
    a. are just like split-brain patients.
    b. can read words in either visual field and name objects that they touch with either hand.
    c. are especially fast at tasks requiring coordination of both hands.
    d. all of the above.

11. Which of the following was *not* proposed by Geschwind and Galaburda to be associated with increased testosterone during development?
    a. left-handedness
    b. deficits in mathematics
    c. dyslexia
    d. immune system disorders

12. One possible mechanism to explain the results in #11 is that
    a. testosterone may decrease the size of the corpus callosum.
    b. migraines in children may keep them from learning to read.
    c. testosterone may inhibit maturation of the right hemisphere.
    d. testosterone may inhibit maturation of the left hemisphere.

13. Pan paniscus
    a. can understand spoken English sentences.
    b. use symbols only to request objects.
    c. are unable to put symbols together in new ways to express new meanings.
    d. have learned to speak English fluently.

14. A patient has great difficulty in articulating words and a tendency to omit endings and abstract words, but little difficulty comprehending spoken and written words. The patient probably has damage in
    a. Broca's area.
    b. Wernicke's area.
    c. the corpus callosum.
    d. primary motor cortex controlling muscles of articulation.

15. A second patient has difficulty naming objects and understanding both spoken and written language; speech is fluent but not very meaningful. You suspect that the patient has damage in
    a. Broca's area.
    b. Wernicke's area.
    c. the anterior commissure and hippocampal commisure.
    d. left visual cortex and posterior corpus callosum.

16. PET scans and functional MRI studies of intact humans showed that
    a. speaking increased activity only in Broca's area.
    b. reading a sentence aloud activated only primary visual cortex and Broca's area.
    c. naming objects activated the temporal lobe in the general area of Wernicke's area, as well as other areas, depending on the specific object named.
    d. all of the above.

17. People with Williams syndrome
    a. have severe difficulties with even simple grammatical rules.
    b. have superior language abilities, but are retarded in nonlinguistic function.
    c. can draw beautifully, but cannot write.
    d. have almost total loss of Wernicke's area.

18. Dyslexic people
    a. are more likely than normal readers to have a bilaterally symmetrical cerebral cortex, larger language-related areas in the right hemisphere than in the left, or relatively unresponsive magnocellular visual pathways.
    b. are sometimes helped by focusing on whole paragraphs at a time, rather than reading one word at a time.
    c. all have very similar symptoms, and all of the symptoms are limited to difficulties in visual perception.
    d. all of the above.

Answers to Multiple-Choice Questions

1. b	6. d	11. b	16. c
2. a	7. c	12. d	17. b
3. c	8. a	13. a	18. a
4. c	9. d	14. a	
5. a	10. b	15. b	

Diagram

Label the following areas related to language processing: Broca's area, Wernicke's area, Sylvian or lateral fissure, visual cortex.

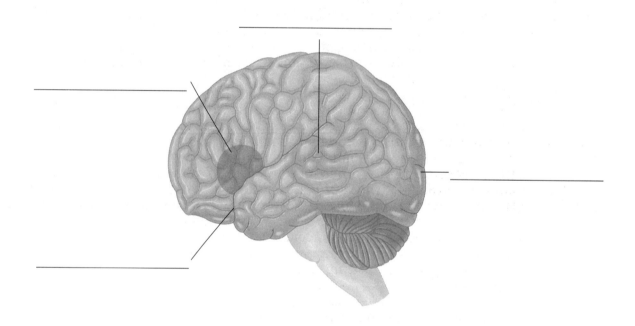

15

RECOVERY FROM BRAIN DAMAGE

INTRODUCTION

Brain damage can be caused by a variety of factors, including a sharp blow to the head; stroke; tumors; infections; exposure to radiation, drugs, and toxic substances; and degenerative conditions. Stroke can result either from ischemia due to a blood clot that obstructs an artery, or from hemorrhage, caused by rupture of an artery. Strokes kill neurons either by depriving them of oxygen and glucose or by overexcitation, which allows excess sodium, calcium, and zinc ions to enter the neuron, resulting in swelling or bursting of the membrane and interfering with normal processes. Cell death can be minimized by the use of drugs that break up clots, block glutamate receptors, or prevent the entry of calcium or zinc. Potential new treatments include the administration of neurotrophins or cooling the brain. Neuropsychologists can infer the location of brain damage by observing the type of behavioral deficits on tests that are specific for damage to certain brain areas or on a general battery of tests. In addition, the neuropsychologist may check for signs of impulsivity, altered emotional expression, or social unresponsiveness.

Even after behavioral recovery from brain damage, the recovered behavior may be disrupted by stress or old age. Recovery may depend on a number of possible physiological mechanisms. Learned adjustments in behavior allow an individual to make better use of abilities unaffected by the damage and to improve abilities that were impaired by the damage, but not lost. Diaschisis, or decreased activity of neurons after loss of input, contributes to impairment following brain damage. It can be reduced by administration of stimulant drugs. Regrowth of axons can be guided by myelin sheaths in the periphery. However, axons in the central nervous system do not regenerate, in part because of formation of scar tissue and in part because of growth-inhibiting proteins. Sprouting of axons occurs in response to normal cell death, as well as after brain damage; axons from undamaged neurons develop new terminals that occupy the vacant synapses. Sprouting can be facilitated by gangliosides, and may or may not be beneficial. Denervation supersensitivity refers to the increased sensitivity to a neurotransmitter by a postsynaptic cell that is deprived of synaptic input. It may explain why people can lose most of their dopamine-containing neurons in substantia nigra before exhibiting signs of Parkinson's disease. Reorganization of sensory representations can occur by postsynaptic adjustments of synaptic strength or by collateral sprouting, sometimes over surprisingly long distances. However, these reorganizations may not be beneficial, as in the case of phantom-limb sensations.

Under some circumstances, damage to infant brains may be less debilitating than similar damage to adult brains. This is because an infant's brain development can be modified so as to compensate for damage. Infant neurons have a greater capability for sprouting, and damage to one set of neurons may allow survival of other neurons that otherwise would have been lost. On the other hand, damage to an infant brain may be more disruptive than that to an adult brain, if it interferes with the organization of the brain.

The effects of brain damage may be less devastating if they occur in several stages (the serial-lesion effect), rather than in a single lesion of the same total size. Serial lesions or gradual degeneration allow learning and collateral sprouting to occur between lesions or during the degeneration. Therapies for brain damage stress teaching people to take advantage of their unimpaired abilities. More recently, researchers have experimented with drug treatments, such as calcium channel

259

blockers, gangliosides, and brain grafting. Because of the unique characteristics of fetal brains, fetal tissue is often used in such transplants. In some cases, the fetal tissue survives and extends dendrites and axons; in other cases, it may stimulate axon and dendrite growth by releasing trophic factors. Difficulties with use of fetal tissue for transplants include ethical concerns, the brief period during development when the tissue is suitable, and the requirement for tissue from 6 or 7 fetuses. Patients receiving such transplants have received benefits, but have not been fully cured. Potential sources of tissue include genetically altered neurons grown in tissue culture and fetuses of other species. In addition, neurotrophins or similar chemicals may benefit brain-damaged humans, as they have in rats and monkeys.

KEY TERMS AND CONCEPTS

Brain Damage and Mechanisms of Recovery
1. Causes of human brain damage
    Blow to head
    Stroke (cerebrovascular accident)
        Ischemia (blood clot closes artery)
            Area of direct damage: loss of oxygen and glucose
            Penumbra: loss of much, but not all, oxygen and glucose
        Hemorrhage (rupture of artery)
            Area of direct damage: loss of oxygen and glucose
            Penumbra: excess oxygen, calcium, blood products
        Penumbra, following both ischemia and hemorrhage
            Waste from dead cells in area of direct damage
            Extracellular potassium
            Edema
            Glial cells release stored glutamate -->
            Overstimulation -->
            Accumulation of sodium, calcium, and zinc -->
            Interference with chemical processes and
            Swelling or bursting of membrane
        Means of lessening damage
            Clot-busting drugs (used for ischemic stroke)
            Glutamate antagonists
            GABA agonists
            Drugs that prevent calcium or zinc entry
            Nerve growth factor and other neurotrophins
            Reduction in brain temperature
    Other causes of brain damage
        Tumors, infections, bullet wounds, drugs, toxins, radiation, diseases

2. Assessment of brain-damaged patients
    Specific tests for areas of known damage
    Battery of tests: vision, hearing, manual dexterity, intelligence, language,
        memory, abstract thinking
    Impulsivity, emotional expression, social responsiveness
    Comparison before and after damage and across tests

3. The precarious nature of recovery
    How stress impairs recovered behavior
        Cold after lateral hypothalamus lesions
        Return of sensory neglect or sensory extinction

260

The loss of recovered behavior in old age
    Lateral hypothalamus lesions in rats
    Brain-damaged veterans
    Parkinson's disease

4.   Adjustments and potential recovery after brain damage
   Learned adjustments in behavior
      Deafferented limbs
         One deafferented limb: lack of spontaneous use
         Two deafferented limbs: monkey learns to use both
   Diaschisis
      Amphetamine (releases dopamine and norepinephrine): enhanced recovery
      Haloperidol (blocks dopamine receptors): impaired recovery
      Benzodiazepines (enhance GABA transmission): prevent recovery
      Treatment of stroke patients to control blood pressure: probable
         interference with behavioral recovery
   The regrowth of axons
      Myelin sheaths as guides
      Inhibiting growth of scar tissue: little effect
      Glia cells in periphery, but not CNS: overcome growth-inhibiting proteins
   Sprouting
      Collateral sprouts
         Locus coeruleus
      Normal condition, not just response to damage
      Cut connections from left entorhinal cortex to left hippocampus -->
      Right entorhinal cortex sprouts -->
      Recovery
      Then cut path from right entorhinal cortex -->
      Impairs recovery
      Gangliosides (glycolipids): enhance collateral sprouting
   Denervation supersensitivity
      Disuse supersensitivity
      6-OHDA (6-hydroxydopamine)
      Amphetamine: increased release of dopamine mostly on intact side of brain
      Apomorphine: stimulated supersensitive dopamine receptors on brain-
         injured side
      Parkinson's disease
         Symptoms only after loss of most dopamine-containing axons from
            substantia nigra
         Compensation by remaining axons
         Denervation supersensitivity
  Reorganization of sensory representations
      Synaptic reorganization
         Fairly rapid for short distances (1 mm)
         Long-term reorganization for longer distances (10-14 mm)
         Phantom-limb sensations

Factors Influencing Recovery
1. Effects of age
    Kennard principle: more extensive recovery after early damage
        Applies only to certain kinds of damage
            Poor nutrition or alcohol exposure: worse impairment in infancy
    Altered connections of spared neurons: greater in infancy
        Collateral sprouting
        Dendritic branching
        Redirection of axons
        Superior colliculus damage
        New connections not necessarily helpful
    Effects on still developing neurons
        Removal of one hemisphere: increased thickness of other hemisphere
        Removal of anterior portion of cortex: less development of posterior cortex
        Early orbital frontal cortex damage: later developing areas compensate
        Early dorsolateral prefrontal cortex damage: effects more apparent later

2. Slow-onset and rapid-onset lesions
    Serial-lesion effect
    Collateral sprouting between partial lesions
    Some normal function of postsynaptic neurons due to remaining connections
    Learning between partial lesions or during gradual degeneration
        May be due to collateral sprouting

3. Therapies
    Behavioral interventions
        Regain lost skills or memories
        Practice impaired skills
        Remove distracting stimuli
    Drugs
        Nimodipine
            Calcium channel blocker
            Prevent damage due to excess NMDA stimulation
        Gangliosides
    Brain grafts
        6-OHDA in substantia nigra
        Fetal grafts
        Adrenal gland grafts: little benefit for most patients
        Difficulties with fetal transplants for Parkinson's patients
            Weak to moderate benefits
            Requires tissue from 6 - 7 aborted fetuses
            Tissue suitable only for brief period in development
        Tissue culture: may cause tumors
        Fetuses of other species
        Trophic factors
            Neurotrophins

SHORT-ANSWER QUESTIONS

Brain Damage and Mechanisms of Recovery

1. *Causes of human brain damage*
   a. What are the two types of stroke and the cause of each?

   b. In what two ways does a stroke kill neurons? Describe the sequence of destructive processes in the penumbra.

   c. What are six treatments that may minimize damage from stroke?

2. *Assessment of brain-damaged patients*
   a. What kinds of tests do neuropsychologists use to locate brain damage? Why does it take so long to arrive at an accurate conclusion?

3. *The precarious nature of recovery*
   a. How do animals respond to cold after recovery from lateral hypothalamic lesions?

   b. What causes sensory neglect? What is sensory extinction?

c. Why may deficits be uncovered by old age?

4. *Adjustments and potential recovery after brain damage*
   a. List six potential mechanisms for recovery from brain damage.

   b. How may learned adjustments in behavior be promoted?

   c. What is diaschisis? How is recovery from diaschisis affected by amphetamine or haloperidol?

   d. How may crushed, but not cut, axons in the peripheral nervous system form appropriate connections when they regenerate?

   e. Under what conditions is sprouting most likely to be useful? What evidence suggests that sprouting produces beneficial results?

f.   What are gangliosides? How may they contribute to recovery?

g.   What is denervation supersensitivity?

h.   What are the effects of 6-OHDA? Explain the differential effects of amphetamine and apomorphine after 6-OHDA lesions.

i.   What evidence is there that sensory representations may be reorganized during recovery? What was the surprise that investigators found when a monkey's limb had been deafferented 12 years earlier?

Factors Influencing Recovery
1. *Effects of age*
    a.   What is the Kennard principle? What evidence supports or refutes it?

    b.   Under what circumstances is brain damage more disruptive to an infant brain than to an adult brain?

c.   What are some ways in which an infant brain may be better able to recover from brain damage?

d.   What are the differences in the time courses of recovery from early damage to the orbital frontal cortex and the dorsolateral prefrontal cortex?

2.   *Slow-onset and rapid-onset lesions*
      a.   What is the serial-lesion effect? Through what means might it affect recovery from brain damage?

3.   *Therapies*
      a.   What are three emphases of effective therapy for humans with brain damage?

      b.   What are two potential drug therapies for brain damage? How may each work?

      c.   What unique characteristic of the brain seems to make it amenable to tissue grafting?

d. Describe the experiment by Perlow and colleagues that used substantia nigra transplants.

e. How successful have brain transplants for Parkinson's disease been?

f. What are four possible sources of tissue for brain grafts? What are some difficulties associated with each?

g. What are two means by which transplants may promote behavioral recovery?

POSTTEST

Multiple-Choice Questions

1. The most common cause of brain damage in young adults is
    a. stroke.
    b. disease.
    c. a sharp blow to the head.
    d. brain tumors.

2. Which of the following occurs in the penumbra surrounding the area of direct damage from stroke?
    a. It is invaded by waste products from the dead or dying cells in the area of direct damage.
    b. Potassium ions and fluid accumulate outside the neurons.
    c. Glutamate released from glial cells overstimulates neurons, resulting in sodium, calcium, and zinc ions accumulating in the cells, which in turn impairs normal processes and causes the membranes to swell or burst.
    d. All of the above are true.

3. Damage from strokes can be minimized by
   a. activating glutamate synapses.
   b. increasing activity at GABA synapses.
   c. creating a fever.
   d. all of the above.

4. Stress, cold, and aging
   a. can cause recovered rats to return to prerecovery behavioral deficits.
   b. do not affect recovered rats, although they cause normal rats to eat more.
   c. can cause recovered rats to become hyperactive.
   d. usually increase eating and drinking in rats with lateral hypothalamic damage.

5. Research on recovery from brain damage has shown that
   a. injections of transmitters can sometimes restore lost memories.
   b. a person has to completely relearn the skills and memories that were lost when brain cells were killed.
   c. the primary means of recovery is having some other area of the brain take over the function of the damaged area.
   d. recovery can sometimes occur when an individual is forced to make full use of remaining capabilities.

6. Amphetamine improves recovery by
   a. reducing diaschisis.
   b. producing denervation supersensitivity.
   c. relieving stress.
   d. stimulating regrowth of axons.

7. Adequate regrowth of an axon does *not* occur if
   a. the damaged axon is in the retina or spinal cord of fish.
   b. an axon in the peripheral nervous system of mammals is crushed.
   c. the damaged axon is in the central nervous system of mammals.
   d. all of the above.

8. Research on regrowth of axons in mammals has shown that
   a. inhibiting the formation of scar tissue is a highly successful new technique.
   b. glia cells in the peripheral, but not central, nervous system manufacture chemicals that overcome growth-inhibiting proteins.
   c. the mammalian central nervous system has evolved advanced chemical stimuli to promote better axon regrowth than that seen in fish.
   d. the reason that neurons in the central nervous system fail to regenerate is that there are no myelin sheaths there.

9. Sprouting
   a. occurs only in response to traumatic brain damage.
   b. is always maladaptive, since the wrong axons make connections.
   c. is enhanced by gangliosides.
   d. is enhanced by haloperidol.

10. Denervation supersensitivity is the result of
    a. increased output from other presynaptic cells adjacent to the one that has been damaged.
    b. postsynaptic neurons producing receptors for a different transmitter.
    c. changes in the chemical composition of the transmitter, making it more potent.
    d. an increased number of receptors on the postsynaptic cell and other changes within the cell.

11. After 6-OHDA lesions were made on one side of a rat's brain
    a. amphetamine increased the release of dopamine mostly on the intact side and thereby caused the rat to turn in one direction.
    b. amphetamine directly stimulated supersensitive postsynaptic receptors on the intact side, causing the rat to turn in the same direction as with apomorphine.
    c. both amphetamine and apomorphine stimulated postsynaptic receptors on both sides of the brain, causing the animal to walk in a straight line.
    d. the primary means of recovery was collateral sprouting of neurons containing acetylcholine.

12. After amputation of one finger of an owl monkey
    a. neurons that had previously responded to it died because of lack of input.
    b. neurons that had previously responded to it became more responsive to other parts of the hand.
    c. reorganization caused the adjacent fingers to feel like the lost one.
    d. no reorganization could occur because connections become permanently fixed during the early critical period.

13. The Kennard principle
    a. states that infants have less ability than adults to recover from brain damage, since their brains are more fragile.
    b. is true only for the peripheral nervous system.
    c. is only partly correct, since children recover less well than adults from poor nutrition or exposure to alcohol or other drugs.
    d. is entirely correct, since infants always have greater ability to recover from any sort of brain damage.

14. Which of the following statements about recovery from damage in infant brains is *not* true?
    a. The main reason that infant brains appear to recover from damage more fully than adults is that they cannot be tested as thoroughly.
    b. Performance deficits may not be noticed for more than a year after damage to dorsolateral prefrontal cortex.
    c. During early development, damage to one set of neurons may alter the survival and connections of other neurons.
    d. Damage to infant brains can result in altered connections by the spared neurons.

15. The serial-lesion effect
    a. refers to the fact that after several consecutive lesions, animals recover behaviors in the same order in which they were lost.
    b. proposes that repeated brain damage is always more harmful than a single lesion of the same total size.
    c. opposes the parallel-lesion effect.

     d.   refers to the fact that sometimes successive small lesions are less debilitating than a single lesion of the same total size.

16.   Nimodipine
     a.   is a type of ganglioside that can decrease the amount of damage caused by a stroke.
     b.   is a calcium channel blocker that can decrease the amount of damage caused by a stroke.
     c.   is a neurotoxin that destroys catecholamine neurons.
     d.   is an immune suppressant that stops rejection of brain grafts.

17.   Brain grafting
     a.   would be more successful if there were no blood-brain barrier.
     b.   is successful only if most or all of the grafted neurons survive and establish synaptic connections.
     c.   has been used with some success to promote recovery of adult rats with a rat version of Parkinson's disease.
     d.   of the adrenal medulla has produced consistently excellent results in restoring function to Parkinson's disease patients.

Answers to Multiple-Choice Questions

1. c	6. a	11. a	16. b
2. d	7. c	12. b	17. c
3. b	8. b	13. c	
4. a	9. c	14. a	
5. d	10. d	15. d	

LANGUAGE AND RECOVERY

Constructed by Elaine M. Hull using Plexus Word Weaver®

Across

1 Molecules composed of carbohydrates and fats that promote recovery from brain damage
5 A severe language disorder
8 Acronym for method of measuring brain activity during naming tasks
9 Area, damage to which produces nonfluent aphasia
10 Hemisphere that is important for speech
12 Number of letters that can be read at one time by a person with optic aphasia
14 Type of glutamate receptor that produces damage after a stroke (abbr.)
17 Hemisphere that is important for spatial and emotional functions
19 Drug that reduces diaschisis

Down

2 A type of function for which left hemisphere is important
3 _____ receptors, ones that mediate increased responsiveness of postsynaptic cells following loss of input
4 Syndrome in which the person has good language skills in spite of extremely limited abilities in other regards
6 Type of function for which the right hemisphere is important
7 Inability to name objects
11 Area, damage to which produces fluent aphasia and anomia
13 Midbrain area containing dopamine neurons
15 A factor affecting ability to recover from brain damage
16 Transplant of tissue to treat Parkinson's disease
18 ___ paniscus, chimpanzees that have considerable language abilities

16
MOOD DISORDERS AND SCHIZOPHRENIA

INTRODUCTION

Depression is typified by episodic sadness and helplessness, lack of energy, feelings of worthlessness, suicidal ideas, sleep disorders, and lack of pleasure. While the cause of depression is not fully understood, a number of possible factors have been identified. Hormonal changes, such as during the premenstrual or postpartum periods, may trigger a depressive episode but are not the underlying cause of depression. Abnormal hemispheric dominance is sometimes associated with mood disorders. Happiness in normal people is associated with activation of the left prefrontal cortex, whereas depressed people have lower metabolic activity in the left, and increased activity in the right prefrontal cortex. There may be a genetic component to depression, since depression and related disorders, such as substance abuse and anxiety, tend to run in families. More recently, it has been suggested that depression may sometimes be caused by exposure to a virus at some point in life.

Drugs that improve affective disorders act in one of three ways: block reuptake of monoamines (tricyclics), inhibit monoamine oxidase (monoamine oxidase inhibitors, or MAOIs), or block reuptake of only serotonin ("second generation" antidepressants, such as fluoxetine). Fluoxetine and other selective serotonin reuptake inhibitors have fewer side effects than do the tricyclics. A major problem with the transmitter hypothesis is that drugs affect transmitter levels almost immediately but exert noticeable effects on mood only after two or three weeks. Alterations of sensitivity of either autoreceptors or postsynaptic receptors may underlie drug effectiveness; however, the mechanism of action is not understood.

In addition to treatment by drug therapy, mood disorders are sometimes treated with electroconvulsive therapy (ECT), sleep alterations, or bright lights. ECT is particularly useful for patients who are unresponsive to antidepressants or who are suicidal and need immediate relief. Sleep- or REM-deprivation therapy is based on observations that depressed persons enter REM sleep much sooner than normal persons, as though their body temperature rhythms were phase-advanced. Earlier bedtimes may allow their activity cycles to become synchronized with their temperature cycles. Total or REM sleep deprivation may also be beneficial for a few days or weeks.

Depression can occur as either a unipolar or a bipolar disorder. A unipolar disorder is one in which an individual displays only one extreme of mood. Bipolar disorder, or manic-depressive disorder, is characterized by cycles of depression and mania. During their manic phase, people are restless, uninhibited, excitable, impulsive, and apparently happy. Manic-depressive cycles may last a year or only a few days. Bipolar disorder has been linked to genes on several chromosomes; however, the specific genetic influences are not understood. Lithium is effective in treating manic-depressive disorder, and if taken regularly, prevents relapse into either mania or depression. It has complex effects on second-messenger systems and may stabilize fluctuating brain systems.

Seasonal affective disorder (SAD) occurs mostly in areas where nights are long in the winter. SAD patients may have phase-delayed sleep and temperature cycles, unlike other depressed people. Exposure to bright lights is usually an effective treatment for SAD.

Schizophrenia is an illness in which emotions are "split off" from the intellect. Its positive symptoms include a psychotic cluster (hallucinations and delusions) and a

272

disorganized cluster (inappropriate emotions, bizarre behavior, and thought disorder). Negative symptoms include deficits in social interaction, emotional expression, and speech. Approximately 1.3 percent of the US population will suffer schizophrenia at some point in their lives; another 1 percent will have a milder schizoid condition.

Much evidence favors a genetic predisposition to schizophrenia. It is more common in biological relatives than in adopted relatives of schizophrenics and is more common in monozygotic than in dizygotic twins of schizophrenics. Also, adopted paternal half-siblings of schizophrenics, who did not share even the prenatal environment of the affected child, have a much greater frequency of schizophrenia than is found in the overall population. Genetics cannot completely explain the occurrence of schizophrenia, however, since the concordance rate for monozygotic twins is not 100 percent, and cases of schizophrenia do occur in families with no previous history of this disorder. Perhaps several genes on different chromosomes may predispose people to schizophrenia. One behavioral marker, which may predict schizophrenia independently of schizophrenic symptoms, is abnormal pursuit eye movements.

The neurodevelopmental hypothesis suggests that schizophrenia results from abnormal early development of the brain. Difficulties surrounding birth or during early or middle pregnancy have been linked to increased incidence of schizophrenia. These include complications before and during labor, severe stress or starvation during pregnancy, Rh incompatibility, and fevers due to viral infections during middle to late pregnancy. A number of minor brain abnormalities have been found in the brains of schizophrenics. The cerebral cortex and overall forebrain are smaller than usual; the ventricles are larger; there are abnormalities in the thalamus. The area of most consistent abnormalities is the dorsal prefrontal cortex, one of the latest brain areas to mature. Some neurons are found in the midst of white matter, and some that do migrate to the correct area are more scattered. Because there is no evidence of brain damage in adulthood, it is thought that the brain abnormalities result from early developmental factors, due either to genetics or problems during pregnancy. Since the most affected brain areas are those that mature slowly, the behavioral problems may not emerge until long after the damage occurred.

Some symptoms of schizophrenia can be temporarily experienced by people who take large doses of drugs that stimulate dopamine receptors. However, drug-induced hallucinations are typically visual, rather than auditory. Antipsychotic drugs, including phenothiazines (chlorpromazine: Thorazine) and butyrophenones (haloperidol: Haldol), block dopamine receptors. On the basis of such observations it has been hypothesized that schizophrenia occurs because of excess activity at dopamine synapses. There are a number of problems with this hypothesis. First, there is no consistent evidence of abnormally high levels of dopamine or its metabolites in schizophrenics. However, amphetamine does cause greater release of dopamine in schizophrenics than in others. Furthermore, there may be abnormal ratios of the subtypes of dopamine recepotrs in schizophrenics. Second, the primary problem may be a deficit in glutamate activity, rather than excess dopamine. Schizophrenics release less GABA and glutamate than do other people, and glutamate has effects that are frequently opposite to those of dopamine. Therefore, any problem observed could be due either to insufficient glutamate or excess dopamine. Finally, neuroleptic drugs block dopamine receptors almost immediately, but take two or three weeks to produce therapeutic benefits.

The decision to administer neuroleptic drugs has been complicated by their potentially severe side effects. The most troublesome effect is tardive dyskinesia, which consists of tremors and other involuntary movements. This condition develops gradually and is more likely to occur in individuals who have taken large doses of antipsychotic drugs and in whom those drugs have the least therapeutic effect. It may result from receptor supersensitivity, although the exact mechanism is not understood. Recent advances in research have led to the use of new atypical antipsychotic drugs (such as clozapine), which appear to control schizophrenia without causing tardive dyskinesia. These drugs appear to control schizophrenia by affecting dopamine receptors in the prefrontal cortex without affecting those in the basal ganglia, which contribute to movement. Clozapine blocks D_4 receptors more than D_2, and also blocks serotonin 5-HT$_2$ receptors. Clozapine's major side effect is a decrease in white blood cells, which leaves the patient vulnerable to infections.

Key Terms and Concepts

Mood disorders
1. Major depressive disorder
    Symptoms
        Sad and helpless for weeks
        No energy, feel worthless, contemplate suicide
        Trouble sleeping
        Little pleasure from sex or food
        Cannot imagine being happy again
    Incidence
        Twice as common in women as men
        Any time from adolescence to old age, peaks in 25-44-year age range
        19% of all people suffer depression at least once
    Triggering depressed episodes
        Precipitation of an episode by life events
        Genetic or other biological predisposition
        Episodic, not constant
        Hormonal changes
            Premenstrual depression
            Postpartum depression
    Abnormalities of hemispheric dominance
        Happy mood: increased activity in left prefrontal cortex
        Depression: decreased activity in left and increased in right prefrontal
            cortex
    Genetics
        Increased risk among biological relatives of depressed people
        Adopted children: more similar to biological than adoptive relatives
        Probably a general risk gene, not just for depression
    Viruses
        Borna disease
    Antidepressant drugs
        Tricyclics
            Decrease reuptake of catecholamines or serotonin --> longer in synapse
            Imipramine (Tofranil)
            Generally more helpful than MAOIs
        MAOIs
            Block monoamine oxidase --> monoamines broken down more slowly
            Phenelzine (Nardil)
        Second generation antidepressants, or selective serotonin reuptake
            inhibitors
            Similar to tricyclics, but selective for serotonin
            Fluoxetine (Prozac)
            Fewer side effects

Implications for the physiology of depression
    Problem of time course
        Rapid effect on reuptake
        A few hours later: stimulate autoreceptors
        Still later: desensitize autoreceptors
        Later yet: decreased sensitivity of postsynaptic receptors
        Effects on behavior: begin a few days to several weeks after starting drug therapy
Other therapies
    Psychotherapy
    Electroconvulsive therapy (ECT)
        Used for patients who do not respond to drug therapy or who are suicidal
        Works faster than drugs
        Administered every other day for two weeks
        Used with muscle relaxants or anesthetics
        Side effect: memory loss; minimized with shock to right hemisphere only
        Half are depressed again within six months
        Increases D_1 and D_2 receptors in nucleus accumbens
        Decreases postsynaptic norepinephrine receptors
        Variety of other effects
    Altered sleep patterns
        Depresssed: REM within 45 min, not 80-90 min
        Therapy
            Earlier bedtime: effective for months
            Stay awake all night: effective for 1-2 days
            REM sleep deprivation: gradual improvement, effective days to weeks

2.   Bipolar disorder
Definitions
    Unipolar disorder: one extreme -- depression
    Bipolar disorder: manic-depressive disorder
        Mania: restlessness, excitement, laughter, rambling speech, happy mood, loss of inhibitions
        Cycle length: days to a year
Genetics
    Apparent linkage to genes on chromosomes 4, 6, 11, 13, 15, and 18
Treatments
    Lithium salts
        May have toxic side effects
        Complex effects on second messenger systems
        May stabilize fluctuating systems
    Anticonvulsant drugs
        Carbamazepine

3.   Seasonal affective disorder (SAD)
Common where nights are long in winter
SAD: phase-delayed sleep and temperature rhythms, unlike other depressed people, who are phase-advanced
Bright lights

Schizophrenia
1.   Characteristics
      Dementia praecox
      Not multiple personality
      Behavioral symptoms
            Negative symptoms
                  Deficits in social interaction, emotional expression, and speech
                  More stable, less responsive to treatment
            Positive symptoms
                  Sporadic occurence
                  Psychotic cluster: delusions and hallucinations
                        Increased activity in thalamus, hippocampus, basal ganglia, and prefrontal cortex
                  Disorganized cluster: inappropriate emotions, bizarre behaviors and thought disorder
                  Difficulty with abstract concepts
            Acute onset: greater probability of recovery than with chronic onset
      Demographic data
            Approximately 1.3 percent of US population: schizophrenia
            Additional 1 percent of population: schizoid condition
            Reported 10-100 times more often in United States and Europe than in Third World
            More common in impoverished areas
            Diagnosed at earlier age in men

2.   Genetics
      The evidence
            Twin studies
                  Greater concordance for monozygotic (50%) than dizygotic (15%) twins
                  Related to concordance for handedness in monozygotic twins
                        Both right-handed: 92%
                        One right- and one left-handed: 25%
            Adopted children who develop schizophrenia
                  Greater concordance with biological than adoptive parents
                  Paternal half-siblings
                        Higher concordance than for general population
                        Different mothers: no shared prenatal environment
            Children of people with schizophrenia and their twins
                  Children of twin without schizophrenia: almost same risk as children of twin with schizophrenia
      Unanswered questions
            Problems due to misdiagnosis
            Combined effects of several genes
      The search for behavioral markers
            Saccadic eye movement
            Pursuit eye movement
                  Impaired in schizophrenics and close relatives
                  Impaired even after drugs relieve symptoms of schizophrenia
                  Not an accurate marker

3.   The neurodevelopmental hypothesis
      Prenatal and neonatal abnormalities of development
            "Nonoptimal signs" around time of birth
            Problems in early or middle pregnancy
            Second Rh-positive child of Rh-negative mother

Season of birth effect
    Winter births: higher risk
    Only in non-tropical climates
    Viral epidemics
        Fever in mother slows cell division
        Higher rate of schizophrenia in babies born 3 months later
Mild brain abnormalities
    Smaller brains
    Thalamic abnormalities
    Enlarged ventricles
    Abnormal dorsolateral prefrontal cortex
        Less task-induced metabolic activity
    Fewer or smaller neurons in some cortical areas
    Some neurons within white matter
    Disorganized arrangement of neurons
    Abnormal amounts of cell-recognition molecules
    No evidence of adult brain damage
Early development and later psychopathology
    Areas that show abnormalities are late maturing

4.   Neurotransmitters and drugs
    Drugs that can provoke schizophrenic symptoms
        Substance-induced psychotic disorder
            Hallucinations (usually visual) and delusions
            Extensive use of stimulant drugs (amphetamine, methamphetamine,
                cocaine)
        Dopamine hypothesis of schizophrenia
            Excess activity at certain dopamine synapses
        Glutamate hypothesis of schizophrenia
            Deficient activity at certain glutamate synapses
        Relationships between dopamine and glutamate
            Dopamine inhibits glutamate release
            Glutamate excites neurons that dopamine inhibits
        Phencyclidine ("angel dust")
            Inhibits glutamate receptors
            Symptoms similar to schizophrenia
            Little psychotic effect in preadolescents
    Drug therapies
        Phenothiazines
            Chlorpromazine (Thorazine)
        Butyrophenones
            Haloperidol (Haldol)
        Block dopamine receptors
            May have effect similar to stimulating glutamate receptors
        Some antipsychotic drugs
            Stimulate glutamate and block dopamine synapses
    Side effects and the search for improved drugs
        Antipsychotic drugs: decrease mesolimbocortical activity --> beneficial
            effects
        Decrease activity of dopamine neurons that control movement -->
            undesired effects
        Tardive dyskinesia
            Tremors and other involuntary movements
            Receptor supersensitivity
            No excess of dopamine receptors

Other mechanisms of supersensitivity
Persistent
Atypical antipsychotics
Greater blocking of dopamine activity in prefrontal cortex than in basal
ganglia
Clozapine:
Blocks D_4 more than D_2 receptors
Also blocks serotonin 5-HT_2 receptors
Side effect: decrease white blood cells
Neurotransmitters and their receptors
Problem not simply excess dopamine
Dopamine levels generally not elevated
But amphetamine --> greater release in schizophrenics
D_2 receptors: normal density
D_1 receptors: below normal
D_3 and D_4 receptors: twice as high as normal
Not clear whether receptor abnormalities are cause or effect
Less GABA and glutamate release
Prefrontal glutamate receptors: altered form
Time course of effectiveness of antipsychotic drugs
Block dopamine receptors almost immediately
Affect behavior over two to three weeks
Complex pattern of effects on pre- and postsynaptic neurons

SHORT-ANSWER QUESTIONS

Mood disorders
1. *Major depressive disorder*
    a.   Describe the symptoms of depression.

    b.   What evidence suggests that hormones may affect depression? What is the
         likely relationship between hormonal changes and depression?

    c.   What patterns of hemispheric dominance have been associated with
         depression? with happy moods in normal people?

d.   What is the evidence for a genetic predisposition for depression?

e.   What other disorders may be linked genetically with depression?

f.   What is Borna disease? What evidence links it to depression?

g.   Name three groups of antidepressant drugs and explain how each exerts its effects.

h.   Why is fluoxetine (Prozac) preferred over the monoamine oxidase inhibitors and the tricyclics?

i.   What is the current status of the controversy about whether fluoxetine increases suicide and violence?

j. Explain the problem of the time course of drugs' effects on neurotransmitters and their effects on depressive symptoms.

k. So, what can we say about neurotransmitters and mood disorders?

l. How has electroconvulsive therapy (ECT) been improved since the 1950s?

m. For which two groups of patients is ECT most often used?

n. What are the advantages and disadvantages of ECT?

o. What are two of the physiological changes brought about by ECT? Can we infer that these changes produce the improvement in symptoms?

p. How does the onset of REM sleep differ in depressed people, compared to nondepressed individuals? How may this be related to body temperature cycles?

q. What three changes in sleeping schedules have been found to alleviate depression? How long do the benefits of each of these last?

2. *Bipolar disorder*
   a. What is the difference between unipolar and bipolar disorder? What is another term for bipolar disorder?

   b. Describe the symptoms of mania.

   c. What is the incidence in the population of bipolar disorder? What is the mean age of onset?

   d. What can we say about genetic factors in bipolar disorder?

e. What is the most effective therapy for bipolar disorder? What can we say about its mode of action?

3. *Seasonal affective disorder*
    a. What is seasonal affective disorder (SAD)? How is it treated?

    b. How are the sleep and temperature rhythms of SAD patients different from those of other depressed patients?

Schizophrenia
1. *Characteristics*
    a. What is the origin of the term *schizophrenia*?

    b. What are the negative symptoms of schizophrenia? How stable are they?

    c. What are the two clusters of positive symptoms of schizophrenia? How stable are they?

d. What is the overall incidence of schizophrenia? of schizoid disorder? Does this incidence vary among ethnic groups, sexes, or economic levels?

2. *Genetics*
    a. What evidence from twin studies suggests a genetic basis for schizophrenia?

    b. What are concordance rates, and how are they used in studies of twins?

    c. What evidence from adoption studies suggests a genetic basis for schizophrenia?

    d. What advantage is there to studying paternal half-siblings?

    e. What conclusions can be drawn about the role of genetics in schizophrenia?

f.　What is one behavioral marker for schizophrenia? How closely correlated is this marker with schizophrenic symptoms?

3.　*The neurodevelopmental hypothesis*
　　a.　What three lines of evidence suggest that schizophrenia may result from abnormalities in the early development of the brain?

　　b.　What specific prenatal conditions have been associated with increased risk for schizophrenia?

　　c.　In which season of birth is there a slightly greater likelihood of developing schizophrenia? What factor may account for this effect?

　　d.　What are some of the brain abnormalities that have been linked with schizophrenia?

　　e.　Why do researchers believe that these abnormalities resulted from developmental effects, rather than gradual brain damage in adulthood?

f. How might one explain the late onset of schizophrenic symptoms, if the brain damage occurred during early development?

4. *Neurotransmitters and drugs*
    a. What drugs can induce a state similar to schizophrenia? What are the similarities and differences between drug-induced psychosis and schizophrenia?

    b. What is the evidence favoring the dopamine hypothesis of schizophrenia?

    c. What other neurotransmitter has been hypothesized to be abnormal in schizophrenia? What are two types of interactions between these two neurotransmitters?

    d. What is phencyclidine? What are its effects on receptors? What are its psychological effects?

e.   What are two chemical families of antipsychotic (neuroleptic) drugs that have been in wide use for many years? What is their major effect on receptors?

f.   Why may blockade of dopamine receptors have beneficial effects, if the original problem is deficient glutamate?

g.   Antipsychotic drugs are thought to exert their beneficial effects on which dopamine system? Effects on which system are thought to underlie the unpleasant motor side effects?

h.   What is tardive dyskinesia? In what type of patients is it most likely to occur?

i.   What is one atypical antipsychotic drug? Why are atypical antipsychotic drugs promising?

j.   Why are they less likely than other neuroleptics to produce tardive dyskinesia?

k.   Which two receptor subtypes are blocked by clozapine?

l.   Why can we not say that schizophrenia results simply from excess production and release of dopamine?

m.   Describe the differences in density of the subtypes of dopamine receptors in schizophrenic, compared to nonschizophrenic, people.

n.   Which other neurotransmitters show abnormal levels of release? What abnormality has been found in glutamate receptors?

o.   What is the problem of the time course of antipsychotic drugs?

POSTTEST

Multiple-Choice Questions

1.   Which of the following is *not* a common symptom of depression?
     a.   excessive sleeping
     b.   sadness and helplessness
     c.   lack of energy
     d.   little pleasure from sex or food

2. Which of the following is true of depression?
   a. A gene on chromosome 11 is now known to be the cause of most cases of depression.
   b. Hormonal changes before menstruation or after childbirth may cause depression, even in people without a biological predisposition to that disorder.
   c. Since a specific genetic abnormality has not been discovered, it is now commonly agreed that depression does not have a genetic basis.
   d. Having a close relative with depression increases the risk for alcoholism, other substance abuse, and anxiety disorders, as well as of depression.

3. Depression is frequently associated with
   a. increased activity in the left prefrontal cortex.
   b. decreased activity in the left prefrontal cortex.
   c. increased activity in the right temporal cortex.
   d. decreased activity in the right temporal cortex.

4. Research on Borna disease suggests that
   a. a virus causes an autoimmune attack on the brain.
   b. any illness that causes a fever also causes depression.
   c. a virus may be one cause of depression.
   d. the viruses that infect animals cannot infect humans.

5. Which of the following is *not* a type of antidepressant drug?
   a. monoamine oxidase inhibitors
   b. tricyclics
   c. serotonin reuptake inhibitors
   d. dopamine antagonists

6. Which of the following is true?
   a. The effects of drugs on transmitter systems are immediate, but their effects on depression are delayed for one to two weeks.
   b. The effects of drugs on transmitter systems are delayed for one to two weeks, but their effects on depression are immediate.
   c. Depression results from having too little of all the monoamine transmitters.
   d. The major effect of fluoxetine is to block serotonin receptors.

7. The general effects of antidepressant drugs are
   a. an increase in the release of neurotransmitter as long as the drug is taken.
   b. an increase in the amount of neurotransmitter in the synapse initially, and with prolonged use, desensitization of autoreceptors, thereby restoring nearly the original rate of release.
   c. a decrease in the amount of neurotransmitter in the synapse initially, and with prolonged use, increased sensitivity of autoreceptors, thereby restoring nearly the original rate of release.
   d. a prolonged decrease in the release of neurotransmitter as long as the drug is taken.

8. Electroconvulsive therapy
   a. is effective because it confuses patients, and they forget their depressing thoughts for several years.
   b. is rarely used anymore because of its bad reputation.
   c. is usually used on patients who do not respond to antidepressant drugs or who are suicidal.
   d. must be administered to the left hemisphere, which produces severe loss of language ability.

9. Depressed people
   a. have their symptoms worsened by REM deprivation.
   b. enter REM sleep more slowly than do normal people.
   c. show an improvement lasting for many months after as little as one night's sleep deprivation.
   d. are sometimes helped by REM deprivation, an earlier bedtime, or staying awake all night.

10. Bipolar disorder
    a. is characterized by cycles between depression and normal moods.
    b. is characterized by cycles between depression and mania.
    c. is much more common than unipolar depression.
    d. is characterized by higher glucose metabolism in the brain during depression, and lower activity during mania.

11. Lithium
    a. has complex effects on several second messenger systems, which somehow stabilize fluctuating brain activity.
    b. is extremely safe because it is so simple.
    c. is helpful for depression but not for mania.
    d. all of the above.

12. People with seasonal affective disorder (SAD)
    a. become more depressed during winter because of the cold.
    b. are frequently helped by sitting in hot sauna baths for an hour or more each day.
    c. show phase-advanced sleep and temperature rhythms, similar to other depressed people.
    d. are frequently helped by exposure to bright lights for an hour or more before the sun rises and after it sets.

13. Schizophrenia
    a. refers to multiple personalities.
    b. refers to a split between the emotions and the intellect.
    c. is caused primarily by stress.
    d. is typically diagnosed in the elderly.

14. Which of the following is true of the *positive* symptoms of schizophrenia?
    a. They consist primarily of visual hallucinations.
    b. They include deficits in social interactions, emotional expression, and speech.
    c. They include two clusters: a psychotic cluster, consisting of delusions and hallucinations, and a disorganized cluster, consisting of inappropriate emotions, bizarre behaviors, and thought disorder.
    d. They are more stable over time than are the negative symptoms.

15. Which of the following supports a genetic basis for schizophrenia?
    a. The season-of-birth effect is greater in families in which there is at least one schizophrenic relative.
    b. The concordance rate for schizophrenia is greater for dizygotic than for monozygotic twins.
    c. When twins are discordant for schizophrenia, the children of the nonschizophrenic twin are no more likely than the general population to become schizophrenic.
    d. Paternal half-siblings of schizophrenics are more frequently schizophrenic than would be predicted from the overall population frequency.

16. Research on possible causes of schizophrenia has demonstrated that
    a. a prenatal viral infection may cause fever, which results in impaired brain development.
    b. abnormal pursuit eye movements may cause schizophrenia by providing unstable visual input.
    c. conflicting messages from parents are a major cause of schizophrenia.
    d. the season-of-birth effect occurs more often in the tropics, where diseases are harder to control.

17. Studies of the brains of schizophrenics have revealed that
    a. they have smaller forebrains, fewer or smaller neurons in various cortical areas, more abnormalities in slowly maturing areas such as dorsolateral prefrontal cortex, and neurons located in white matter that should have migrated to cerebral cortex.
    b. they have shrunken ventricles.
    c. they have a large proliferation of glia cells, indicating that much of the damage was caused gradually during adulthood.
    d. all of the above

18. Drug-induced psychosis
    a. is usually permanent and causes a full-blown state of schizophrenia, complete with auditory hallucinations.
    b. is caused by drugs that increase the stimulation of dopamine receptors.
    c. is caused by drugs that block dopamine receptors.
    d. is caused by drugs that stimulate glutamate receptors, especially in young children.

19. Which of the following is *not* an effective neuroleptic drug?
    a. haloperidol
    b. chlorpromazine
    c. L-DOPA
    d. clozapine

20. According to the dopamine hypothesis of schizophrenia, people with schizophrenia have
    a. excessive activity at dopamine synapses.
    b. deficient activity at dopamine synapses.
    c. glutamate in neurons that should release dopamine.
    d. too little dopamine activity in the mesolimbocortical system and too much in the basal ganglia.

21. Tardive dyskinesia
    a. recedes completely once all traces of antipsychotic drugs have left the body.
    b. usually occurs soon after beginning antipsychotic drug treatment.
    c. is more likely to occur in those who have taken larger doses of antipsychotic drugs and in those for whom those drugs had the least therapeutic effect.
    d. develops because of increased numbers of dopamine receptors.

22. Atypical antipsychotic drugs
    a. include haloperidol and chlorpromazine.
    b. decrease dopamine activity primarily in the mesolimbocortical system.
    c. decrease dopamine activity primarily in the basal ganglia.
    d. should be avoided because they produce more tardive dyskinesia than do typical neuroleptics.

23. Clozapine
    a. blocks dopamine D_4 receptors more than D_2.
    b. also blocks serotonin 5-HT_2 receptors.
    c. has undesirable side effects, including a decrease in white blood cells.
    d. all of the above

24. Which of the following is true?
    a. In many brain areas, dopamine inhibits glutamate release; in others, glutamate excites neurons that dopamine inhibits.
    b. Since there is too much glutamate in the brains of schizophrenic people, a good way to improve their symptoms is to block glutamate receptors.
    c. Unlike antidepressants, antipsychotic drugs produce beneficial effects on behavior almost immediately.
    d. All subtypes of dopamine receptors are present in abnormally high numbers in the brains of schizophrenic people.

Answers to Multiple-Choice Questions

1. a	6. a	11. a	16. a	21. c
2. d	7. b	12. d	17. a	22. b
3. b	8. c	13. b	18. b	23. d
4. c	9. d	14. c	19. c	24. a
5. d	10. b	15. d	20. a	

MOODS AND PSYCHOSIS

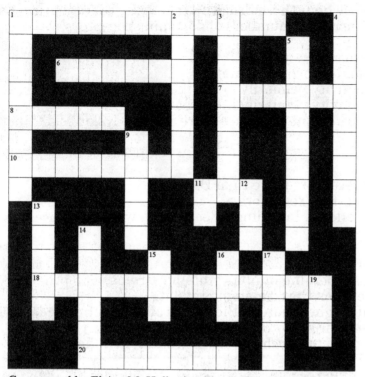

Constructed by Elaine M. Hull using Plexus Word Weaver®

Across

1 Slow maturing area of prefrontal cortex, damage to which produces delayed behavioral effects

6 Season when increased numbers of schizophrenics are born and when people suffer from SAD

7 Selective serotonin reuptake inhibitor used to treat depression

8 State characterized by restlessness, excitement, happy mood, and loss of inhibitions

10 Type of schizophrenic symptoms characterized by deficits in social interaction, emotional expression, and speech

11 Stage of sleep, deprivation of which sometimes relieves depression

18 A positive symptom of schizophrenia in the psychotic cluster

20 Drug used to treat bipolar disorder

Down

1 Transmitter whose receptors are blocked by antipsychotic drugs

2 _____ dyskinesia, a side effect of prolonged use of typical, but not atypical, antipsychotic drugs

3 Neural process that is blocked by tricyclic drugs

4 A class of drugs used to treat depression

5 Fraternal (nonidentical) twin, who shows lower concordance for depression or schizophrenia than a monozygotic twin

9 An effective treatment for SAD

11 Blood factor, which can increase the likelihood of schizophrenia, if the mother and fetus have different subtypes

12 Sex in which schizophrenia is diagnosed at an earlier age

13 Hemisphere that shows increased activity during depression

14 A typical antipsychotic drug

15 Acronym for a treatment for depression that is used when patients are suicidal or did not benefit from drugs

16 Acronym for a disorder that is common during winter where nights are very long

17 A potential cause for some cases of depression

19 ___natal, a period when oxygen deprivation or other abnormalities may predispose an individual to schizophrenia

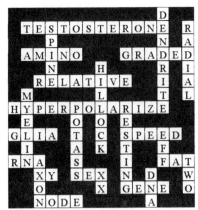

1 using Plexus Word Weaver®

1 using Plexus Word Weaver®

1 using Plexus Word Weaver®

1 using Plexus Word Weaver®

1 using Plexus Word Weaver®

1 using Plexus Word Weaver®

1 using Plexus Word Weaver®

1 using Plexus Word Weaver®

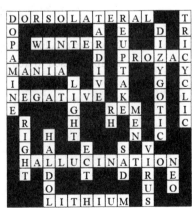

1 using Plexus Word Weaver®